£1.50

CW00734843

BIRDWATCHER AT LARGE

BRUCE CAMPBELL

Birdwatcher at Large

drawings by Donald Watson

J. M. DENT & SONS LTD
London, Toronto and Melbourne

Photoset in VIP Bembo by D. P. Media Ltd, Hitchin
Printed by Biddles Ltd, Guildford
for J. M. Dent & Sons Ltd
Aldine House, Welbeck Street, London

British Library Cataloguing in Publication Data

Campbell, Bruce, b.1912
    Birdwatcher at large.
    1. Campbell, Bruce, b.1912
    2. Ornithologists – Great Britain – Biography
    I. Title
    598.2'092'4   OL31.C/

    ISBN 0–460–04373–0

Contents

List of chapter illustrations by Donald Watson

Drawings 2, 6, 14, 15, 16, 17, 18, 20, 21 previously published in *Wildlife* magazine; 3, 4, 11 appeared in *The Countryman*.

Acknowledgements   It has been impossible to write this account of my ornithological life up to the end of 1978 without drawing on matter already published elsewhere, mainly in magazines. I therefore acknowledge with gratitude permission to reprint various extracts given by Crispin Gill of *The Countryman*, with which I have been happily associated since 1952, by Michael Wright of *Country Life*, to which I have contributed for many years, by Nigel Sitwell of *Wildlife*, whose Birdwatcher at Large I was from 1971 to 1978, and to Colin Rose of Topaz Publishing, Great Missenden. The Royal Society for the Protection of Birds has also kindly given permission to quote extracts from *Bird Notes* and its successor *Birds* magazine. 'Birdsmanship' first appeared in *Bird Notes* in 1951 and has been reprinted or adapted in *The Bird Notes Bedside Book*, in Stephen Potter's *Oneupmanship* and in three American magazines.

My brother and sister-in-law, Niall and Moira Campbell, read through the first draft and made many useful comments; to the rest of my family the book will, I hope, come as a pleasant surprise, all the more so for the illustrations by Donald Watson, with whom I have collaborated over so many years. Between them Anne Bell and Susan Digby Firth typed the whole text with their usual speed and efficiency. Finally, on the publisher's side, I must thank Malcolm Gerratt, who suggested the whole idea and has presided over its embodiment so sympathetically.

Bruce Campbell   Wootton by Woodstock   May 1979

1
Beginnings

My first recollection in this world, or so the curious data retrieval system which we call memory informs me, is of standing by my father in my mother's parents' house at Shawford near Winchester. He was sitting by the fire, convalescing from a wound received in the autumn of 1914. He made a complete recovery, for my next image is of him lowering me to look into a grey wagtail's nest by a weir on the Itchen the following spring. His diary is both brief and ambiguous but this event must have taken place early in April 1915 when I was six weeks short of my third birthday.

The next nest I remember was a moorhen's by a stream at Blatchford near Cornwood in South Devon the following year, though I cannot confirm this from my father's diary. At roughly the same period he pointed out a tree near the skyline where ravens had once nested, but long before he came to know the area in the early 1900s.

Psychologically it is no doubt significant that my first avian memories are of nests; but this interest in

7

what many people nowadays consider should be left undisturbed was fostered by paternal reminiscences which had for their scene the town of Bedford and its surrounding villages, the superficially pretty prosaic East Midlands. But there my father and his three brothers had been brought up, after their father had died young, by a devoted mother on the proverbial shoestring; and there they roamed the unremarkable farming countryside in search of birds and their eggs.

So Bromham and Turvey, Sharnbrook and Kempston, Honey Hills and Rowney Warren, Ampthill and distant Olney became my Bokhara and my Samarkhand. In a series of bedtime stories my father made them come alive, as he told me of chases by gamekeepers and farmers and, rather surprisingly, by gangs working on the railway, led by the formidable Surly Buck, who could be roused from his lunchtime nap by a yell of 'Surly Buck on the Line!'

In general my father and his friends did not ask permission to go on anyone's land, unless they wanted to investigate old trees right by the house for owls' nests. The ever-present likelihood of bumping into a keeper was part of the fun. On the whole each brother belonged to a gang of school friends of his own age and operated with them. These gangs did not appear to keep to a territory and were often keen rivals. 'Having carefully put them away,' runs my father's diary, referring to a clutch of nightingale's eggs, 'we were startled by voices, but they turned out to be Fielder, Clode and young Jarvis. When we knew this we shouted at them. They turned and ran the whole way back.'

At the finding of a teal's nest on Bedford Sewage Farm, a unique occurrence, my father and his brother 'Baggs' seem to have acted in concert. A companion, who in their view wanted to come back and scoop the clutch, tried to prevent Baggs, the actual finder, taking any eggs. 'But I slipped two into my pocket while Baggs took one.' All three evidently went back to complete the raid but could not find the nest again.

The farthest point in my father's expeditions was Olney, twelve miles from Bedford. His transport varied from trains, when he had funds, to an unreliable bicycle and his two good feet. Even if he got to his destination in some sort of conveyance, he and his friends – referred to almost always by surname or nickname – had walked miles by the end of the day.

The stout notebook in which he recorded all the nests found, descriptions of their sites and accounts of particularly long or successful days, begins in 1890 when he was twelve and at school near Portsmouth, but the brief notes on the early years seem to have been copied from an older book. There are several laconic complaints about the lack of 'anybody to come out'. Of his great friend Louis Finlinson, who later became my godfather, he writes, 'Finlinson was too keen on cricket, so consequently most of the season was wasted'. That year, 1896, he was back at Bedford School and took his first kingfishers' eggs from the river bank near Bromham, a well-known site, and he shows one of his few twinges of feeling for the birds: 'After this haul we vowed never to disturb the ill-treated Bromham kingfishers.'

My father and his friends robbed nests because, although there were by then bird protection laws, egg-collecting was still a reputable branch of ornithology. Also, if they did not empty the nest, another gang might come along and be no more forbearing. Most towns then had a taxidermist's shop which also sold eggs and in Bedford there was 'Covey' (Covington) whose main line was hairdressing. My father often described the excitement when a fresh consignment of eggs arrived and were exposed in the shop window, nestling in cotton wool.

Once there was a clutch of golden eagle's eggs, priced at £2 and bought by a wealthy parent for his son. Covey also bought eggs from the boys and one of my uncles offered him an apparently attractive package deal: on lifting the lid of the box the rich reds and browns of kestrels' and sparrowhawks' eggs could be seen. Only after the deal was done did it emerge that the lower layers were composed of jackdaws and magpies eggs. But probably not crows; perhaps due to efficient keepering carrion crows were scarce round Bedford; not until 1897, his last full season in the area, did my father get up to a nest near Turvey, to find the young hatched.

At the end of this season, when he was nineteen and, incidentally, playing for the East Midlands at Rugby as a forward, he wisely committed outstanding memories of his boyhood to paper. They begin with a long day in April 1895. He set out with the Finlinson brothers to Turvey, where they had a glass of beer, and then on to Olney, looking mainly for tawny owls. But another gang had been there first, 'Finny' fell down a tree and they only found one nest of young owls. My father 'surprised' himself by climbing to a high magpie's nest. He was also sent up the owl's tree and comments, after the twenty-seven-mile walk, that 'it was the longest and hardest day I ever had'.

Perhaps because it was freshest in his mind the 1897 season rates five expeditions. On 12 April he and Finny went by train to Olney where they had a useful friend: Baxter. My father, after a fatiguing search, found his first lapwing's nest, which suggests that these birds were not common even then round Bedford. The luckless owls yielded up three eggs and, after parting with their friend Baxter, who on another occasion did them 'grandly' at lunch, they walked home to make it at least a twenty-mile day. Next morning they were out in another direction, to visit a friend called Lock at Wootton Hoo, where they also, in a phrase somehow reminiscent of a Western, met 'old Jake Parker on our way, he seemed surprised to see us at that quarter'.

Lock went up to some rooks' nests. 'He had barely come down when a keeper appeared. We bolted down, Lock leading. We went so fast that he never even saw us. From here we went to some owl trees but they had gone.' Later they crossed the railway line to look at a likely elm in front of Ampthill House. 'When I got up and saw there was nothing, the great bough I was standing on fell with a crash, so we quickly cut across and joined Finny.' My father's verbal account was even more dramatic: according to this version, Lock bolted when the bough fell and, as he moved home soon afterwards, my father never set eyes on him again, following his dereliction of *cave* duty. I was tremendously impressed by this, as by another story, of how my father's gang trained for the football season hurdling over the stooks in the corn fields by night. Once they landed on two tramps, who had dossed down behind a stook. The tramps fled and, 'my dear old boy', my father used to conclude in a significant tone, 'for all I know they may be running still'.

On 22 April, still after owls, my father was out with a new figure, Ben Severs, on a long walk to Staughton Moor. Hearing of a house called the Priory, they 'thought it an old place, perhaps with owls, but it was merely a modern dwelling. While we were looking at the trees, the daughter of the house met us and showed us round, we pretended we had come to photograph it'. Later 'Ben went weak although over six foot and wouldn't come to get a tawny's nest a little way off'. So they went down Ravensden Hill into the fields.

'Here some horses looked at Ben, he was so angry and ill-tempered that he threw his new silver-mounted cane at them. The crook end caught in a horse's tail. A minute before he had said he was too tired to walk, but he gave chase. The noise of the stick on the horse's hoofs made them go faster, so he never got it back.' The only nest they found was a starling, a poor reward for a thirty-mile walk and the loss of the cane.

15 May saw my father out with his former rivals, Fielder and Clode. They found a goldfinch's nest, then quite a rarity due, it is usually said, to the activities of bird-catchers. This was sufficiently exciting for the day to be singled out. On the 24th he was at Olney again with Baxter who, like Ben Severs, said at one point that 'he couldn't walk another yard'. Remembering my father's remorseless pace on the Hill in middle life, I am not surprised that he exhausted all his youthful companions. This time he asked Baxter to watch while he knocked a small ash tree with a magpie's nest in it. 'A kestrel flew out. So I said "A ———— hawk!" Baxter put his head down and charged thro' the undergrowth and was pushing me up the tree in a "shake".' After this success, they 'trudged' back to Olney where the unreliable 'bi' or 'grid' was having its chain mended. It was not ready until two hours after the last train for Bedford had left. My father had no lamp and after a mile the chain broke again. So he walked via Turvey, not liking to wake the blacksmith 'as I had no money. Got home about twelve. Baggs had come home about eleven after some adventure with a keeper.'

The atmosphere of search and grab which pervades the diary seems an age away from the modern birdwatcher with his binoculars, camera and tape-recorder, and all-the-year-round observations. My father's and his friends' interest was seasonal: birds-nesting in spring, catapulting in winter. They made their own 'catties', preferably of privet which produces the right narrow Y-shaped forks. In spring they used to shoot pellets close to high nests to flush a sitting bird or make it peer over the edge. In winter came the sport of 'hedge-hopping', when two or three 'guns' would work either side of a suitable, not-too-thick hedge, shooting at the flustered birds within it.

When my father returned from the South African war, having been commissioned on the battlefield, he had not lost his taste for this boyhood pastime and the diary records three days hedge-hopping in January 1902 with a total bag of fifty-eight birds, thirty-two of them blackbirds, but including a jay and a skylark, the victim of a long shot in the open. I think my father's defence would be that they ate the thrushes and blackbirds and skinned the others for their collections of stuffed birds. He could not afford to shoot game, but the language he used is not so different from that of the posh shoot or, for that matter, the fox hunt: 'Began operations at Bromham House lodge . . . the birds were very wild . . . drawing blanks in many good hedges, we went towards Waite's farm . . . after working without a kill for about two hours . . .'

By the early 1900s my father had become friendly with Jannion Steele Elliott, historian of Bedfordshire's wild life and with a national reputation as an ornithologist. On 4 June 1903 they visited Southill Park, a few miles from Bedford, and found the occupied nests of twenty-seven kinds of bird. At the diamond jubilee of this event, Steele Elliott's nephew Denis, James Ferguson-Lees and I attempted to emulate them and reached twenty-six species. But 1963, after the cold spell, was not an ideal season. Two years later we got to thirty-five species, with the reassuring feeling that our common birds still compare in numbers and diversity with the situation sixty and seventy years ago; also that the fruits of our search survive on nest record cards and not in cottonwool. My father would have approved; by the end of his long life he was as keen on conservation as the rest of us. But he continued to enjoy the sight of a nest and eggs, the bird's inmost secret revealed.

When I was six and a half and he was back from the war my father drew up an ambitious programme of joint studies which I still have. First came birds, then 'animals', then 'you insects, we shall find out and put down all about your different lives, what is your purpose in life, how you help us and how we can help you . . .' Flowers got a short final paragraph. I do not think Julian Huxley would have approved all the terminology (he loathed the phrase 'birds and animals'), but his concept of 'the patient humility of free enquiry' seems to have been there all right.

At the time of our manifesto we were living at Farnborough in Hampshire, and so was Douglas English, a pioneer nature photographer. He was a fine naturalist and took me out in the still unspoiled heathland where he corrected some of the bias caused by my father's primary enthusiasm for birds. Incidents that stick in my mind are his beating into a net off a flowering may tree the first green hairstreak butterfly I had seen, my bringing home a nestful of young moles which he and my father painstakingly replaced, and finding a cuckoo's egg in a meadow pipit's nest on my seventh birthday. There are also memories of glittering dragonflies, slow worms and lizards, frogs and toads in a habitat that is quickly vanishing from southern Britain with irreparable loss.

Although my father was so keen on birds, he never acquired the *Practical Handbook*, forerunner of the classic five-volume *Handbook of British Birds*. When we returned to the Highlands, our guide was T. A. Coward's *Birds of the British Isles and their Eggs*, first published in 1920 and the book on which most of my generation of ornithologists was brought up.

I have always regretted that I did not meet Coward who, after an early retirement, spent nearly half his life in the field and writing about natural history. To Manchester's Literary and Philosophical Society in 1921 he gave a presidential address, subsequently published in his book *Bird Haunts and Nature Memories*, which anticipates most of the modern conservation ethic, falling then on deaf ears. But we did have some connection: he was one of the judges for the Royal Society for the Protection of Birds essay competition in 1930 when I was a winner.

The return of our family unit to Argyll came quite by chance. In 1919 my father's great friend 'Chas' Nairne married, and among the places he and his bride considered for their honeymoon was the school-house at Kinlochteacuis in Morvern. Their final choice fell elsewhere but I can remember Chas asking my parents if they would like to take it on. So in August, after a visit to my formidable great-aunt Jane at Kingussie and a journey by train across the Highlands to Oban, we sailed to Lochaline by the *Lochinvar* and I did the last ten miles across Morvern to Kinloch by horse and trap, while my parents cycled. Two years later the T-model Ford had invaded the Highlands.

Although we had started 1919 with such high-sounding intent, our journal petered out some time in May; but my father did keep a pencil diary of our first visit to Morvern, from 22 August to 21 September. Red and roe deer, seals, buzzards, peregrines and ravens attacking a golden eagle punctuated what was mainly a fishing trip. On 25 August I was only able to 'half-catch' a small trout, on 3 September I landed one on a worm, on the 9th came my first two on a fly (trolling, not casting, I hasten to add) and by the end of the visit my total was fifty, mostly from Loch Doire nam mart, a mile inland from Kinloch. It is no effort to recall our ceaseless circuits by rowing boat, my eye on the bob-fly, but sometimes roving to the green slopes of Beinn na Uamha above or to the *doire* of oak and birch, behind which towered the black-avised basalt of Aoineadh Mòr and Aoineadh Beag.

We also often borrowed his boat from Ronald Gillies the shepherd at Ardantiobairt, the cottage nearest the schoolhouse, or went with him down Loch Teacuis. Once my father shot two ducks from the boat; I suppose now they were juvenile eiders; they were certainly inedible. More peacefully and mysteriously we rowed to a beach where Caol Charna widens into Loch Sunart and spent an idyllic day picnicking, bathing and finding all sorts of marine creatures, including oysters. Some alchemy was at work; never again did we find that beach in its pristine state, although we must have passed it scores of times. Another time my mother 'stripped' and dived to rescue a bag of winkles covered by the tide. She had learned to swim in the warm waters of Bermuda, where she met my father.

The Morvern holiday proved a great success but next year both my mother's parents died and it was not until June 1921, with the country in the throes of a coal strike and the sun shining even over Glasgow, where we stopped a few nights on our way north and saw an appetite-whetting egg collection, that we got to Morvern again and I met the breeding season bird life of a sea loch.

2
My Double Life

The outcome of our second visit to Morvern was the beginning of a sort of double life for me. England meant primarily school, an institution for which I never cared; Argyll meant holidays, freedom and a degree of adventure. But until my father retired from the army early in 1924, we spent Christmas and Easter holidays in the south, mainly in the suburban atmosphere of Farnborough near Aldershot, where in those days there was still a lot of soon-to-be-spoiled wilderness about.

One of my father's (latterly I always called him Pa and intend to do so henceforth wherever it seems more natural) unorthodox ploys as Inspector of Physical Training* was to set up allotments alongside the gymnasium and swimming bath in Aldershot. This was a follow-up to the farm he had started in France towards the end of the 1914–18 war as a means of rehabilitating wounded or 'shell-shocked' soldiers, and he did not see

* His biography, *Prophet in Plimsoles* by John G. Gray, was published by the Edina Press in 1978 at £4.50.

why the idea should not be continued in peacetime; there were also hens and a pigeon loft; Pa maintained that everyone had an instinct to 'nurture' young animals (and babies), which was usually stifled; I would like to have seen him argue with a modern sociobiologist.

The allotments and their addenda attracted bird life; stonechats bred in 1921 and just beyond was an area of heath, bog and scrub where in the years 1921–3 we found tree pipit, yellow wagtail (a 'first' for Pa), whinchat and grasshopper warblers nesting. This haven was turned into no doubt much needed sports grounds for the army soon afterwards, but the allotments survived, and many years later, on my birthday in 1936, I saw a cock red-backed shrike there, not even then a very notable event.

We lived in Farnborough from 1919 to 1923 just east of what became the A 325. West of it were commons stretching to Cove reservoir and Fleet Pond, areas which my father had 'worked' in the early 1900s. One hot May day in 1921 I stumbled after him among enormous tussocks of *Carex paniculata*; we called it 'pampas grass'. All we found were four whitethroats' nests and I remember wishing that I had a magic wand which would respond to nests. Now that animals can be fitted with minute radio transmitters and fed on radio-active substances, the idea ceases to be far-fetched. Although most of our expeditions were during the nesting season, we noted seventeen species on Laffan's Plain on 3 January 1921; these included what must have been a female or immature hen harrier, 'a large brown hawk with a heavy flight and a white patch over its rump'. The magazine to which we sent this description replied that it was 'in all probability' a female peregrine, which prompted Pa to surround the cutting with derisive exclamation marks when we pasted it in our diary.

I have already mentioned Blatchford as the place of one of my first nest memories. This was an estate on the edge of Dartmoor; its owner, Miss Deare, had been very kind to Pa when he was a young officer on sick leave after the South African war's legacy of dysentery, and we paid fairly frequent visits up to the time of her death, which must have been around the end of the 1914–18 war. Disjointed recollections include making a spoof nest by the lake to take in Pa; his rushing down a steep bank in Hawns and Dendles Wood (now partly a national nature reserve) to stop me chewing an ivy leaf; seeing my first *Cladonia* lichens with their grey cups (podetia) and red apothecia on the granite boulders by the river Yealm; our hostess's fear of a bat getting into her wonderful white hair; and learning the facts of life when I saw a small foetus in the gralloch of one of her herd of fallow deer, which (as we should now euphemize) had just been culled.

Two fallow deer skins accompanied us to Swanage, where my mother and I spent the last year of the war. We left them behind when we moved to Farnborough and I worried about their loss intermittently for years. Living in the same house was Dr Penrose, a well-known naturalist of the day. Once on Durlston Head he announced dramatically, 'Ah, a kestrel is going to treat us to a display of hovering.' It was helped no doubt by the upcurrents of air from the cliffs where, at the Tillywhim Caves, I saw my first nesting seabirds. But my most vivid memory is of a mild concussion sustained by jumping clumsily off a rock below Ballard Cliff, and how Pa miraculously whistled up a taxi when we got back to the edge of Swanage. That day I also associate with my first painted ladies feeding on what must have been the flowers of marjoram, a plant notably attractive to butterflies.

Butterflies and moths were always a fairly close

second to birds. My father brought back from France a small glass-fronted case which included a swallowtail, a red underwing and a set of clouded yellows, some of which had been caught, or so the saga has it, by Jimmy Driscoll, the Irish-Welsh boxer who was featherweight champion of the world and one of Pa's team of itinerant physical training instructors. On another leave, when we were staying with my mother's parents at Shawford, he tried to catch marbled whites on the slippery downs above Compton. The family tradition is that he used his glengarry, but I think he must have had a net. At any rate I rolled helpless with laughter among the anthills, and the marbled white, paradoxically a member of the 'brown' family, remains one of my favourite butterflies, whose abundance depends today so much on relict areas of chalk and limestone grassland.

More early butterfly memories take me to the Wyre Forest. Although Jannion Steele Elliott (see p. 13) was brought up in Bedford, he became an ironmaster (not inappropriate metaphorically either; he could be a man of iron) in Dudley, and early in the century he bought the unspoiled little Tudor manor of Dowles about a mile from Bewdley and by the brook of that name which drains a large part of the Forest. Here in the long hot summer of 1921, after our stay in Morvern, I saw my first commas (then considered quite rare) and tradition again says that I tried to catch one by bringing my net down over a whole hollyhock on which it had settled.

On this visit we went to tea with the Chases. J. F. Chase was a bird and egg collector in the sense that people collect china or pictures: he did not go into the field but bought his specimens. When I told him that I had been given a rather curiously marked cuckoo's egg, he at once offered me a shilling for it, which I refused. His collection, which includes some great British rarities, went to the Birmingham Museum, where it was put on special exhibition in the autumn of 1977 and I was asked to give a talk based on it.

This cuckoo's egg came from near Stowmarket in Suffolk, where Great-aunt 'Dovie' (another imposing lady with white hair) lived with peppery Uncle Eugene Wells at Buxhall Vale. The local rector took the egg from a pied wagtail's nest in the creeper on his rectory; for once the cuckoo had erred, the egg was fresh while the wagtail's were about to hatch. The rector also took me looking for reed warblers' nests (all this in that wonderful summer of 1921). We got very hot and only found an addled egg but I have been hooked on their meticulously neat nests ever since, each one a lucky dip that may have a cuckoo's egg in it.

Uncle Eugene was a keen hunting man and used to rear cubs each season, in an artificial earth enclosed in a wire cage, to supplement the local wild population of foxes. His excellent keeper Haggar (I never discovered his forename) used to take me out sometimes looking for pheasants' nests and was responsible for my first little owl's nest in an orchard tree; he caught the tight-sitting bird in a net and dispatched her while I had the eggs. On another visit I took a single deserted part-ridge's egg, which prompted Uncle Eugene to a heavy practical joke, disguising himself as an outraged gamekeeper; my reaction was a mixture of fright and embarrassment. Although he authorized the destruc-tion of all birds of prey and their nests, he was shocked at my taking a full clutch of, I think, blackbird's eggs and made me put them all back except one.

His death in June 1925 took my father down from Argyll for the funeral, which Pa combined with noting the songs of fifteen species, finding nests of stock dove and wren and hearing a late cuckoo call before he started back on the 29th. Aunt Dovie lived on for some years, latterly bed-ridden and sustained in part by the visitors to her window bird-table; these included nuthatches of which I suppose I had my first good view from her bedside.

We spent much of the Easter holidays of 1923 at Buxhall and this was the first season of which I kept a full record myself, having begun a diary – 'The year opened fine with slight frost' – on January 1, something which, apart from a short period during my student days, I have managed to maintain ever since. The forty-four nests recorded at Buxhall included not only the little owl's but my first long-tailed tit's nest, in epicormic shoots on a leaning willow in one of uncle Eugene's game coverts. Its unusual site and entrance at the top made me think at first that it was an outsize chaffinch's nest.

But on 3 May my whole life was changed. Hitherto I had attended a series of day schools. On that fateful day I joined a carriage full of other inmates bound for a boarding prep school at Cirencester: Oakley Hall, of which my cousin Francis Letts was the junior partner in the headmastership. That night I reckon as the most unhappy of my life. This chronicle is not a record of my private sorrows, but it is relevant that no one in authority at the school, in spite of all the senior headmaster's wife had told my parents, had the slightest interest in or knowledge of natural history. When a grass snake appeared in the swimming pool, it was immediately slaughtered. Francis Letts, for whom I came to have the deepest admiration and affection, had a passion for cricket and, like Roger Peterson on birds, could be guaranteed to get any conversation round to it in five minutes.

So the long days of May and June were spent either in the classroom or on the cricket field. Actually the

policies of Oakley Hall, which had once belonged to
the white Rajah Brooke of Sarawak, were full of birds.
Even on my first dismal day I managed to see a song
thrush on its nest and my diary records a few others,
including young starlings audible from inside the
school chapel. By 13 May, which I called a 'red letter
day', I had recovered enough spirit to form a 'nesting
gang', thus trying to carry on Pa's Bedford traditions
in my confined space. We did not find many nests, but
on the 22nd came the 'great news' of the grasshopper
warblers at Aldershot. My parents, perhaps unwisely,
came down for half-term, which coincided with my
eleventh birthday. At the end of their visit my diary
comments 'only 5 weeks and 4 days more to the holidays'.

The diary is interspersed with the imaginary
histories to which I was much addicted and to 'dab
cricket' matches, but there is one double spread of the
nests of British birds which surprises me by its exe-
cution. Very few bird artists have been able to draw
nests which are remotely credible, yet William Henry
Hunt showed many years ago by his 'Bird's nest and
Apple Blossom', a reproduction of which I keep by my
desk since a thoughtful daughter found it for me, that it
is perfectly possible to paint even the relatively complex cup nest of the dunnock.

My diary for the last weeks of that interminable
summer term contains two observations not concerned with nests: 'the woodpigeon's cry does not
seem to have gone off since the first night of term' – it
called from the beeches across the road long after our
early bed-time – and 'swifts came out after the disturbed flies', when a thunder-storm (I was extremely
frightened of storms until the air raids of the 1939–45
war put them in perspective) had cleared.

At last came 26 July. After a day in London with my

devoted Aunt Kitty Brockman, who had lifted me up to my first blackbird's nest at Shawford in 1919, I left King's Cross, on my own for the first time, by the night train for Fort William and freedom.

Although I knew that, apart from a few late tern nests, the breeding season, my main period of interest, was over even in the West Highlands, this may be the point at which to enquire how well equipped I was to identify birds. I have already mentioned that 'Coward' was our field guide. But my father had also percipiently bought Archibald Thorburn's four volumes of *British Birds* as they came out in 1915–16. As the plates in 'Coward' were reproduced from Lord Lilford's *Coloured Figures of the Birds of the British Isles*, many of which were painted by Thorburn, I can be said to have learned my birds the Thorburn way. Joseph Wolf has his champions (the plate of the red-footed falcon in 'Coward' is signed 'A. T. after J. Wolf') but Thorburn was the first realistic painter of British birds to reach a wide public and it is arguable that the majority of ornithologists see their birds through Thorburn's eyes and that many of the artists and illustrators who have succeeded him have been profoundly influenced by his approach.

Thorburn's birds (incidentally the title of James Fisher's one-volume revision in smaller format of the 1915–16 books) look alive, their plumage seems soft yet serviceable. The contrast is well brought out in 'Coward', in which the other main artist was J. G. Keulemans, whose birds appear to be cut out of wood, although their colours are perfectly correct.

Yet Thorburn was primarily an artist and not an ornithologist, which makes his success all the more remarkable. The text of his great work is ridiculously meagre and with dimorphic species he unashamedly preferred the more colourful male. His hen blackbird peers apprehensively over the back of the ebony ouzel-cock, and he does not even show the hen chaffinch (or linnet or siskin for that matter). My father used to complain that his birds were out of proportion to the backgrounds but I do not agree; I find the flowers that surround many of them very attractive. It is noticeable, however, how Thorburn avoids depicting nests; in the whole of his *British Birds* I think you will find only two.

The first bird I recall identifying from my knowledge of his plates was the goldfinch, by no means common in my youth, when I saw a party on Shawford Downs. Then there was the great spotted woodpecker on a birch tree and the cock bullfinch, both in my grandparents' garden. These three were colourful subjects after Thorburn's heart. He loved the nominative case, the adult male; not for him the accusative, genitive, dative and ablative: the females, juveniles and immatures with which the illustrators of modern field guides strive to make us familiar.

Nevertheless, I do not regret being a child of the Thorburn era; my golden eagle is forever planing down the hillside, its talons clutching a mountain hare, and my rock pipit stands up against flowering thrift on a ledge partly orange with *Xanthoria* lichen.

Of course, even granted the excellence of Thorburn's paintings as a grounding in British bird identification, they were no help in recognizing the voices on which so much depends in the field. For this we had to rely on Coward. He used descriptions and verbal renderings of songs and calls, which was the best that could be done before the arrival of disc and then tape-recording. Being both unmusical and unmechanical I have been comparatively happy with the verbal system even when it leads to phrases like 'a simple *see, see, see, sissy-pee*' for the song of the treecreeper. I chose this example from Coward because my father maintained that treecreepers sang very little. I believe he got this idea from W. Warde Fowler, the Oxford don whose books appeared during his boyhood and who is said to have been slightly deaf. This shows how important the dictum of an 'authority' can be; Pa, though as lacking in musical sense as his son, had an excellent aural memory for songs and calls, and passed on as much as he could to me. So, in spite of all modern developments, I still think that there's no substitute for a knowledgeable companion in the field to help you learn what are now called bird vocalizations.

3
The Sea Loch

The end of Chapter 1 left my nine-year-old self at midsummer on the shores of Loch Teacuis, about to enjoy nearly eleven weeks of a notably fine summer and incidentally the second longest continuous period that I have ever succeeded in spending in the West Highlands.

Loch Teacuis, by way of kyles on either side of the large hilly island of Carna, is joined to Loch Sunart, Sweyn's Fjord, one of the longest of the sea lochs that snake inland into the backbone of the West Highlands. They are agreed to be drowned valleys of an ancient river system which drained before the ice ages into a great river flowing along the floor of what is now the Minch.

When I first became aware of the sea loch as something different from shores elsewhere, it was the tawny stretch of seaweeds between the tide-lines that impressed me. Ecology was then a word unknown, but I realized, as I slithered over the rocks, that there were several kinds of weed and that they grew in regular zones parallel to the water. It was years before I knew any names for the little tassels of channelled wrack, which spend more than half their life dry among a thinnish rash of barnacles and mingle at their upper limit with lichens and the lowest tufts of thrift and sea plantain in the rock crevices. Below the channelled wrack lie the larger flat wrack and bladder wrack, then the wide band of knotted wrack, marching with the thin but innocuous blades of serrated wrack, which appear only at low tide, above the heaving kelp or *Laminaria*, the 'tangle o' the Isles'.

At half tide and higher the strands of knotted wrack float upwards, buoyed by bladders which it is difficult to pop. Between the hold-fasts of each plant little fish – cuddies, codling, pink and gold poor-cod and razor-toothed ballan wrasse – nose their way over the pebbles or the boulders. At low tide the wrack zone is the place for big periwinkles, so characteristic of the loch shore that Ossian called it *Traigh na faoch*, 'strand of the winkles'. Under the weed-covered stones is a teeming life: sea anemones, sea urchins, starfish, mussels, small eels, spotted gunnels or butterfish, cobbler fish, shore crabs and hermit crabs. Some of the same creatures live in the rock pools with their pink coralline wall-coatings; here blennies, gobies and tiny flatfish hide in the shell debris on the bottom, translucent prawns dart over them and occasional larger fish are trapped between two tides. The higher brackish pools, often clogged with green flocculent *Enteromorpha*, are the home of the three-spined stickleback and of swarms of shore-skippers. Other pools look rusty-brown with rotting seaweed and seem lifeless. My brother Niall points out that, apparently confined to the mid-West Highland coast, is a benign and unrecorded version of these 'dead' pools, usually backed by a peat bank: here are toads, palmate newts, whirligig beetles and the skating water-bug *Gerris*. When the toads are not there, you may find their tadpoles.

Most of this richness was to be found immediately in front of the schoolhouse at Kinlochteacuis, which faced north-west towards Ben Hiant, the fairy hill, in Ardnamurchan. Between the house and the almost flat, weed-covered shore, through which a small burn wove its braided way to the loch, were 'saltings' mainly of sheep-cropped thrift, divided by muddy channels over which I enjoyed trying to jump. The head of the loch attracted various birds which we could watch at ease from the front window. Here a duck red-breasted merganser brought her brood, soon reduced from eight to three by predators, and here, after their breeding season, I saw my first redshank and greenshank.

The nests of the sea loch birds are found mainly in the vegetation caps of the islands or on low rocky headlands which alternate with shingly, muddy and weed-covered or occasionally sandy beaches. We wasted no time that first evening. 'After supper', wrote my father, 'nested down Barr side of loch; found meadow pipit 5 eggs, saw several pairs of sandpipers.' The pipit was in heathery ground on a headland, pressing close to the narrow zone of the rock pipit, a bird we did not seem to notice much on this visit. It must have seemed small beer compared to the spectacular and noisy oystercatchers. These, with the mergansers, are to me the essential sea loch birds, though I have met both of them since in many other habitats.

It was nearly a week, however, before we were able to use Ronald Gillies's boat, propelled by formidable 'sweeps' for which we substituted lighter oars in due course. On this trip we landed on the headlands and little islands of Loch Teacuis and I saw my first nests of oystercatchers, common gulls and what Pa then called common terns. We got as far as Barr beach, of sand and fine shingle, and I am pretty certain he let me go ahead and find our first ringed plover's nest, the splendid camouflage of the four eggs undone by their symmetrical point-to-point arrangement which catches at least the human eye. Even if I was allowed this little triumph, I had two or three days before I spotted a sandpiper getting up from the edge of a field at Kinloch and Pa had gone back later and found the nest, a first for him too.

Using not very effective binoculars, we swithered about in our identification of the terns between common and arctic, their eggs being in most people's view indistinguishable. Eventually we decided that both species nested on the Loch Sunart islands. The maps in *The Atlas of Breeding Birds of Britain and Ireland*, based on field work in 1968–72, show far more 'proved breeding' dots locally for the common tern; there are only two for arctic, one covering Loch Teacuis and the other the upper part of Loch Sunart; some of these dots derive from my own observations. I have also looked through the bulging box file labelled North Argyll, which contains notes kindly sent me over many years by visitors to the area. Some are cautious and do not commit themselves; the majority plump for common tern but, terns being capricious creatures, I think it is quite likely that one species may replace the other in succeeding years and fairly certain that both may be found on the same island in the same season, though in May there can be confusion with birds on passage.

Recently new criteria for distinguishing this difficult duo have been published, but I have not had a chance since these pronouncements to visit Loch Sunart and make a fresh personal assessment. In theory quite enough points of difference have now been described to enable a competent observer to decide on the species in breeding plumage; in practice, under the weather often obtaining in Argyll and if, in addition, you are bobbing about in a small boat, it is surprisingly hard to come down on one side or the other.

Here perhaps is a good point at which to introduce J. J. Dalgleish, the friend of W. H. Hudson and for many years tenant of the Ardnamurchan estate. He published a 'List of the birds which have been observed in the district of Ardnamurchan, Argyllshire' in the Proceedings of the Natural History Society of Glasgow in 1877 and added further notes in 1896. We are therefore luckier than most Highland districts in having records going back well over a century, but on the terns he was not to be drawn; of each he writes, 'Visits Loch Sunart but in sadly diminished numbers'.

The only other tern recorded to my knowledge on Sunart was a pair of roseate terns seen at Strontian near the head of the loch in August 1954 by Vernon van Someren. If they had bred, which he was not able to establish, they were miles north of any other British nesting place.

I had almost added common gull to my short list of typical sea loch birds, but it also breeds even more characteristically on the hill lochs. On Loch Sunart solitary pairs may nest or colonies form, usually on a different island to the larger gulls, whose acquaintance we made two days later on a longer row, to Risga. This island bestriding Glenborodale Bay is well known to archaeologists for its cup marked rocks which I have never been able to find.

Risga was then the main stronghold of the lesser black-backed and herring gulls, though on my last visit (in 1971) their numbers seemed much reduced. Whereas there is not much difficulty in telling these two species apart (I do not intend to go into their curious relationship, which keeps several systematists

31

happy), but their eggs, like those of the two terns, are indistinguishable. Over the years we decided that, both on Risga and on Garbh Eilean, their mixed colony higher up Loch Sunart, herring gulls usually nested just above the splash zone or close to exposed outcrops of rock, while 'LBBs' built their equally simple saucers of grass and debris in quite deep cover. On this first visit we made no such distinction and took away sixty eggs, apparently intending to eat some, only to find most of them very well incubated as indeed the date should have warned us.

My mother distinguished herself by finding our first merganser's nest, with thirteen hard-set eggs, still, I think, the family record. On the way home we landed on a smaller, also heather-clad island and to my delight I flushed another merganser off eight fresh eggs. We christened this Merganser Island, the first of a number of namings which add confusion to my diaries; it is really Eilean nan Eildean, 'island of the hinds'. Whether because we had not a sufficiently large-scale map or because we found their Gaelic names too complicated, we bestowed our own commemorative titles. Years later, when we lived in Gwent, we discovered that many fields had original Welsh names, superseded by old English names which might themselves be overlaid by new ones when a new farmer took over. So we were probably only copying a widespread but, to the seeker after accuracy, extremely annoying practice.

'Merganser Island' soon saw us back again for the first of two nights camping; the second was spent on Oronsay, another archaeologically famous island, which encloses the sheltered anchorage of Loch na Droma Buidhe. Although the weather was 'soft' at times, the light rain did not deter Pa from his traditional camping method, which was simply to lay an enormous valise on a bed of cut bracken, and to cook on an open fire which it was a point of honour to light with dead heather and not paper. Actually the rain was less of a trial than 'Monty Midge and his Millions', as we called them, surely the most potent factor operating against tourism in the West Highlands and one on which the glowing brochures are silent. Anyway, Monty broke up our camp effectively and we joined the Newtons of Rahoy for a picnic on Carna before getting a tow from their motor launch most of the way home.

The Rahoy estate is now partly a nature reserve of the Scottish Wildlife Trust and partly an experimental deer farm. In 1921 it was one of the properties of the Newton family, who owned much of north Morvern. A predecessor at Rahoy had been Dr John MacLachlan who, though a Gaelic poet, allowed himself to become involved in the evictions of the nineteenth century, for which, it was said, 'Naething but dockens ever grew on his grave'. Anyone who wants to know more about the social changes in the district should read Philip Gaskell's *Morvern Transformed* (Cambridge University Press, 1968).

On 13 July we took advantage of a 'perfect day with fresh south wind' to make one of our longest rows. After lunching on pillaged Risga, we landed at Glenborodale to see Mr Armstrong, the Ardnamurchan estate factor, about the possibility of renting a cottage. He told us of one at Glenmore, a mile or two to the west, but it evidently did not appeal because Pa rowed on to Sligneach Mhor, most 'oceanic' of the Sunart islets, lying where the loch broadens out towards the Sound of Mull. Here a colony of 'common' terns had eight nests of eggs and we disturbed what was evidently a mallard in flightless eclipse plumage. On the way back we chased a razorbill and its chick, which had probably come from the Treshnish Islands, their nearest breeding station.

We continued our search for a Highland foothold some days later, this time up Loch Sunart, which we crossed, with a strong following wind and the help of my mother's umbrella, to land at the Dunghallain group of islands, where another small tern colony still had six nests of eggs. This group, apart from the crumbled ruins of the dun, is notable for an islet with a climax vegetation of woodrush *Luzula*, a plant found on most vegetation caps and headlands along Loch Sunart, emphasizing the relatively sheltered sea loch habitat. After Dunghallain we had a very hard row with the wind now across our bows and Pa was forced to put into a small bay with a cottage at Tarbert, a mile west of Salen. These were the days of unquestioned Highland hospitality and we were welcomed by Willie Mackay, a retired gamekeeper with a wooden leg, and by his wife who gave us the meal of scones and tea which seems to be eaten at any time of day. But she regretted that she had no accommodation (probably her longest word in English) and so we spent two nights at the Salen hotel. In the afternoon we looked over Alma Cottage, a hundred yards above the head of Salen Bay, a house built by C. D. Rudd, Cecil Rhodes's partner and the previous owner of Ard-namurchan, for the captain of his yacht, which he kept in the bay. The decision to take it was made and we celebrated with another meal at the Mackays. Willie knew a good deal about the local birds and some years afterwards I found two clutches of eggs taken by him, probably for J. J. Dalgleish, in the Cotton collection at Winchester. He was also the local piper for dances, at which he would be suitably refreshed but latterly complained of modern proprietary whiskies that 'there wasna a headache in a bottle of it'.

Our return journey to Loch Teacuis was described by my father as a 'hard and risky row'; he and my mother each took an oar, while I crouched, chilled and wet (as on so many occasions when too small to row) in the stern. The crossing from Dunghallain to the Morvern shore was the worst stretch but, once we were sheltered, the wind dropped to a dead calm and we made a fire, without which my parents did not regard an outdoor meal as complete, on the shore at Carna, after getting milk from another family of Mackays who still worked a croft on the island. We rowed home fishing, slowly and somewhat euphorically, as Pa recorded seeing a 'smew' (probably a juvenile black guillemot, of whose presence on the loch we were then unaware) and 'three carrion crows', a most unlikely sight on Morvern in 1921; they may have been wandering rooks.

This hazardous trip was one of the most important in my life, for it gave us a base in Argyll for the next thirty-four years. I can only finish the story of that magical summer by recalling another *al fresco* meal on Carna, this time with Ronald Gillies himself. After it we fell in with several cauldrons of silver fry, attacked from below by mackerel and saithe and from above by 'swarms of gulls', on the edge of which we saw at least two arctic skuas, showing both light and dark colour phases, and the first we had seen of these rakish – no bird writer can resist the adjective – pirates. They probably came from Coll, their nearest breeding place, as did the four I saw years later flying down the Sound of Iona, just like a line of rugby three-quarters in training.

We got home at midnight in the mild midsummer glim with fifty-three fish, forty-six of them mackerel, having seen, more vividly than any textbook could describe it, a predator-prey relationship in violent action.

The sea loch during our first summer holidays at

Salen in 1922 and 1923 was mainly the scene of fishing exploits, with very casual bird observations. Pa and I did succeed in getting ourselves capsized when being towed by a motor launch in August 1922; fortunately by then I had learned to swim and our loss was mainly of fishing tackle, for we were intending to visit the Morvern lochs and burns that we had found rewarding in 1921. My first Easter holidays at Skipper's Cottage, as we had renamed the house, were in 1924 and about this time we formed SCAN, the Skipper's Cottage Amalgamated Naturalists, which held meetings at irregular intervals up to 1929, and had a nominal existence for many years afterwards. Pa was president, I was hon. secretary and kept the minutes, my mother was culinary expert and friends and relations floated in and out of various grades of membership; chief of these was Freddie Webster, my father's ward, who was at school in England but whose home was the Argentine. Brother Niall, born at Salen in 1924, formed the Junior SCAN. I think SCAN was one way in which Pa sought to rationalize our collection of birds' eggs and skins and later of butterflies and moths.

The justification for taking whole clutches of eggs is that the robbed bird normally lays again, sometimes even a bigger clutch, and at a time – the lapwing is often given as an example, by gourmets rather than collectors – when it stands a better chance of raising a brood. But some large birds, like the golden eagle, seldom lay again and for many species the eggs must be fresh or only lightly incubated if a replacement is to follow. No one has produced any serious scientific reasons for 'oology' though old collections did unexpectedly provide a useful comparison when the effect of ingested residues of toxic chemicals on shell-thickness was being studied, an outcome the original 'eggers' can hardly have foreseen.

If egg collections have any appeal, except as trophies like the heads of big game, it is aesthetic. As T. A. Coward put it: 'It is seldom that a clutch of eggs is unattractive.' Today photography, by presenting the nest in situ and the eggs in colours that do not fade, is a far more effective means of recording them. I can only write in extenuation of our collecting and shooting of small birds that it was something that my father and his friends accepted as boys and that SCAN did have rules which we tried to keep. Every specimen must be recorded with full data. There were certain rare birds we regarded as tabu and others of which we were content with a single clutch; we also tried not to take hard-set eggs. Later there were areas at Salen which we regarded as 'sanctuaries'. At our worst we did not take more than one clutch in four or five of what we called 'non-noxious' species; on gulls and the crow family I admit we let ourselves go.

All this is by way of introduction to the season of 1924 when we had just acquired our own new locally built dinghy, inevitably called *Merganser*,* though our first expedition connected with the sea loch was in fact by road on 22 April when we walked five miles east to locate a heronry of which we had been told. This was on the west-facing headland of Rudha an Daimh, which for many years we called Rookheronry, because on this first visit both species occupied the Scots pines; by 1928 the rooks had gone, perhaps to the much larger colony at Strontian. By 22 April one heron's nest at least had large young whose constant clacking I likened to 'an electric saw'. There was a strong wind blowing up the loch and Pa, after scaling one tree with

---

* Niall reminds me that this was Hugh Connell's first (clinker-built, larch) boat, made as a journeyman at £1 a foot and £1 for the oars. Niall's *Merganser II* was his last boat; it was powered by a 'Seagull' engine.

an old nest, could not manage the slender one he chose next. But the following day *Merganser* went on her first long voyage. Freddie shared the rowing with my father and we made our first landing on Garbh Eilean, the island closest to Rudha an Daimh, and on which we found two rock pipits and many common gulls building.

The slender tree yielded its three chalky-blue eggs to Pa's second assault, with climbing irons. In 1925 Freddie got up a tree, as did Bill Smythies, my one friend from Oakley Hall days, now distinguished both as author of the standard works on the birds of Burma and of Borneo and as a leading authority on the flora of south-western Europe. I finally mastered a tree in 1928, and in 1929, the first year of the Scottish heronry census, made a complete count, poking my head Alice-like above the canopy of pine needles to look into the great shallow nests, added to year by year, with their lining of birch twigs and bracken. Margaret, then my fiancée, climbed two trees without using irons in 1937, much to my father's surprise.

A completely contrasting heronry was that on Eilean nan Eildean. This we did not find until 1929, hidden in a grove of large, contorted sallow trees which Arthur Rackham might have designed. The deceptively large island has quite a hinterland, with ruined buildings; willow warblers sing and I have even seen a long-tailed tit on it. On Eilean Mor, west of Glenborodale, it was possible to look down into the few herons' nests, which were in trees below the out-cropping rock. Over the years 'Rookheronry' declined, not recovering from the 1963 winter, while the herons down the loch had consolidated by 1971 into a rectangular block of conifers on the sheltered side of Carna, planted some time in my boyhood but now mature. The largest heronry I found in 1929 was on Loch Moidart's conifer-clad Riska, to visit which Dr Macdonald Macvicar provided me with a boat, his Angus as oarsman and invited me to lunch. After an hour's stumbling over fallen trunks and boulders, I arrived at a total of twenty-eight occupied nests, which my host assured me must be an exaggeration since he had never, from his house about half a mile away, seen more than fourteen birds over Riska. As he was a world authority on liverworts and I was a schoolboy, his figure was, as Bottom would have put it, preferred.

In 1951–3 my brother Niall and I ringed a dozen young herons at Rudha an Daimh and Eilean nan Eildean, but my only recovery is one of twenty young, ringed with Emlyn Evans's help on a blazing June afternoon in 1967 at the island heronry in flowering rhododendrons on Loch Druidibeg in South Uist. It is relevant here because its remains were found nearly two years later by Loch Sunart, probably within a couple of miles of Rudha an Daimh.

A sea loch bird which escaped us entirely in 1921 was the eider. Where the ducks had taken their broods I do not know, but we were soon made aware in April 1924 of the crooning parties of drakes wooing their ducks close to Salen. We found our first nest on Garbh Eilean on 8 May, the flushed bird depositing her odorous faeces over the eggs as she left. It has been argued that this is a protective adaptation, rather than an involuntary action which also lightens the flying bird. On 22 May we found seven nests on the heathery islets joined to Risga at low tide and in succeeding years we have found nests on headlands and, since the coming of the Forestry Commission, in young plantations close to the shore. Other regular sea loch ducks are the mallard and the shelduck, which is scarce and whose breeding on Sunart we only proved in 1969. Actually the eider, though now so numerous, is the newcomer, starting to breed in the last years of the nineteenth century.

We did not find black guillemots nesting on Sunart until 1926, when there was a large young one under a boulder on a small island. As Pa extended his hand to me in mutual congratulation, the chick came in on the act and nipped his finger. There was a nest under the same boulder forty-two years later, but this is a species which has declined locally, though *Atlas* gives it two big dots on Loch Sunart.

One of the charms of the sea loch is the juxtaposition of the marine habitat, where the black guillemot nests a few yards from a favourite hauling out spot of the common seal, and the scrubwoods of birch and oak whose branches just clear the splash zone. Often common sandpipers nest some yards inside the woodland, darting out over the rocks when disturbed. We called them *eedle-odles* from the spring song of the males as they chased prospective mates round Salen Bay. Rock pipits also nested close to the village; in 1924 a meadow pipit built a nest in what must have been a desirable site on a steep bank because a pied wagtail dispossessed it and next year a rock pipit took over. This was close to where we moored *Merganser* and the squeaky chant of the birds became associated over the years with the start of expeditions to 'the islands'.

If Sunart be accepted as a typical sea loch, I think I have covered the principal birds which make up its characteristic breeding community, except for the great black-backed gulls, of which we found only single pairs, usually building their large nests on the summit of an island, as though they scorned concealment and wanted to show their position literally on top of the pyramid of lesser breeds.

If large islands are included, there is a case for adding

raven, buzzard and certainly hooded crow, which has
nested on Garbh Eilean and close to the herons on
Eilean nan Eildean. Of small passerines I have already
mentioned the willow warbler; several others might
stake a claim, especially pied wagtail, song thrush and
twite, which I have watched in the heather on Risga.
Once I put a barn owl out of the rocks of Garbh Eilean
and watched it fly the gauntlet of the gulls; there was
also a roost close to the shore of Dunghallain. But *Atlas*
shows no sign of it in 1968–72.

The list of non-breeding visitors to the sea loch
could be a long one. Red-throated divers fish there for
their young hatched by some remote hill lochan. The
great northern is a winter visitor, gradually changing
into spring splendour. In April 1954, the year I persuaded Niko Tinbergen and Uli Weidmann to look at
the common gulls on one of Sunart's 'dry islands',
there was a magnificent great northern in Salen Bay.
Early on the 6th I watched it circle high above the bay
three times anti-clockwise, then dive down to the
water again, and supposed it was nerving itself for a
migratory flight.

We saw our first two Slavonian grebes in full breeding plumage on 10 April 1925, about two miles west of
Salen; this was a bird then verging on the fabulous.
Later we found both they and little grebes wintered
regularly. Black-headed gulls (scarce breeders locally
on hill lochs), cormorants and, much more frequently,
shags are to be seen, the shags having a perching place
on Carna where for years we hoped to find a nest.
Gannets, kittiwakes, razorbills, guillemots, occasionally puffins and Manx shearwaters come some way up
Sunart. Among the ducks wigeon used to be regular
visitors, perhaps still are, outside the breeding season;
teal may nest occasionally and on 25 September 1930
John Duncan and I saw a duck scaup with three young

ones near the head of the loch: where had they been hatched? There is very little wader passage to be seen: redshanks (which now nest, according to *Atlas*), occasional greenshanks, more rarely turnstones and even a purple sandpiper at Salen which became the first victim of the .22 rifle I had been given for Christmas 1927.

Much of this chapter has been written in the past tense, recalling a time when it was rare to see another small boat on the loch, rarer still not to recognize its crew. Now, with the advent of the boat-trailer, the little islands are no longer undisturbed; they are all quite near the shore along which the road runs, and what is more eye-catching or attractive than a column of gulls or terns over one of them? No particularly rare birds are at stake on Loch Sunart, but is it only a question of time before the unwitting interference that has driven breeding oystercatchers and ringed plovers from the Cornish mainland becomes equally oppressive along the West Highland coast?

If these seem crocodile tears in the light of our own raids, we at least did work for them by foot or by oar. Pa would never have an outboard engine on *Merganser* and, as late as July 1937, Margaret and I rowed from Salen to the vitrified fort near Rahoy and back round the outside of Carna; with liberal stops it took us about twelve hours, but must have been the best part of twenty miles. As a last tribute to the age of the oar, Emlyn Evans and I in May 1968 rowed from Salen to Glas Eilean off Laudale and back. On the island, which is surrounded by tide races, we had glimpses of a foxy red vole among the riot of wild hyacinths and gulls' nests. The sea loch still has its secrets.

4
North Argyll: the First Spring

In the Highlands, until the quite recent massive conifer afforestation programme, pretty well everything away from the vicinity of the lochs and rivers, with their margins of cultivation and scrub woods, could be called 'The Hill', a vast arena of adventure, mainly peat-covered, strongly contoured, studded with lochs of all sizes and dominated by frequent outcroppings of usually ancient rocks.

The special features of the part of the West Highlands that I know best are, apart from the sea lochs, the great mosses, one now a national nature reserve, at the western end of Loch Shiel and around Kentra Bay, the basalt caps of the hills of Morvern, and the majestic peak of Ben Resipol, straddling between Shiel and Sunart and surveying the whole wild domain. Scrub woodland of oak and birch is still quite extensive along the loch sides and, though I did not realize it as a boy wandering through them in search of hoodie crows'

43

nests, the woods along the north side of Loch Sunart are especially rich in mosses and lichens, attesting to their freedom from pollution: a large part is now a Grade 1 site in the Nature Conservancy Council's classification.

Anticipating the plantations of the Forestry Commission was a fine wood of European larch stretching almost all the seven miles from Salen to Glenborodale. Felling began in the First World War and continued into our time at Salen, so that my early memories are of cleared hillsides to the west and of scrub woods behind our cottage ('all round us like a football crowd', my father used to say) and then along most of the ten miles to Strontian near the head of the loch.

Although there were once three or four crofts, there is practically no flat ground in Salen, which in modern terms is a service centre, having doctor, policeman (during our time), post office, store and (up to 1925) two hotels, as well as a stone pier or jetty and, by our day, the remains of a wooden one visited by tourist steamers before the first war. Salen, in rosy retrospect, seems full of beautifully kept gardens, by 'Grannie' McPherson at the Post Office, by 'Daisy and Dunky' at Tarbert and by Aunt Kitty and my parents at Skipper's Cottage. Both hotels and the doctor's house had tall conifers and thick shrubbery, whence rhododendrons have invaded the whole village hinterland.

The bayhead itself empties for over a hundred yards at low springs and is surrounded by a variety of rock formations of no great height, some becoming islets at high tide. Two fishable burns run into the bay and there are two natural and a system of artificial (Salen once had a bobbin mill) lochans in and above the scrub woods. The whole Salen 'basin' was and, I hope, still is, an excellent mixed habitat for birds. During the years we knew it intimately, it is likely that some fifty-five species, forty of them passerine song birds, bred there and the total list, including visitors to the bay, was well over the hundred.

Some of the nesting birds have been gone for years, like the nightjar whose eggs a fishing friend came on as he walked down one July evening in 1925 from a hill loch, the moorhen, whose old nest with eggshells I found by Lochan Refollan in 1927, and the stonechats which bred in 1924 but doubtfully thereafter. Newcomers are collared doves, chiffchaffs (so often associated with rhododendrons in the north), possibly sedge and garden warbler, and the common gull which I watched back to three eggs on Rudha Bhuailte in May 1971. There are puzzles like the woodpigeon, regularly to be seen but with no occupied nests recorded, and the odd herons' platform in the trees of An Cnap, the eastern bastion of the bay. Salen's claim to fame is that in 1951 a hen pied flycatcher laid an infertile clutch in a nestbox that Pa had put up on one of the 'football crowd' of oaks that had survived his axemanship: the first record for Argyll. The eggs are now in the Royal Scottish Museum, as is a juvenile turtle dove which I shot by the cottage in August 1929; it was acknowledged by James Ritchie who, years later when he was Professor of Zoology at Edinburgh, supervised my Ph.D. thesis.

It must be confessed that shooting of small birds figured largely in my early diaries, at first with catapult, then with .410 gun, .177 air and .22 rifles. As well as such unusual visitors as the turtle dove, the purple sandpiper mentioned in the previous chapter and the crossbills which invaded Salen in July 1927, we pursued the local sparrows and bullfinches, ostensibly because of their depredations on the gardens. There was a harrowing incident in 1925 when I clumsily dispatched a juvenile common gull and reacted violently and tearfully. This must have been awkward for Pa, who was very kind-hearted, yet had been brought up to believe that boys and men must shoot and fish. He succeeded in rehabilitating me, always with the proviso that any bird shot (except sparrows) must either be eaten or skinned as a specimen for the SCAN collection.

Although I have not skinned a bird for years, the ability to do so is useful for an ornithologist to whom accidentally killed birds may be brought. I envied Hugh Elliott a few years ago when I saw the neat job he made of a wryneck, victim of a cat while looking for ants on an Oxfordshire lawn, and I still remember with pride the redpoll, admittedly shot, that I skinned over fifty years ago. But eventually moths got our collection and we did not replace it. At Marlborough my industrious son Robert taught himself to skin from a book and started a taxidermy club, whose ambitions became larger and larger. His dabchick, found dead in the Kennèt, adorned a mantel-shelf for years.

I was always a poor shot and not much more successful as a photographer, though I did get quite a nice portrait by remote control of a cock chaffinch at our bird table. Chaffinches held their own with sparrows at the several village tables and were joined by the usual habituées all over Britain: blackbirds, robins – both 'very aggressive', notes Betty Paterson, who now stocks the Tarbert table when in residence – great, blue and coal tits. Yellowhammers were rather a speciality at Tarbert and I am glad to hear that one still turns up occasionally, because my impression was that they had almost vanished as Salen birds. Dunnocks also regularly visited the tables, which they are shy of doing in some areas. In a cold spell early in 1929 'Dunky' (Miss E. A. Duncan) reported to me a 'plover' at Tarbert and Betty tells me that some summers ago they were visited three times a day by a gull, which 'strutted up and down on the grass, pausing to look in the window very pointedly'. It also jumped up to get bacon rind which her husband Alex hung on a birch tree for the tits. Gulls, of course, are notorious scavengers elsewhere. Away from Salen, Dr Macvicar attracted many chaffinches to feed by his secluded house on Shona Beag, getting some of them hand-tame. On one occasion our admiring group was broken up by an attack from a sparrowhawk, which is a regular bird table visitor one up the food chain. Well into May 1966 Mrs Pern had about thirty chaffinches (mostly cocks, and most probably winter visitors) at food she put out in her garden at Arevegaig. At the other extreme, the only tree sparrow I have ever seen in Argyll appeared on the Skipper's Cottage table on 20 August 1953 with a cock house sparrow. Apparently it had been seen once or twice in June by Ian Holroyd. This was the period when tree sparrows were in a phase of expansion but, as far as I know, it was the first recorded in Ardnamurchan since 1880 when J. J. Dalgleish found about twenty pairs nesting in the old church and in the thatch of cottages at Kilchoan, twenty miles west of Salen.★

In August 1953 and again in early April 1954 I marked with coloured and numbered rings about forty birds caught by means of potter traps on the cottage bird table. Nine out of eleven chaffinches in 1954 were cocks, thus agreeing with the disproportion among Mrs Pern's birds and suggesting that they too were Linnaeus's Scandinavian 'bachelor finches'. But my Salen ringing was too desultory to show anything else,

★ In the late 1930s Niall put an injured greenfinch (from Edinburgh) in a cage on the lawn. It called loudly and a wild bird, very seldom seen at Salen, 'appeared from nowhere'.

except that the scrub wood tits came to feed at the table.

The woods were the home, summer and winter, of the woodcock, which we soon heard and saw roding over the cottage when we arrived in April 1924. I once worked out that we spent about sixteen hours searching for each of our first three nests, in 1924, 1925 and 1928. I have come to the conclusion that the breeding population of the Salen woods was very low because, compared to Oxfordshire oakwoods, the cover was sparse, only dead bracken with no brambles, and should not have been too difficult to search thoroughly. (When some of the woods were enclosed and converted into conifer plantations, brambles appeared, showing that their absence was due to the previous heavy grazing.) In 1924 it took from 2 to 30 April to find our first nest, on An Cnap. We went back the next evening, jubilant after seeing a buzzard's nest across Loch Sunart. 'We found the place,' my diary records, 'but I only saw a broken branch. D. pointed it out: "The bird's just like a piece of wood". "It is a piece of wood," I replied. Then the wood assumed the shape of a bird and I saw it just like a huge moth, sitting motionless.' A woodcock on her nest has now been photographed innumerable times, but remains one of the great sights of British woodland.

The woodcock's nest came only halfway through a somewhat protracted 'Easter' holiday. Somehow I managed to persuade my parents and our doctor, Duncan Fergusson, that May would be much better for me at Salen than at Oakley Hall. There was no weapon – illness, real or imagined, even a coal strike – that I would not use to keep away from school, and my record of returns on time was abysmal.

So the whole of the Merry Month was added to April and by the end of it I had seen sixteen new 'first

nests'. These did not include the golden plover, a real
hill species, of which we only located a single, baffling
bird one afternoon late in May. Pa went back next day
and found the nest, apparently just where we had been
looking. More spectacular but much easier to find was
the red-throated diver. 'Diver Lochan' (I really don't
think it has a Gaelic name), though only about 850 feet
above sea level, was always a hard slog to reach, up a
steep hillside and then over rocky ridges and boggy
hollows. On 3 May, when we located the divers, we
were met by a violent hailstorm, a fit welcome to this
wild countryside. But it was to be what I called a
red-letter day: we had already found a stonechat's nest
with deceptive ease in long heather and now, in a level
stretch of bog with heather tufts standing up on mossy
hummocks, we flushed a duck teal off six eggs,
another first. Although my diary is explicit that we
saw a pair of divers, it does not confirm that we actually reached their lochan. But, three weeks later, on the
afternoon of what had been a wet day, we were
accompanied there by my mother, who plainly
thought we needed a good walk. This was a considerable feat on her part, as Niall was born just four
months later.

As we approached the area where we had seen
divers, the unmistakable cacophony of a colony of
common gulls assailed us and soon we could see their
white forms floating against the dark hillside.

We came down to the lochan to find a red-throated
diver on the water, sticking its slightly *retroussé* bill in
the air. Suddenly a second bird surfaced and we
guessed that it must have submerged at once after
leaving the nest. None of us had ever seen a diver's nest
before but we knew it must be very close to the water
and, while the islets were the best bet, it was worth
making the circuit of the lochan first. This produced

three gulls' nests on little headlands, green from years of enrichment by droppings. Then my father and I waded to the islets over the stony bottom and my mother took a photograph of us in shirt-tails when we returned in triumph, having found seventeen more gulls' nests, a mallard which with the optimism of youth I tried to make into a gadwall, and, just as we had begun to despair, a single long greasy-looking dark brown egg with black spots, in a 'scrape' at the water's edge. Five years later, this time convalescing from German measles, I was at the lochan on 10 May, to see gulls in strength and a pair of divers; later Pa found the nest with two eggs. Then came a long gap of twenty-one years before I was at the lochan again in May, at 5.30 a.m. on the last morning of our 1950 trip. Near it a diver flew over, then a pair spiralled down. When I eased myself over the rocks to view the water, there were four birds on it. One pair soon left, but the remaining male, judged by his stouter neck, uttered the famous wailing cry shared by all the family, then gave a short *gruk* of alarm when he saw me. Both birds began sipping at the water and occasionally flapping their wings, probably distraction displays; they were too aware of me to put on a real show, with a 'plesiosaur race' or a 'snake ceremony'. They dived each time I showed myself and finally flew off. There were only three common gulls about, but I decided to land on the islands, and found to my surprise that, whereas I had waded to them as a boy, I now had to swim several yards, and this has been necessary on each visit since. Of course, we had made no careful examination of the shore line but it all looked much the same, the islets seemed the same size and there was a free-running outflow burn.

There were no nests for my trouble and, on my next visit one June evening two years later, no divers and only a pair of gulls. But ripples on the Lily Lochan (which holds trout) alerted me and I rounded a rock quickly to see an otter dive across the shallow end, visible all the way. It surfaced to look at me, dived again and made off some fifty yards up the lochan, turned for a final look and then disappeared. Although we had often seen their traces on the shores of the sea loch, this was my first good view of a local otter.

Mysteriously fourteen years passed; by my next visit my brother Niall was the authority, I was indeed the émigré. He had decided that Diver Lochan, enriched by the gull colony and attracting both frogs and newts, yet with no suitable ground for spawning, would be the ideal water in which to test his view that, to get heavy trout quickly, they should be at a low density, have good feeding but not be able to spawn. So we carried two plastic bags full of tiny baby trout up that ever-formidable slope and across the rocks and the peat hags. The gulls were back in some numbers – we found nine nests – and there was a pair of divers again. They moved off to Teal Lochan, while we enlarged the alevins into their experimental home, and then followed the birds. One flew off into the north wind, but the other hesitated and had to swim towards us before turning for its take-off 'run'; it only just cleared the north bank. Then came a burst of the quacking flight call as it joined its mate.

Two years later the gulls were in strength, with twenty nests and two small young on the last day of May. The divers were there again but apparently had not laid: there was a large damp scrape at the tip of one islet. This visit was memorable for the discovery of a colony of bog violets close to the lochan, their pale beauty standing out against the brown peat: how had we missed them before? On my last visit there were no divers, few gulls and a deserted duck's nest. But Niall and his son Ronald each landed a fine trout of nearly two pounds, thus vindicating his theory; what is more, they proved to have pink flesh and newts in their stomachs.

Much of our time in 1924 was spent exploring Loch Sunart in *Merganser*, but we did visit Caisteal Tioram, the old Clanranald stronghold where the Shiel enters Loch Moidart. For years a vestigial colony of jackdaws held out on the battlements: one was entering a hole on 29 May 1968. This is a very local bird in north-west Scotland and the nearest colonies we knew in the 1920s were about ten miles from Tioram at Glenhurich, which runs into Loch Shiel, and even farther off in another ruin, Mingary Castle near Kilchoan. There is still work to be done on the distribution of common 'southern' species in the Highlands. The greenfinch is another more or less commensal bird in the north, found in very small numbers in the townships of Ard-namurchan. The twite is in rather a different position: outside the breeding season it is found close to what cultivations there are, and it may nest near them in whin bushes, but it also breeds on 'the Hill'. We found our first and only Ardnamurchan nest on 18 May 1924 when Pa sent me to search the heathery ledges on a rocky outcrop above Acharacle. Out flew a small brown bird which I assumed to be a meadow pipit. But the small nest was lined with wool and the three eggs were of linnet type, one of them a dwarf freak.

On our way home that day we visited a possible sparrowhawk's nest in a glade of birches by Allt an t-Sailean. I got stuck in my attempt to reach it and had to be extricated; Pa then went up and found four eggs. This was our second sparrowhawk that year close to Salen, something that did not occur again. The next day saw another fairly inglorious exploit of mine when we decided, on the way back from a pillage of the gull islands up the loch, to reach the buzzard's nest found on May Day. It was decided that a rope was necessary: the nest was in a favourite West Highland site on the base of an oak tree growing out of a rocky outcrop in a wooded glen. My father stood on top of the minuscule cliff holding the rope to which I was attached below, where my mother stood by to encourage my ascent. As my reluctance for the task grew, her sympathy waned and Pa maintained it was only her threat to stimulate me with a hat-pin that finally sent me scrambling up.

During May the woods come alive, not with a great burst of flowers but with delicate blossoms of primrose, violet, wood anemone and wood sorrel, followed by bluebells. This delicacy is rather due to the heavy grazing already mentioned than to anything climatic: where protected, West Highland primroses are as fine as any and profuse quite early in April. The winter bands of tits have broken up; chaffinches appear to proclaim their territories from spreading oak boughs or lichened birches; and great spotted woodpeckers, a Salen acquisition since about 1935, drum and call. Soon the first of the summer visitors filter in: willow warbler and redstart, tree pipit and wood warbler are the outstanding quartet, with spotted flycatchers along the woodland edge. In 1929 a pair of redstarts arrived at the cottage and subsequently bred in a nest-box outside the garden. But first they treated me to several days' intensive image-fighting, the hen leading. Even though they trapped themselves between the two sections of the old-fashioned window, they would continue the frenzied routine as soon as released. Five years earlier, on 23 April 1924, I had been introduced at Salen to another now well recognized but baffling form of behaviour: 'Saw a pair of starlings eating ants; however it look [*sic*] as though the

ants were eating them, for the cock threw . . . weird
antics . . . as though he had had his neck broken.'
Apart from an unsatisfactory glimpse of a rook, this
remains my only observation of passive anting in
the wild, years before it attracted the attention of
ethologists.

On 19 May 1950 I walked over the hill from Salen to
Loch Laga, making contact with fifty-one birds,
thirty-five of them meadow pipits, in three hours. It
took me only twenty minutes when I reached the road
through the Loch Sunart scrub woods to score a half-
century of contacts. But the volume of scrub-wood
song does not compare with southern woodland
because, though mistle thrushes, robins and wrens
retain their independence, song thrushes and blackbirds are largely commensal in the West Highlands.
Yet even in Salen with all its rhododendron cover you
can pick out the individual blackies: there is not so
much a dawn chorus as a mingling of soloists.

In 1924 we also sampled (in the tentative rather than
the strictly scientific sense) the most difficult local
habitat of all, the mosses of Loch Shiel. Seen from the
top of Resipol, Claish Moss looks like a vast pudding
of peat stirred by giants; if the sun is out, the narrow
ribbons of water have a burnished gleam in contrast to
the dark strips of deerhair sedge and heather. Near
Acharacle, on ground that had probably once been
reasonable grazing, several pairs of lapwings bred,
their nests extremely difficult to see. Farther into the
moss there were mallard, teal, odd pairs of curlew, a
few red grouse, a small pocket of dunlin, and the
ubiquitous meadow pipit. The density of birds must
be extraordinarily low and it seems remarkable that we
found two curlews' nests that first season. Even if you
get a good mark – they usually rise at least a hundred
yards away – you have then to thread your way

through the mosaic of quaking peat and sphagnum-filled pools, keeping your eye the while on the distant mark. Fortunately curlews' nests are large saucers, usually open to the sky, and the sight of four beautifully marked, pear-sized eggs is worth a pair of wet feet.

Although we used rubber boots on the sea loch in winter, changing to bare legs and plimsolls in summer, Pa was a great advocate of leather boots on the hill, in which general category the mosses also fell. But no boot could stand up to a day on Claish and chronically wet feet added to our trials. Not for years, when I found that Pennine shepherds and naval commandos alike used rubber boots, did I have the courage to make the change. Although rubber boots are heavy, the comfort of dry feet is well worth the extra weight. Leather boots were, of course, suitable for tree-climbing with irons. I have only owned one pair of these, inherited from my father. They are short irons, the upright member only reaching above the ankle, not right up the shin as in the type used by post office engineers. The iron continues under the instep to the downward-pointing spike, which fits into the inside of the foot, the whole being secured by leather straps. When the straps decayed, I used football boot-laces and latterly, by wrapping a handkerchief round the ankle, used them with tough shoes, which could be painful but reduced weight.

Climbing irons are valuable when coping with branchless trunks where a long swarm would be exhausting. Unfortunately the technique involves making small jabs in the bark as you progress upwards and these are unpopular on trees of timber value. Also, only the best and fittest climbers can avoid gashing the trunk on the way down, because the foot has to be lifted up and out of the nick, and then lowered carefully to make the next. To avoid this, we often took off the irons on reaching the canopy and came down by swarming, only sliding when exhausted. A rope can be used effectively with irons (see p. 85) and James Manuel and I also used one to pull a slender ivied oak with a buzzard's nest close to a bare tree which was an easy climb and whence I could reach out to the nest.

We usually carried rucksacks or haversacks with camera, notebooks, collecting tins, food, maps, possibly a torch and spare stockings. Our binoculars were old Zeiss 8 × 30 which were light but in my view lacked sufficient magnification. Our clothing varied with the weather and the season: on the sea loch we usually wore shorts but on the Hill, when rock or tree climbing might be involved, breeches or long trousers were the rule. Alas for romance, we did not wear kilts. A shepherd's cromag or a straight hazel stick which we cut ourselves was essential, especially in places like Claish, to test the ground and assist jumps over the pools, to lay over barbed wire, to act as a marker and, in thick cover (rare in Argyll) as a probe. It also had a defensive role against over-attentive dogs or cattle. I have to admit that we did not carry a compass and I cannot recall that we ever needed one. In August 1953 when sons David, then eleven, and Robert (seven) climbed Resipol with us, we found the summit in cloud, so laid a trail of orange skin on our way up, collecting the pieces on our return.

5

DW

North Argyll: the Rolling Years (1925–71)

There could not be another 1924. The Easter holidays of 1925 were largely a repeat performance though this time it was Freddie Webster who spun a convalescence into May and visited the Sunart islands in *Merganser* with Pa. Then came two springs in the south. The summer of 1927 was Freddie's last with us and we celebrated it by rowing up and down Loch Shiel. This was primarily a fishing expedition with a touch of drama thrown in as we were storm-stayed for two nights on our way back to Acharacle. My diary noted 'an extraordinary lack of birds' even in the wooded country round Gaskan where we camped: only robins, wrens, passing tits, grey wagtails on the burns and '10 hoodies – perhaps this explains it'. A cock sparrowhawk and a scavenging juvenile common gull are the only other species mentioned.

By the Christmas holidays I was fifteen and a half and well able to undertake longish days on my own.

What I dramatically called the Great Frost set in, and on 28 December I set out with a packed lunch and the newly repaired family binoculars for Acharacle. Where Loch Shiel narrows into its eponymous river was a party of waterfowl: wigeon and coots, surprisingly both first records for the North Argyll list we had begun compiling in 1921. The local status of the coot remains a mystery; there is certainly no suggestion that it breeds. Nor nowadays does the moorhen, of which I saw two farther down the river. A rap of my stick on ice and some resting duck on a sand bank resolved themselves into a volatile spring of teal; near them was another 'first', a drake tufted duck with what I called his harem. The fifty years that have passed have seen a general increase of 'tufties' as breeding birds, but only odd spring records from North Argyll as we defined it.

Kentra Moss, when I reached it, was not easy going even when frozen, but a lot easier than in its usual state. Its only inhabitant was a wren. Life was concentrated on the bay, where the tide was out, and I drove before me a medley of herring, common and black-headed gulls; curlews and oystercatchers; and hoodie crows and herons.

Where the water began, so did the red-breasted mergansers, already game for a bit of courtship chasing, and a few shags, fishing in the outgoing tide. On a mud bank were seven geese, the only ones I saw all day, driven from their haunts on the moss by the frost. Cautiously I did not give them a species, but have little doubt that they were Greenland whitefronts, a race then undescribed. A greenshank and a redshank, neither of them common winter birds locally, enlivened the scene before I sat down to eat my 'piece' on a dry island near the mouth of the bay.

Crouched in the springy heather I watched the birds

at my and their ease, before retracing my steps over the now deserted sands and working northward along the edge of the moss to Newtown Ardtoe; I then slithered over rocky headlands – where a pair of hoodies nearly flew into me and I dropped the precious field glasses – until I reached the tidal waters of the River Shiel as it enters Loch Moidart.

On the Inverness-shire side stood the grey bulk of Caisteal Tioram on its rock; behind it fir-clad Riska, and Eilean Shona, where Barrie is said to have written much of *Mary Rose*. But I had eyes only for the round pool into which the Shiel pours its offering. Wigeon and teal flew over; and on its waters were mallards and mergansers, a raft of domestic ducks belonging to one of the crofts, and a drake goldeneye with a bevy of red-heads (another new species for our list). Eclipsing them all were nine drake goosanders and a single pair, the first I had ever seen alive.

Brought up on Thorburn, I had often gazed at his magnificent portrait of the drake, emphasizing the pale salmon-pink breast and underparts. Now I was looking at the real thing in an unforgettable setting. The nine bachelors flew off, but the pair stayed on to delight me for several minutes.

After that climax the walk home seemed uneventful. I passed below the vitrified fort of Shielfoot, saw a fellow-clansman miss two tufted ducks on the river with both barrels, cut across the lifeless moss again to the outskirts of Acharacle, raised a lift in the post van for the last two miles (a valued bonus in those car-less days), and was back before the long winter's night descended.

The holidays did not continue on this high note; this time the agent I employed to prolong them was jaundice, which had its disadvantages, and the Great Frost soon reverted to the usual wind and rain. When I did get up and about, the main ploy was shooting with my new rifle at the birds on Loch Sunart, which I do not now find very edifying. But on my return for the Easter holidays on 30 March, our activities took on a new dimension, symbolized by finding our first raven's nest, an easy climb on a crag just behind Salen, our first peregrine's eyrie on a magnificent rock looking west in Moidart, our first pair of ptarmigan on Ben Resipol, and a night at Ardnamurchan Point lighthouse.

Most of our detailed information about migration came in those days from the lighthouse returns of the Eagle Clarke era, so in my young mind the words 'migrants' and 'lighthouses' were so closely associated that I believed where there was a lighthouse, there must be – at the right times – hordes of migrating birds. I easily persuaded my father that it was our plain duty to spend at least a night of vigil at our nearest lighthouse, some thirty miles away. We took advantage of Dr Fergusson's weekly visit to that end of his enormous practice and one exceedingly chilly morning he put us down where the roads to Achosnich and Achnaha divide, in a wilderness of rocky moorland whose acquaintance we had first made on our walking tour of Ardnamurchan in September 1924.

The road was enlivened by what my diary calls 'masses of starlings', by a cheerful postman who looked like Garibaldi (we had just been doing him at school) and by a snow shower so fierce that we had to take cover behind a rock. Eventually we reached Achosnich, caught up the local carrier who had brought on our packs, and met the lighthouse keeper. He told us that we would be welcome to spend the night below the light but couldn't come inside it without a permit, which had not entered into my sketchy preparations for the trip.

We accompanied him along the rocky road to the light. At the last farm we parted, to search the wild country north of the lighthouse. Tree growth was reduced to a tight scrub of hazel and sallow cowering against the windswept hillsides, but in sheltered corners we found a surprising concourse of small birds feeding: song thrushes, blackbirds, robins, yellowhammers, dunnocks, and wheatears which had recently arrived in strength. Pheasants, relics of the estate's great days, still held out in this bleak habitat. On a bog near the farm, lapwings flew up, but we pushed on to the coast where we found a raven nesting high on a dark north-facing crag, with shags flying in and out below.

Going back to the farm where we had left our packs, we looked round the lapwings' bog more thoroughly and found two nests with eggs, not on tussocks in the bog itself, but in patches of dead bracken in what had been cultivated land just above it. I have never seen lapwings' nests since in quite that sort of site.

But our observations were interrupted. We had been aware of several cows and calves on the bog close to us. Now a flaysome noise made us aware of their lord and master in a commanding position on the bank just above us. My father started running down the little valley; at his yelled orders I ran up the opposite bank. With the optimism of youth I had covered myself in binoculars, cameras and a singularly cumbrous tripod on a strap. In the moment of panic these inanimate objects took on a life of their own and seemed to fly into obstructive pieces around my flapping knees. Clutching them to me, I staggered to the top of the bank and saw that the bull, having ambled down to his herd, was taking no more notice of us.

Circuitously I joined my father, we collected our packs and made our way – with a good many glances over the shoulder – to the lighthouse whose outer walls, I was delighted to note, were strong enough to hold out an elephant.

'A fine tea followed', says my diary, but the hospitable lighthouse keeper was not very encouraging about the chance of seeing migrating birds. Indeed, allowing for his Highland courtesy, his report could be read as negative. I refused to be discouraged; about 10 p.m. 'we heard a bird call' outside his cottage and began our watch in the lee of the lighthouse doorway. I can't remember now quite what I had expected would happen but certainly not the interminable chill hours that followed, with the sea slapping at the low rocks of the headland and the north wind moaning round the cone of the lighthouse. Then, at last, I heard it – a quiet, screeping call somewhere behind us. I went round the doorway into the wind: nothing to be seen. Back to our slightly more sheltered stance and again the mysterious call. It must have happened four or five times before we tracked it down to the flap of my father's raincoat beating against the rough granite blocks of the lighthouse. Later in the long night we took half-hour spells on duty each; at the end of one of them my expectations rose once more; but the whistle was only Pa's intimation that my time was mercifully up.

When pale dawn broke, the actual birds heard were only the oystercatchers and gulls on the rocks and 'alleged geese'. Soon after 5 a.m., warmed by a last cup of tea from the lighthouse keeper, we gave it up and started on our long journey home. We eluded the bull successfully and reached Kilchoan at the hungry hour of 7.30 a.m. Although I should by then have known my touch was out, I glibly assured my father that a private hotel had recently been opened in the village. So we walked up to the substantial house, were received with the customary politeness and asked for breakfast. During the excellent meal of eggs and black pudding it was borne in upon us that my information was more than premature and that we were, in fact, in a private house. Fortunately our host did have a car for hire, so my father hastily booked it to help us on our way and save face a little. I was too young and far too embarrassed to study the superbly discreet way in which our host carried off the situation.

In conjunction with increasing activity in the field, my diary for 1928 became more elaborate, with marginal illustrations, passed through a laconic, note-form phase in 1929, expanded again in 1930. Another parameter was indicated by the number of hoodies' nests found: from one in 1925 to three in 1928, eleven in 1929 and seventeen with eggs in 1930. Since nests are usually well separated, these totals represent a fair mileage covered. In the summer holidays of 1928, pursuing the idea of a career in forestry which then seemed the only domestic avenue for a field naturalist, I got to know William Anderson, the Commission's first forester at Glenhurich, reached by steamer up Loch Shiel to Polloch pier. This led to frequent visits in 1929 and 1930. I saw for myself the fillip that the early stages of conifer afforestation can give to birds as different as the kestrel (I climbed to my first nest, with a beautiful clutch of six, in a crevice above Polloch) and stonechats.

Having tracked the rooks to a clump of tall spruces at Strontian, we raided them in 1929, 1930 and 1931, amassing a good deal of data which, I am afraid, being several years before the nest record scheme of the British Trust for Ornithology started, has not been available to ornithologists in general. We also counted the heronry at Rudha an Daimh, usually with most of the nest contents, and these data went to the Scottish heronry census, for which I was supposed to cover our area when it began in 1929.

Since most of our Easter holiday discoveries were concerned with large species, because they are the early nesters in the Highlands, it is nice to have one exception: the long-tailed tit, which may be found building from the end of March. We found one nest of young in 1924 in the fork of a birch tree. On 31 March 1928 we watched a pair each take a feather to a very well hidden nest in another birch. Two days later one was moulding the start of a nest high in the fork of an oak; the same day my father found a nearly complete nest in what would be regarded as a normal southern site, seven feet up in a beech hedge. Subsequently we found two more high in birches and realized that this was the usual local site to which the lichened exterior of the nest seems ideally adapted. Years later David and Elizabeth Lack found that both high and low sites were used by long-tailed tits in the Wytham estate near Oxford, and that the same birds might switch from one type of site to the other after nest failure. Although the nest is often conspicuous in brambles and blackthorn, it must derive some protective benefit from their thorns, in contrast to the camouflage of a tree-fork site.

After I returned to school in May 1929, Pa fed me with letters full of bird news. He had a very good season, finding young ptarmigan on Resipol, and young dunlin on Kentra Moss, successes never since repeated. It must have been a great effort for him to sit down and write a long letter to me after a hard day on the Hill or sea loch. I am afraid I was always urging him to revisit places where I had earlier located birds, or to break new ground: only with the years do I realize how grateful I should have been to him.

Also in 1929 John Cameron, one of the Ardnamurchan gamekeepers, showed me my first occupied eagle's eyrie. Ten years later the same inland crag was in use and Eric Hosking immortalized the nest and birds from a robust wooden hide, still visible after the war. We found an eyrie for ourselves at the end of April 1930 and had a magnificent view of the bird sweeping off the nest just below us. This was a fitting end to my boyhood apprenticeship in North Argyll. Earlier in the holidays John Pringle and I had visited the ravens of Carna, and had taken a clutch of five from quite a difficult rock in Glenhurich, one of our first rope descents. 'What a dose, man!' cried one of the remaining non-forestry inhabitants when we told him of our success.

A fairly short visit to Salen in September 1930 brought me for the first time into touch with H. F. (Harry) Witherby, the colossus of British ornithology, founder and editor of *British Birds* journal, chief editor of the two-volume *Practical Handbook* and subsequently of the five-volume *Handbook*. On 20 September 'a large brown hawk', which we dismissed as a buzzard, sailed west to east across the bay. That evening it was circling over the loch and I was struck by 'its elongated appearance both in body and wings' and realized that it could be an osprey. I followed it, with inadequate hastily borrowed glasses, up to its perch on a dying oak but could only establish that it had 'bare feet [*sic*] and a pale head'. It flew off and then (how casually I noted it) a peregrine flew across. More inconclusive observations next day, but on the 22nd I found the bird 'hovering quite beautifully below Boghill, motionless and its tail down'; a buzzard flew by to give a comparison and later I saw it hovering several times, once violently pursued by two kestrels. The last report was from 'Dunky', that it had made a bad landing on the shore at Tarbert.

I reported my observations to Witherby and, although I cannot now find the correspondence, I remember that he turned the record down on insufficient evidence. But a short while later he wrote again to say that so many more records had come in, all about the same date, that he was now ready to accept mine, and it duly appeared, my first 'scientific' publication, in the November 1930 number of the journal (an indication incidentally of the speedy turn-round of material in those days). The odd feature of my observations, of course, is the hovering over land. Ospreys hover over water when hunting and, George Waterston tells me, over land in spring when picking up nest material. But he considers autumn hovering to be quite exceptional. On the other hand the rough-legged buzzard regularly hovers, but would be ruled out if my noting 'bare feet' embraces the legs and is valid. Most of these ospreys were probably young birds and this makes slightly aberrant behaviour a bit more likely. The whole incident, apart from the light it sheds on 'H.F.W's' criteria, is an instructive example of the difficulties we experienced fifty years ago in making what would now be a routine identification.

After 1930, spring visits were much shorter and I usually relied on some sort of transport provided by long-suffering friends. In 1931 Tony Legard and Bernard Keeling at least saw a clutch of three eagle's eggs for their trouble and we located a 'new' raven site in the basalt west of Loch Teacuis. John Pringle and I celebrated my Finals in March 1933 by finding the eagle again and seven ravens' nests (reaching six of them). Sometimes we had help in our descents, more usually we let each other down (John doing all the hard ones) and hoped for the best. Actually, with a guide rope attached to a crowbar at the top, a doubled body rope held by a firmly seated companion, and remembering that none of the descents we attempted were more than fifty or sixty feet, we were not taking undue risks. In 1934 Archie Macpherson and I penetrated farther up Glenhurich than before and he did a tricky descent to a new raven site, releasing half the doubled rope after he had passed the nest. We now knew at least fourteen raven sites used over the past five years in Ardnamurchan, Sunart and north Morvern; I wonder what the full total was and how many it is today.

My next spring visit was in April 1937 when I introduced Margaret to North Argyll. A day which involved scrambling up the rocky, precipitous western side of Carna put her firmly against my wild idea of buying the island. Swinging the other way, Niall and I then showed her the easiest eagle's eyrie I have ever found. This decided her that there was nothing much to field ornithology, an astringent attitude which is of inestimable value in her appraisals of my work. She has, in fact, absorbed a surprising amount of knowledge over the years without letting on: but an unquestioning yes-woman would have been intolerable as a wife.

The war made the first great break in our links with Salen. When we returned, in August 1945, it was with Emlyn Evans and a party from the Fochriw Youth Centre in Glamorgan, where I had been helping him for several years. Surprisingly we had a week of glorious weather on one day of which, leaving the campers prostrated with sunburn, Emlyn and I rowed across Loch Sunart and climbed Ben Iadain to enjoy on its basalt cap a wealth of wild life which included eagles, ravens, ring ouzels, wheatears, twites, golden plover and a wild cat following a line of sheep up a track. In 1946 there was another Fochriw party with which I climbed Ben Nevis. Immersed in mist on the summit plateau, I was aware that some of the party had strayed from the path, and I found myself bellowing into the gloom: 'If you don't come back at once, I shall ask Mr Evans to send you all home'. I have seldom felt more foolish, and unrighteousness was rewarded to the extent that the wanderers were the only ones to see ptarmigan. Years after, Derlwyn Lewis and Stuart Davies came back to Salen with their wives, so their first visit must have meant what we hoped it would to them.

During 1945 I managed to revisit many of the old favourite places. George Waterston and Iain Munro turned up and took us to see shags' nests near Ockle on the north coast; they also told us that David Lack had been appointed to succeed W. B. Alexander as Director of the Edward Grey Institute at Oxford, one of the first big moves in post-war ornithology. Then on 1 September came one of those days of calm that turn the West Highlands into a Daniell print. Margaret and I cycled over to Ardtoe pier, where we had hired a rowing boat. There were porpoises, puzzling divers and rafts of red-breasted mergansers at the entrance to Kentra Bay and we soon caught our first mackerel. My father and mother with David, then rising three, joined us at Ardtoe, whose shell-sand beaches had been one of our favourite picnic places for years. A grey seal watched us lunch and the first whale rose out of a dead calm that stretched all the way to the Small Isles, transparent in the distance. Margaret looked after David while my parents and I rowed out to the gathering of birds and cetaceans; there was a raft of shearwaters on the water, the nearest I have ever been to them off Ardnamurchan; fulmars, terns and gulls crisscrossed overhead and more gulls crowded on Sgeir an Eididh where Pa and I eventually landed, leaving my mother to row round it, unaware that a whale was surfacing on the other side. On our way back we caught mackerel, lythe and saithe, and attracted a following of up to ten dogfish, one of which jumped up close to the boat. In a similar situation the intrepid 'Dunky' once hauled two or three out by their tails for their presumptuousness, but we were not so skilful.

Two days later Margaret and I went back for a second helping, augmented by gannets, and a turnstone on little Dubh Sgeir. The divers continued to tax my powers of identification, as did the terns, but who doesn't have trouble with them in September? For once I was inclined to agree with Margaret's view that it is not necessary to identify a plant or animal to enjoy it: our urge to know their names may not be scientific but a relic of the belief that such knowledge conferred dominance.

After the war some or all of our family visited Salen annually until my parents sold the cottage in 1955 and went to live near and later with Niall and his wife Moira in Perthshire. In September 1948 I paid a short visit for Pa's seventieth birthday and at Kentra added bar-tailed godwit to the North Argyll list which we kept going, now swelled by notes from a number of friends and other bird-watchers who visited the area. Among these were John and Enid Foster, John Gibb and Christina Godfrey who camped at Salen in August 1949. The two Johns turned out a neat little paper on feeding rock pipits as a result. We also visited Kinloch-teacuis again in an attempt to pick up an old scent: a mysterious 1921 record of 'three marsh tits' seen by Pa up the Kinloch burn. No enlightenment came our way but we got suitably wet investigating Ben Iadain's bird-rich cap again; we did not know then about its remarkable flora.

My May 1950 visit was memorable in several ways. Theed Pearse, Pa's old Bedford friend, who had emigrated to British Columbia early in the century, made his first flight back to Europe at the age of seventy-nine, *en route* for the International Ornithological Congress at Uppsala. On the way he stayed with us in Oxfordshire and then he and I travelled by the traditional route – King's Cross to Glenfinnan and down Loch Shiel by steamer – to Salen, where Niall and his friend Cliff Simmons as well as my parents were in residence. From the 17th to the 24th, assisted by Niall's skill with the outboard motor, we visited most of the old haunts along Loch Sunart, searched the Salen woods, had a look at Kentra Bay and Ardtoe, and finished with my early morning visit to Diver Lochan already described.

Altogether we found the nests of thirty-two species, mostly the sea loch community; but luck was with us inland too. Landing at Camasine, half way between Salen and Strontian, I heard a song already very familiar to me in the Forest of Dean. I followed it up the burn to see my first Argyll pied flycatcher. On the way back I spotted a woodcock's round eye among the bracken and Theed Pearse was able to photograph the nest. We also let him see into a sparrowhawk's nest not far away by means of the mirror on a stick which I carry mostly for lower nest inspections. For once the Salen redpolls allowed us to find two of their beautiful lichened nests on the ends of birch boughs, and on my way back from Diver Lochan a wood warbler sang so pointedly at me that I had to stop and find its nest with an incomplete clutch. As a result of this successful trip Theed Pearse presented us somewhat embarrassingly with the egg collection he had amassed before emigrating and which is now in the Oxfordshire Museum at Woodstock. He lived to be the oldest member of the British Ornithologists' Union and to publish a book (*Birds of the Early Explorers in the Northern Pacific*, 1968) when in his nineties.

Two years later I spent 7–10 June at Salen on my pied flycatcher tour of Britain. The bird that had tried to nest by the cottage in 1951 did not reappear, but I had a big day with Niall on Loch Sunart. The last of this run of visits was in 1954, when Niko and Liese Tinbergen and Uli Wiedmann drove David, Robert and me up in an Oxford Zoology Department Landrover and had a look at the common gulls of Eilean an t-Sionnaich, a convenient *tioram* or 'dry island'. Niko, however, could not wait for the tide to ebb, whipped off his shoes and socks and waded out to set up the hide. I am always glad that this prince of field ornithologists visited Loch Sunart. Uli achieved remarkable results with the gulls in a short time and duly published a paper on their behaviour. On our way south, crossing Corran Ferry on Loch Linnhe, I saw what I was sure was an unusual gull. But I was trapped in the back of the Landrover by bicycles and had to call on Niko, who confirmed that it was an Iceland gull, still my only Scottish sighting.

My parents came back to stay in Salen in 1959 and we joined them for a few days in early August. My old enemies the sparrows were nesting at Skipper's Cottage; more encouragingly there were some house martins about the village, while by Loch Shiel a single shoveller, a duck whose status in North Argyll is somewhat vague, was feeding beside a mallard. This brief visit was the end of an era. My father died in 1963, my mother in 1965: on a flying visit that December Niall and I scattered their ashes in what Pa had called his chapel, in the woods behind the cottage. I noted that the scrub seemed generally thicker and the rhododendrons 'massive'. Conifers were showing to the east of the bay and above Tarbert to the west. But the change was not only vegetative. Time was claiming my parents' contemporaries in the village, while new wooden chalets for week-end and holiday visitors were springing up round the bay and elsewhere.

In May 1966 Grant Lee and I drove up to meet Niall and Marshall Pugh the writer. We had a day on the loch with them and Grant and I spent two days looking for eagles. We got very wet in Morvern but met a family of the St Kildans settled there in 1931: not having seen trees before, they were given work by the

Forestry Commission. The other day took us to Sanna, the village backing a sandy bay and dunes north of Ardnamurchan Point. Here, through my association with *The Countryman*, I had got to know John Maclean, who after a life at sea had returned with his wife and daughter to work the family croft. Three years later, John took Emlyn Evans and me past the rock dove droppings deep into the cave at Rudha Carrach. After John's untimely death, his son Alasdair continued our family association. His poems, collected in *From the Wilderness* (Gollancz, 1973) and *Waking the Dead* (Gollancz, 1976), turn a sharp light on Ardnamurchan and, both by inference and directly, on its wild life.

After our call at Sanna, Grant and I returned to Ormsaigbeg, the westernmost 'suburb' of Kilchoan, to work along the cliff tops. To hearten us, a cock wheatear disappeared into the shale scree, where there was a nest with six fresh eggs. But we failed to find the cliff heronry known in Dalgleish's day and seen by Derek Ratcliffe on his epic solo coastal survey in 1961, of which he kindly gave me a copy of his notes. A colony of shags was some compensation for our foray into some of the wildest country in Britain.

The next three years, 1967–9, saw Emlyn Evans as my companion. In 1967 we joined forces with an extra-mural party from Cardiff led by Mary Gillham, in an attempted survey of the sea loch habitats. Allowing ourselves a day off on the hill, we all climbed Ben Iadain and I was entertained to find that the birds in the minuscule colony of common gulls on Lochan Iadain attacked me with as much zest as their presumed ancestors attacked Pa in 1921. In 1968, the first year of field work for the *Atlas of Breeding Birds of Britain and Ireland*, we climbed the sister basalt cap of Beinn na h-Uamha, being mocked by golden plover and finding the 'used nest' of a ring ouzel; more evidence of the relative richness of these grass-covered caps compared to the acid, peaty lower slopes. Perhaps because I had a geologist with me, I made more notes on sand martin colonies than ever before. Besides sites occupied to my knowledge for over forty years at Acharacle and Blain in Moidart, we found one of about twenty holes in the dunes at Sanna; a small one of four holes in a solifluction layer running across a roadside quarry above Loch Mudle, several in a quarry and new cuttings of the improved road through Morvern, and one of about sixty holes in a narrow band of sand in a big roadside quarry at Ardgour. Also under Emlyn's influence was our visit to the vitrified fort at Shielfoot, which I had known of for years but only ascended with Grant Lee in 1966. Tightly covered with a maquis largely of hazel, the little hill commands a superb view over the moss to Kentra, Ardtoe and away to the Small Isles. There is little bird life but it is a stronghold of the speckled wood butterfly. Since Emlyn's and my views on the fort and vitrification in general seem to command no expert support, I will only say that we felt the fusing could have been carried out deliberately to increase the defensive strength of a site partly protected by natural rock.

My short visit at the end of March 1970, when I stayed with James and Peggy Manuel, who were also our hosts in 1969, was memorable for a snow fall early on the 28th when I was due to visit the 'fish farm' which had taken over much of Ardtoe. By the time I reached Caisteal Tioram to eat my lunch in the doorway, it had declined to a light smirr and I sat watching a shag fish in the clear water between the castle rock and Riska in what seemed an oasis in time, from which the barks of two contending ravens aroused me. On my way back to the car, parked by the policies of the (literally) fallen house of Dorlin, I saw a siskin peck at the roots of a wind-thrown Corsican pine, then fly up into one of the crowns. Because of the early date, it took me some time to realize that it was taking rootlets to its nest. There was a humiliating moment here as a hinge of my spectacles parted, and for once I blessed the increase in human visitors when one of them kindly effected running repairs with elastoplast. There was no sign of jackdaws at the castle but next day when I took Jim Manuel and his son Andrew to visit the Macleans, we found about a dozen at Mingary and two occupied rooks' nests at Kilchoan, a new rookery we had missed in 1969 and unarguably the most westerly on the British mainland.

So to the most recent visit, at the end of May 1971, when Margaret came with me and we stayed in Joy Dixon's comfortable Cedar Cottage and were joined by Niall and Ronald and later by Emlyn, with whom we spent an idyllic 1 June, partly on Eilean Fhionnain, the burial island in Loch Shiel on which I had never landed in spring. It is a reputed nesting place of black grouse, which seem to have vanished from the district. On this occasion a whitethroat's nest, the first I had found since the 'crash' of 1969, was reasonably notable, and we took away a little azalea plant, one of myriads seeded from the mother bushes, and which now adorns the peat trough in our Oxfordshire garden. This and the rhododendron from the bank above what will always be to me Andrew's sward at Salen are reminders that 'North Argyll' is still there: the reader will have realized by now that more than ornithological ties bind me to the place I have looked on as 'home' for nearly sixty years.

6
Hampshire Lad

Although, in terms of days, weeks and months and in almost continuous contact from birth, most of my childhood and boyhood was spent in the Winchester area of Hampshire where my maternal grandparents lived and are buried, I don't think I ever felt for it as 'home', as I did for Salen: the paternal Highland influence and glamour were too strong. But ornithologically it was certainly more than a good second-best, richer by far in passerine breeding species than North Argyll and giving opportunities for predicaments almost as exciting.

Early and indeed continuing memories are much concerned with the thrushes. In my grandparents' garden a neighbour's son and I climbed to my first song thrush's nest when I was rising seven. Because this is such a common species in Britain, its unique (for Britain) nest and eggs tend to be underrated aesthetically. But I still find the eggs' deep blue against the hard light brown lining enormously attractive, though admittedly the appreciation is greatest at the beginning of the season, after being starved of such sights for months.

As opposed to childhood memories, in which heathy north Hampshire figured larger than the southern chalk, my first boyhood contact was when Pa and I walked down the Itchen valley to Compton from Winchester, where he had been acting as my 'manager' in an assault on a scholarship examination, on a blazing mid-June afternoon in 1925. This is a path I was to follow many times in the next five years, but I would not attempt it today, since the intimate nature of the landscape has long been sacrificed to the Moloch of the motor car.

After searching, with permission, a reedbed for reed warblers, we retired to St Cross village and lowered two ices and five bottles of lemonade and gingerbeer. Evidently I did not explode, because I then climbed to nests of swallow and spotted flycatcher; we saw little grebes, probably with young, near where Pa had found the nest in 1915, and totted up nine more reed warblers' nests in another reedbed. Finally, I climbed to a goldfinch's nest, my first, and we met a distant relative armed with binoculars and regretting that he had not learned to identify birds when young; he added that we seemed to have seen more species in one day than he had in three years, which prompted Pa to write: 'What an indictment against our system of education'.

That afternoon was just a curtain-raiser to the next five breeding seasons, most of which, except when holidaying at Salen, I spent in this rich area. Looking back on 1926 and 1927, when we spent the Easter holidays respectively at Compton Manor and in a small house opposite the Shawford golf links, it is hard at first sight to believe that bird life then was not more profuse, though it is impossible to effect a comparison on a scientific basis with present conditions, and impressions based simply on numbers of nests found may be misleading.

Heartened by the chiffchaff's song as I dressed in the morning of 29 March 1926 at Oakley Hall, I lost no time in getting into the countryside on reaching Compton and remarked, after finding one blackbird's and four song thrushes' nests, that there was 'a wonderful abundance of Turdidae here'. By 28 April, the end of the holidays, for much of which Freddie Webster and my father were active too, we had recorded the occupied nests of seventy-six blackbirds (twelve alone on 22 April), sixty-five song thrushes and twenty-four mistle thrushes. These were supported by fairly comparable totals for 1927: about eighty blackbirds, seventy song thrushes and twenty-eight mistle thrushes.

Granted that these are probably (excluding swans and rooks) the three easiest nests to find in English countryside in early spring and that we seldom revisited a nest, the numbers seem large, though admittedly the habitats we searched were extremely favourable; for example, from Compton Manor a lane led to the Itchen valley, both sides lined with ivy-clad trunks and bushes, beyond which lay pasture fields presumably full of worms and other accessible soil fauna. The valley itself was crossed with thick hedges and its marshy areas studded with bushes, mostly of hawthorn. In the other direction we soon had access to the chalk down slopes where Pa had chased the marbled whites (p. 20) and to the fields above them, still bounded by attractive hedges, often with standard yew trees. There also the large shrubby and tree-clad gardens of our friends in Shawford and Compton.

On the other hand, my intensive searches at Hordley in recent years (pp. 192–9) several times showed some fifteen pairs of song thrushes and more than twenty pairs of blackbirds on eight acres of similarly optimum habitat, suggesting densities as great as in Hampshire if not greater. But nowhere have I come across equal numbers of mistle thrushes. Their stronghold in 1926 was the Pilgrims' Way, which snaked along the foot of Compton Downs. Here on 1 April Freddie and I found five nests in less than a mile; all had outer cups of green moss and were in the old yews, four of them out on spreading branches; their contents ranged from hard-set eggs to young nearly fledged. During the seasons 1926–30 I have records (of varying clarity) for fifty-nine mistle thrush nests; of these twenty-four were in yews, nearly all on horizontal branches. The next most frequent tree was elder, with only five nests. One of the elder nests had an egg on 27 April and was close to a hatched-off nest in a yew. It is possible that yew is popular for first nests of this early species because of the protection given by its thick foliage, and that late nests are more often in deciduous trees. A new analysis of the British Trust for Ornithology's nest record cards might confirm this. The previous analysis, published by Tim Myres and David Snow in 1955 (*Bird Study*, 2: 2–24; 73–84), did not deal with this aspect. 'Just for the record', the other sites recorded in 1926–30 were apple (four), hawthorn and 'fir' (three each), oak and beech (two each) and singles in cherry, ilex and a pagoda in the Japanese garden at The Malms, Alfred Bowker's wonderful estate down river from Shawford to which we paid many visits. No site was given for thirteen nests, which is a great pity and stresses the value of nest record cards in making the observer put down these important details.

The cherry nest I remember with a mixture of shame and sly satisfaction. It was in a friend's garden, built in a favourite position, where the straight trunk spread into flower-bearing branches. The clutch was of four superb eggs, like miniature sparrowhawks', so I managed to substitute them for four blackbirds' eggs, three of which hatched, though my diary does not record their ultimate fate. None of these Hampshire mistle thrush nests held clutches of five, which seemed most likely to occur in late April or early May when perhaps our interest was shifting to other species. But those early years left me with a great affection for the 'missler', one of our least studied common birds. I find their territorial behaviour baffling and their disappearance after breeding even more so and hope that someone will soon get to grips with the bird.

Apart from the thrushes, a closer examination of the nest totals is tolerably reassuring. I would certainly expect in Oxfordshire today to find more robins' nests than the two and five recorded in April 1926 and 1927 and I certainly see (though do not necessarily examine) more than twelve and seventeen lapwings' nests in a season. As I have hinted earlier, I wonder on what basis the supposed pristine abundance of breeding lapwings in southern Britain is based. W. B. Alexander used to say that the bird got its special protection because the senior ornithologists consulted were so senior that they were no longer able to hear its calls. I think he also probably originated the identification tip that, if you are over sixty-five and can't hear a bird reeling, it is a grasshopper warbler; if you can, then it is Savi's warbler.

Early in our 1926 season came what my diary calls '*the* incident'. Freddie and I were nesting rather far along the Pilgrims' Way and saw, through a thick hedge, what we took to be my father and my mother's sister, Aunt Edie, who was visiting us. Hiding behind a bush, I shouted: 'Hi you, what are you doing here? You're not allowed here!' not pausing to wonder why they had come so far from home. I ran forward to enjoy my *coup* and was confronted by the shooting tenant, out rabbiting with his wife. When, still red in the face, I trailed home, Pa rang up to apologize and we called that evening and got permission to go on the estate. We were also told of G. M. Mathews, the authority on Australian birds, who lived at Fishers Pond and on whom we subsequently called.

'The incident', which I could not recall for years without a slightly sick feeling, showed the difference between Argyll and Hampshire, which was still well-keepered. The shooting tenant's keeper did not really care for us on his land and a year or two later got our permission rescinded. But the situation was not as raw as in my father's Bedfordshire boyhood. We usually trespassed only when we had failed to get permission, though in 1930, with all the assurance of eighteen-year-olds, John Pringle and I started to drag a clover field where we had heard a quail, bringing out the farmer in his dog-cart like an inflamed hornet. He threatened to see our 'master', who, we assured him, would be delighted to meet him, and we heard no more.

In 1927 I hit on the idea of entering for the public schools essay competition of the Royal Society for the Protection of Birds, something which the tide of democracy long ago swept away. Under its cover and with my housemaster's sympathy and support, I was able not only to get permission to go on several properties but, by taking up rowing as well, to avoid interminable afternoons of compulsory cricket. Half an hour down river before lunch and I was free for the rest of a long half-holiday afternoon, which could be stretched well into the evening. The subjects on which I intended to write might bear little relation to bird life round Winchester but I did not let anyone worry about that. Actually my senior subject was a comparison of migration dates between Hampshire and Argyll, so to some extent my local wanderings were justified. I chose as my prize A. Landsborough Thomson's classic *Problems of Bird Migration* and, emboldened by this, persuaded the College Natural History Society to invite the author to speak at one of its meetings in my last term. So I met the man who, many years later, became one of my father figures.

On our first visit in April 1927 to one of the estates to which my RSPB activities had gained me an entrée, my father reverted to his youthful habits by killing a large buck rabbit in its form in the field where we were looking, with some success, for a snipe's nest. The owner appeared for a chat and Pa made some excuse to depart, leaving me to retrieve the cached rabbit and get it home, where it proved to be too tough to eat.

A radius of two or three miles kept us pretty well occupied those two distant Aprils. As well as the nests of twenty-six species, we identified some fifty more which, except for the wryneck, probably survive in the area today, though the cirl bunting has decreased generally. In 1926 I saw my first water rail and corn bunting, a bird for which, like the mistle thrush, I have a deep affection without, I am afraid, having added notably to our knowledge of its habits. Other 'new' birds belonging to this period were my first cock brambling, appropriately feeding with chaffinches under beech trees at Compton, and the great grey shrike which Pa and I saw, again characteristically on top of a hawthorn bush, in the Itchen Valley beyond The Malms. This was the first of what may be called 'bird report rarities' to come my way and the date, 5 March 1927, remains memorable.

The only expeditions of any distance that we made in April 1926 were due to 'Chas' Nairne, who had introduced us to Morvern and was now living at Milford on Sea with his wife, 'Aunt Speedie' to me, and young family. By 1927 they had moved to Shawford Down while their house on Compton Down was building. The property was carved out of a field where lapwings nested and they called it Plover Hill instead of the more arty 'Lapwings'. This, with its magnificent view north to Winchester and the Cathedral, became our base. A cirl bunting often sang in the adjoining hedge and larks sometimes nested inside the boundary fence.

How Chas realized that the Lymington area was 'good for birds' I do not know, but early on 14 April he met us at the station and led us down to the saltings where we soon found ourselves surrounded by redshanks, the chief object of our quest. But we were too early and had to be content with some likely scrapes and a lapwing's nest. A 'mileometer' recorded that we walked 15 miles 325 yards in our searching. But we were back on the 26th and this time everything went right. A nightingale sang as we walked down the road, a cock stonechat drew off his mate from a nest in the bank of a ditch and we flushed two sitting meadow pipits, one giving a fine 'broken wing' distraction display. It was left to Chas to find the first redshank's nest when a bird whipped up behind us from a grass field. The next nest, which I found within a yard of Chas's mark – for a professed non-ornithologist he was doing very well – had six eggs, plainly the product of two hens, and was within eight yards of a lapwing's nest. Farther on we found another such pair, and our fourth redshank's nest had a canopy of criss-crossed grass stems over it. So in a few minutes I was introduced to three recurring phenomena among breeding waders: polygamy, the apparently protective association between two species, and the use by a minority of birds of an 'optional extra' whose advantage in giving cover seems to be outweighed by its obviousness to a potential enemy. Chas ended his contribution by putting his elbow on one of the redshank's eggs we had taken and were about to pack: he was engrossed in a story – he was a superb raconteur – and gradually edged nearer my father while I sat in dumb apprehension.

The next year we paid two more successful visits to the saltings and fields, finding six redshanks' nests each time. On our first visit an angry farmer and his dog appeared but Pa's humble apology completely mollified him and he said we could go 'anywhere'; the second visit finished with what I can only call a raid on the black-headed gulls nesting in the cord-grass off Keyhaven, but it made a highly satisfactory finale to the holidays. Since schooldays, I can only trace one spring visit to the area, in mid-April 1969 with Rosemary Jackson when we actually saw fewer redshanks than spotted redshanks, but eleven kinds of wader altogether, including two pairs of oystercatchers which first bred on the Hampshire mainland in 1934. We saw three little terns, also now nesting in the area and my first for Hampshire. So I did not feel that change had been for the worse.

Winchester, which I entered in September 1926, though not exactly the home of liberty, was *largior aether* after Oakley Hall. This was due a great deal to my housemaster, R. M. Wright, who believed in encouraging all 'healthy' enthusiasms, and to the discovery that, whereas at a prep school there is no escape from the rules, at a public school, even fifty years ago, there were ropes which could be learned and twisted to one's advantage. The menial task of 'watching out' at Mill to retrieve balls kicked over the wall from College 'canvas' (the curious pitch on which the primitive game of Winchester football was played) was enlivened by looking for the kingfishers, other birds and fish which visited this 'fine bird observatory', a phrase I used when the first British bird observatory was still some years off; obviously I had been reading about Heligoland.

Although our object in SCAN had been to study all forms of wild life, it was not until I reached Winchester that references to plants and animals other than birds become numerous in my diary. This was partly because of the varied activities of the NHS and partly because, in the summer terms of 1928–30, something like a fever of butterfly-collecting gripped several of us and my diary is full of accounts of successful visits by others as well as John Pringle and myself to noted haunts for particular species; at Winchester we were about as well placed as anywhere in England for chalk, heath and woodland lepidoptera.

Our farthest excursion from school was actually to see the total solar eclipse of 29 June 1927 with John's parents in a field near Southport. I was somewhat disappointed with the ornithological effects of the phenomenon: 'Birds kept on flying across the sun and once a yodelling redshank passed.' When the great moment came, my camera fell over and I spent precious seconds righting it. But it was something I am very glad to have seen and again R. M. Wright must be thanked for making it possible.

Next in distance from Winchester was John's and my visit to the undercliff near Ventnor, where alone in Britain the Glanville fritillary flies as native stock. Our terms were dotted with leave-out days, when in practice one could leave as early as the spirit moved and not be back until 9 p.m. The leave-out day on 11 June 1929 was just right for the emergence of the Glanvilles and John and I made good use of fourteen hours. We saw thirteen other species of butterfly and contented ourselves with eleven fritillaries out of about forty seen.

Normally bicycles were our transport and our longest ride by this means was in our first year, on 9 July 1927, when we reached Midhurst in Sussex in time for lunch. More ambitious plans were foiled by a flat tyre – shades of Pa's Bedfordshire days again. Altogether we rode fifty-seven miles and were pretty tired at the end of them. One of our objects was 'orchid hunting' and, when nostalgia depicts a past chalkscape bright with their inflorescences, it is perhaps reassuring to read that we only found 'two bee orchids, and a quantity of pyramids, fragrants and spotted'. But I will not yield my olfactory memories of the downs at Shawford and their aromatic abundance of summer blooms.

Each year our ornithological knowledge of the Winchester district increased and, though our main objective was still to improve our collection of eggs, we inevitably learned more about the birds and began making annotated lists on important outings. In 1931, the year after I left school, John and I published a long paper on the local birds in the transactions of the NHS, which I hope has been of use to subsequent generations. Our climbing skills improved and in 1930 we began to use a rope to reduce the effort of swarming up a bare trunk with or without irons. Our simple technique was to throw a stone on the end of a string over the first bough (real pros used a bow and arrow), tie the rope to the end of the string and haul it over. The climber then tied one end of it round his waist and the partner kept the tension on as he swarmed; this meant that he could take rests without losing height gained, although it was impossible for one to haul the other up bodily, owing to friction over the bough. By this means we were at last able to get to rooks' nests in tall beeches. On 1 April 1930 I reached five out of seven nests in a tree which had twice defeated us. A farmer came up but 'did not object'; probably he was glad to see the rooks harried. If he had been difficult I had complete confidence in John's ability to sort him out. In *Finding Nests* (Collins, 1953) pp. 33–8, I described more advanced techniques, including those pioneered by Myles North, but we never did much good with them and the coming of the tree-bicycle has revolutionized all tree climbing.

In my last year at school I became a ringer. No training or other qualifications were then required; I simply wrote to Miss E. P. Leach at the Natural History Museum in South Kensington and received a consignment of rings and the cardboard schedules on which to enter my ringing data. No pliers were supplied and we affixed the rings as best we could (teeth were often useful). Few adults were ringed before the days of small traps and mistnets, and my only success was an unfortunate little owl which I extracted from its nest hole at Ampfield, for us primarily a butterfly place, but where I also found the only cuckoo's egg I have seen in a wren's nest and on the same day a young cuckoo in a robin's nest. Ampfield had most of the New Forest specialities: white admirals, silver washed and high brown fritillaries, even purple emperors (though we never caught one).

The New Forest itself usually demanded more sophisticated transport than a bicycle and, though cars were still frowned on by the authorities, especially on Sundays, things could sometimes be arranged on weekdays as on 25 June 1929 when John Pringle's accommodating aunt took us to a heath near Sway, where we found a family party of six Dartford Warblers and were able to compare them with a family of whitethroats, 'flickering in the furze'. We also flushed a nightjar, not the event I should consider it today. Next year, taking our bicycles by train to Beaulieu Road, we timed things better on 29 May, soon found a churring Dartford Warbler holding a large worm and followed it until it disappeared and the churring died away. My second tap on a whin bush dislodged it from four large young and John, who had now become a competent photographer, took the first session. This was long before the days of Special Schedule birds and licences: I simply ensconced John as inconspicuously as possible within range of the nest and left him to his vigil. He was reasonably successful but, of course, when my turn came, I jammed the shutter. Still, I had wonderful views of our one 'Lusitanian' bird.

Much nearer to Winchester was another rarity, the stone curlew. We were shown our first birds in 1928 on stony fields near Micheldever. Then in 1929 John found a nest, when butterflying alone near Farley Mount, traditionally its haunt on close-cropped flinty downland, dotted with juniper bushes: on each of two visits both birds ran away from the nest area, possibly because the eggs were hard-set. The next year W. A. S. Lewis came over from Oxford, found and photographed a nest which he kindly showed us; I found one on my own, marking the bird across a wide dry valley and at least one more was known. Even then Farley Mount saw plenty of human visitors and I should be very surprised to hear there were stone curlews there today. This certainly goes for Old Winchester Hill, now a national nature reserve and one of our farthest points east, where we also found young long-eared owls and climbed to a crow's nest, something that the keepering of those days made quite a rarity, as in my father's Bedfordshire. The woodlark is a habitat associate of the stone curlew and in May 1930 I found my first nest on the way to Farley Mount in a scrape which seems to have persisted since 1927. I think the use of such traditional sites may be quite common, not only among birds of prey and waders like the oystercatcher.

The woodlark is one of a small group of 'south-eastern' species that has become much scarcer since my boyhood; others are the wryneck and red-backed shrike, whose nest we regarded as not uncommon though always worth finding. Shrikes, stonechats and nightingales all nested on occasion on 'Arethusa', a scrub- and heather-clad gravel cap on the downs south of St Catherine's Hill. When the nightingale sang there in May 1930, Edward Malan and I got permission to try to hear it at night. Apart from this unusual concession, the evening was a failure and we returned to find that R. M. Wright had been listening on the radio to a Surrey bird, accompanying Beatrice Harrison's 'cello.

But the most important – 'seminal' is the word now, I suppose – event in my school days was a lecture by Tom Longstaff, the climber and explorer, to the NHS on the Oxford expedition to Greenland. He showed us maps of the breeding territories of some of the few passerines and I realized that there was something you could do with nests other than emptying them. So my absorbing interest in the climax of the bird's annual cycle gradually gained a new, ecological aspect. The maps were the work of E. M. (Max) Nicholson, who had inspired the national heronry census and was soon to get the British Trust for Ornithology going, with unforeseeable effects on my own future.

Over the next ten years I paid occasional visits to the Winchester area, notably in 1936 when I was based at Farnborough and also exploring again the heaths of my childhood and being rewarded by my first garganey at Fleet Pond. A week-end with the Nairnes at the end of May included avian old friends as well, a cock cirl bunting, a shrike already with young and what was apparently my first occupied kingfisher's nest at The Malms. A day visit the following week-end with Rodney Butler produced nests of sixteen species, including a shrike with six erythristic eggs on Arethusa and three cuckoos: egg and young in reed warblers and an egg in a dunnock. Perhaps cuckoos really were commoner then. My last pre-war visit was with Margaret on 21 May 1939 when we walked from Twyford to The Malms and back all the way to Winchester: nests ranged from mallard to long-tailed tit and a grasshopper warbler sang near the red-brick railway viaduct across the Itchen Valley, a landmark I had always accepted because it was there 'when I came in'. After the war my Hampshire visits had a new orientation, to the Cohens' hospitable roof near Sway, and really belong to another chapter.

7
Alumnus Edinburgensis

If Winchester represented a big step towards freedom after Oakley Hall, Edinburgh University, whose Forestry Department I entered in October 1930, offered a degree of emancipation almost undreamed of, far freer than Oxbridge at that period. It was some time before its heady waters took effect; my diary is a good indicator of this: in the middle of the summer of 1931 it breaks off and scribbled notes on crumpled bits of paper had to be deciphered years afterwards and entered up. The record for 1932 was even worse, though I kept brief notes on nests found, thus showing what was still my main preoccupation. By early 1933 some equilibrium was restored and the chronicle has continued unbroken to the time of writing this, though varying in the degree of detail it contains.

My connection with Edinburgh predated (used here in its correct dictionary sense, not – as by so many today – as jargon for 'preyed upon') my arrival as a student. After the death of Great-aunt Jane at Kingussie, her daughter 'Aunt' Minna moved to Edinburgh and I stayed with her several times at Garscube Terrace in Murrayfield, where, when Rugby Internationals moved to the new ground down the hill, she kept open house on match days. Ornithologically the sacred turf was noted for the parties of finches and snow buntings which fed on straw scattered in frosty weather before the days of underground heating. On 6 February 1932 some thirty buntings compensated a little for Scotland's 0–6 defeat by Wales. A few days later there were three at Craiglockhart, the University ground, and on the 13th a flock competed with our efforts, as EURFC 'B', to play Watsonian 'B' on their ground at Myreside. One of Winchester's defects in my eyes was that the school did not (still does not) play Rugby, the only major game for which my physique and lack of speed fitted me in any way. Eventually, after three seasons in the University's junior teams, I did reach the fringe of first-class Rugby and have always believed that the opportunism which should be one of the features of a successful player, even of a lumbering forward like myself, has something in common with that of the bird-spotter; and I minded less, when age terminated my chequered career, because I had bird-watching to fall back on. In other words, birdwatching to me has always been a sport rather than an art or even a science, though, of course, a scientific structure can be built on it.

Aunt Minna also organized my first visit to an island in the Firth of Forth on a holiday visit at the end of July 1927. Inchkeith is perhaps the least known ornithologically and at that date we could expect nothing spectacular: 'linnets and pipits etc' are all I recorded, which prompts me to add that 'etc' should never appear in a scientific context: it is lazy and tantalizing. We got back early enough to pay another visit, to Duddingston Loch, that splendid bird sanctuary on the southern edge of the Kings Park, the winter haunt of one of the largest concentrations of pochard in Britain. On this quick look I recorded coot, moorhen, mallard, curlew (on passage I suppose) and sedge warbler. Next day I travelled north in a crowded train to stay a few days with George Brooksbank, of whom more below, *en route* for Salen.

I spent some days at New Year 1929 with Aunt Minna, learning my way about the city I was soon to know so well. Not much birdwatching was done: at Garscube Terrace I only noted seven species, three of them gulls on the grass field behind the house, but I saw the pair of magpies that had recently occupied Inverleith Park. Magpies, reduced in Hampshire by gamekeepers and absent from North Argyll (though Dalgleish recorded a pair which tried to breed at Kilchoan for 'four or five years after 1856'), were comparatively scarce birds to me then, and their distribution in Scotland is still patchy, Edinburgh being on the eastern limit of their centre of population in the Forth-Clyde area. I saw several more on New Year's Day at the Edinburgh Zoo, one of their strongholds.

After this visit I commented in my diary: 'Now animal photography is so good and stuffed specimens may be seen in any museum, it should be unnecessary to keep creatures in confinement any more.' Fifty years later, in the age of the safari park, I have heard the 'anti' argument put in exactly the same terms.

That afternoon Aunt Minna, whose energy caused George Macleod to nickname her affectionately 'First Citizen', and I made a ritual ascent of Arthur's Seat. This was actually my first meeting with snow buntings. There were two flocks in the park and I noted their habit of leap-frogging as they moved forward over the rough grass, like 'beaten leaves'. A few days later I came into even closer contact when staying with

John Duncan, nephew of the redoubtable 'Dunky' of
Tarbert, and his parents at North Berwick, shooting
four. out of a flock in a stackyard. These I gave to
George Lodge, the bird artist, who lived at Hawk
House near my Aunt Edie Haynes in Camberley and
whom I visited many times. I sent him several other
birds, including a cock merlin shot by one of the
Ardnamurchan keepers, some small recompense for
the hours he used uncomplainingly to devote to my
questions. It has been said that he made all birds look
birds of prey, but who has ever painted better birds of
prey against tremendous natural backgrounds? He was
also a first-rate taxidermist and would spend hours
setting up old skins after they had been relaxed. His
studio was a museum and, next to my father and
George Brooksbank, I learned as a boy more about
birds from him than from anyone else.

George Brooksbank, when my father first met him
in Argyll in 1924, had been retired a dozen years from
the headmastership of Aysgarth, the Yorkshire prep
school where, according to his autobiography,
Richard Meinertzhagen had found him almost the only
sympathetic schoolmaster in an unhappy boyhood. I
started to correspond before meeting him, which I did
at Strontian in 1926, having walked five miles from
Camasine. 'So you're Bruce Campbell', he said, and
we continued a friendship until his sudden death in
1934 at the age of seventy. To me he was at first
primarily a lepidopterist, and we spent many summer
evenings treacling posts and searching the ragwort
heads for moths. Meinertzhagen, however, dismissed
his collecting as amateurish and said he really knew
more about woodcock than anyone else, an acquaintance he improved every year by taking a small winter
shoot in Argyll. He published in *The Scottish Naturalist*
for 1919, pp. 95–6, what must be the first credible

account of a woodcock carrying her young. He was also a keen fisherman and knew most of the leading ornithologists of the day; W. P. Pycraft and Archibald Thorburn often stayed at his Aberfeldy house, called Handa after the Sutherland seabird island which is now an RSPB reserve.

Like George Lodge, John Duncan collected bird skins, specializing in waterfowl. He also painted with sufficient skill to hold an exhibition in Edinburgh before the war. The atmosphere at North Berwick, where the family stayed in winter, moving in summer to Kilcamb near Strontian (the house whence, towards the end of the war, Frank Fraser Darling ran the West Highland Survey), was markedly different from Garscube Terrace, though no one could accuse Aunt Minna of not being a sport. But we spent the short hours of daylight in pursuit of wildfowl of some sort, from the pink-footed geese that flighted in with the dawn from Aberlady Bay to the stubbles, to the ducks and waders of the Dunbar Tyne estuary.

If poachers really make the best gamekeepers, is it arguable that my taste of wildfowling and rough shooting, let alone egg and skin collecting, has made me a more understanding conservationist? If so, then the process should be repeated in each generation, a proposition manifestly absurd as regards collecting. And the delights of early morning birdwatching are just as heady whether you have a gun in your hands or binoculars. I am not arguing here against 'field sports', on which we all have our own boiling points: mine even changes according to which side of the Border I am. But I do not believe that a baptism of fire is necessary either for an understanding of the field sports point of view or as 'training' for conservationists.

During my student years I continued to shoot, with various companions and my usual lack of success, on the Lothian coast and on a farm on the outskirts of Edinburgh of which Jim Verney, a red-headed giant from Southern Africa whose brother Dick became my parents' doctor, had the run. In January 1931 and 1932 I joined George Brooksbank for a few days at Ellary, the shoot he had taken in Knapdale. My inability to hit woodcock distressed his accurate mind. The only shooting feat on which I look back with pride and some shame is a right and left at hen capercaillies when, after a dance which had lasted most of the night, I was lent a gun for a few drives at Craighall Rattray near Blairgowrie in January 1934. 'I think we'll stick to cocks now,' said my host. The day was equally memorable for meeting John Berry, who became the first Scottish Director of the Nature Conservancy fifteen years later. On this occasion he kept us in laughter between drives; when a rather elegant guest, festooned with a cartridge belt, tripped and measured his length in the bog, John cried, 'Ah, adopting the prone position, I see'.

There are so many stories about Colonel Richard Meinertzhagen that I will confine myself to one, which is relevant to my arrival at Edinburgh University. A fellow fresher was his cousin Theresa Clay, perhaps best known for her joint authorship with Miriam Rothschild of the New Naturalist volume *Fleas, Flukes and Cuckoos*, and a world authority on parasitic fauna. My stock with R.M. was quite high because he was then interested in seaweeds and I had sent him, at George Brooksbank's suggestion, specimens of the curious unattached *Ascophyllum nodosum f. mackaii* confined to mud and gravel bays along Loch Sunart and neighbouring sea lochs. In his letter of thanks (I think), beautifully executed on a special typewriter, he invited me to make myself known to Miss Clay but added that if, when in my company, she came to any harm, he would 'take a ticket to Edinburgh and commit murder'. This, from what I heard of his exploits from George Brooksbank, would be no idle threat and it was months before I nerved myself to approach Theresa.

The Edinburgh University Rover Crew contained a number of other forestry students with a general interest in nature. So I joined and, full of zeal engendered by Tom Longstaff's Greenland lecture, tried to get going a study of Edinburgh's birds which could be made along the routes we travelled to classes and other regular occasions. Alas, the attractions of noting the daily dunnock or blackbird soon palled, and our main activity became walks over the Pentlands, Edinburgh's wonderful montane lung. On 27 October we climbed Scald Law, the highest point, and were rewarded by two views of a peregrine, once chased by ravens, a woodcock from a peathag, a skein of twenty geese, and red grouse 'all the way'. The Pentland reservoirs, in a variety of situations, from narrow glens to open moorland, were also often productive of ducks. The Kings Park continued to be worth a short visit for its snow buntings but early in 30 November we 'saw little but a man with a ferret and a thick fog over the city out of which the spires rose'.

Another Pentland companion was Percy Honeyman, my father's comrade in arms. His family lived handily at Juniper Green and, after our walk, we were regaled by stories from 'Honey's' father, who had been one of Lochiel's factors. He once gave a friend a day's fishing on Loch Arkaig. Asked how he had got on, the guest replied that he had lunched on an island and climbed a tree to a bloody big nest from which he had taken 'these', a clutch of osprey's eggs. 'For God's sake bury them,' cried Honey senior, 'they're worth my job to me!'

Against the freedom of Scottish university life had

to be set the constraints of living at home after seven years of being habituated to boarding schools. In May 1930 my father had become the first Director of Physical Education at Edinburgh and early in 1931 we moved into 54a George Square (acronym Livags), a comfortable two-floored University flat on the east side of the square. From the dormer window of my bedroom I could see Allermuir and Caerketton, the nearest of the Pentlands; from the back we looked towards Arthur's Seat. Niall started at Edinburgh Academy at the age of six; we had many friends and kin in the city and soon found more. So, although there were periods of difficulty for both of us, Livags became 'home' on a par with Salen and the mutilation of the square, including the demolition of the flat, as part of the University's post-war development, distressed and infuriated us.

George Square is reputedly the largest in the city (patriots say in Europe) and an oasis for bird life, yet – perhaps because it was so close to us – I seem to have made very few observations on it. In 1944 a survey by Pa suggested that, in the many trees and shrubs, deciduous and evergreen, of the square gardens and in the houses themselves there were half a dozen pairs of house sparrows, three making open nests in hawthorns, four of starlings, one of jackdaw, greenfinch, chaffinch and dunnock, up to five of blackbird and three of song thrush. Tawny owls may well have nested in one of the chimneys, a favourite urban site, and blue tits in the chink of a stone wall, as they did more than once in the tiny garden of Livags. A mistle thrush sang, but probably nested in the adjacent Meadows, ecologically similar to the steppe-like London parks where they are at home. Londoners will miss the woodpigeon from the George Square list and the collared dove did not arrive in Britain for another dozen years. The absence of any summer visitors is less surprising: surely, before the days of smokeless zones, Auld Reekie's insect repellent fumes would have kept the most likely, house martin and swift, away? In fact, house martins were nesting in Melville Street, which is as central as George Square, in 1945, and in 1948 spotted flycatchers nested in the square gardens, building on a notch in the trunk of a lime tree. All the same, lack of nest sites, especially for warblers, and of food, since most small summer visitors are insectivorous, are probably the chief reasons why they do not nest in city centres. Or should this be in the past tense? The *London Bird Reports* show that several warblers as well as the spotted flycatcher now breed in its central parks.

From February 1931 George Square became the point of departure for my 'explorations' of the Lothian countryside, at first mainly inland. In spite of the Firth of Forth's fame as a winter haunt of ducks and other water birds, I only paid one visit that winter to Portobello by tram, to see my first velvet scoters, with goldeneye, mergansers, three great northern divers and three razorbills 'fishing close in'; they have long been known as winter visitors 'far up the Firth', according to the great ladies of Scottish ornithology, the Misses Rintoul and Baxter (*A Vertebrate Fauna of Forth*: 311).

My longest Pentland walk was a preliminary to the 1931 breeding season, on 5 March, the day Winston Churchill delivered his Rectorial Address and therefore a holiday of which full advantage could be taken. Starting from Balerno, I walked south-west up to the Borestone, to set foot in Peebles-shire for the first time in my life. Crossing the Cairn Muir, I climbed Byrehope Mount, then by way of the ridge of The Pike I entered Midlothian again and reached the Lanark road at Crosswoodhill. As I was due to fence against the RAF in the evening, 'Home became the pressing

condition and so, after consultation with a perfect
Pictish type, I walked along a splendid tarred road over
desolate grass slopes, far wilder than any Highland
moor, to Harburn (6.15 p.m.). No luck with trains
there (only a derisive tawny owl) and so two more
miles – a flock of fieldfares passing over with their wild
calls – to West Calder.' Two bus rides eventually
brought me back to Edinburgh where, not surprisingly, I only won one of my four fights. I estimated
that I covered at least twenty-two miles (fourteen of
them on the hill) in seven walking hours. As the
ground was snow-covered, the ornithological value of
the walk was limited – snipe were the only waders I
saw – but no doubt it was good training. I recorded
thirty-three species of bird and four mammals: rabbit,
brown and mountain hare, and roe deer.

At the end of the spring term we spent ten days
doing forest nursery work at Dreghorn, with the Pentlands above us, the dark shelter belts of fir, where later
I saw my first long-eared owls' eggs, beckoning as
well as the moorland slopes. The call of the curlew told
me that the hill was waking up at last and on 29 March
Honey and I found four species of wader present. After
a fortnight or so at Salen, I returned for a summer term
in which it is difficult to believe much work was done
as my diary records major outings on nineteen days
between 24 April and midsummer: six of these were to
the Pentlands, eight to the Moorfoot Hills to which I
was introduced by Tom Edwardson, the prizeman of
our year and now living not far away from us in North
Oxford. Most of my subsequent visits were with
Geoff Rouse, another forestry contemporary with
whom I am still in close touch. Pa also came whenever
his University duties allowed. The area on which we
concentrated included Portmore Loch and Gladhouse
reservoir, very much in the ornithological forefront

today as a goose haunt, the narrow glen of the South Esk which fed the reservoirs, and the rounded hills on either side of the glen. This was wader country *par excellence*: on 13 May, Geoff and I found nests of lapwing, golden plover, curlew (two), snipe and redshank. Altogether that season we found sixteen curlews' nests, mostly by surprising sitting birds in boggy pockets. But the two golden plover we found were by flushing close-sitting birds (one even ran round and got up behind me) and therefore a matter of luck, compared to the technique worked out by Derek Ratcliffe for marking the majority that rise at long range. Auchencorth Moss west of Penicuik was our bogey area: on it were at least five pairs of golden plover that mocked us. One bird would pipe from a tussock as we approached, then fly on ahead while its mate started up behind us.

Actually our most successful Moorfoot day was in 1937 when we celebrated George VI's Coronation on 12 May by a family expedition in the green Riley I had recently acquired. The total of nests of twenty species all with eggs remains our Scottish best. Here they are (in Voous order): mute swan, mallard, red grouse (two), partridge (two), moorhen (two), coot, golden plover, lapwing (two), curlew, black-headed gull (two), tawny owl, skylark, pied wagtail, dipper, ring ouzel, blackbird (two), jackdaw (six), crow, starling (two), house sparrow (three), with meadow pipit building. We saw twenty other species, including pairs of great crested grebe and goosander on Gladhouse reservoir. Margaret flushed the golden plover just where we had stumbled on our first nest in 1931 and we could watch the bird's return from the car. On its way back it found a curlew's eggshell we had dropped and flew off with it before coming to sit, thus anticipating what it would do when its own eggs hatched.

Our early expeditions were facilitated by the excel-

lent country services then offered by Scottish Motor
Traction; it was more convenient not to be encum-
bered by bicycles if we were going on the hill and
might come off it several miles from where we started.
But we had many hair-raising races to catch late con-
nections. I can still feel the glow of sitting in the snug
fug of the bus, almost certainly with wet feet, our
generally dishevelled condition a source of polite interest to our fellow travellers.

It was an official botanical excursion on 30 May 1931
that introduced us to Aberlady Bay, now known as a
highly successful local nature reserve declared by the
former East Lothian County Council. I paid three
more visits that summer, the attractions being a common tern colony and several pairs of dunlin nesting
with lapwings, ringed plover, redshank, larks and
meadow pipits on saltings heavily grazed by rabbits.
This left cosy little tufts of grass which we searched as
we quartered the shore with something of the sensation of a lucky dip. I saw dunlin at Aberlady up to 1947;
then came a break in my visits during which myxomatosis appeared and it is generally held that the resulting luxuriance of the grass did not suit the dunlin and
they disappeared as a nesting species. The ternery, on a
sand and shingle spit, then became the great summer
attraction with, if I read *Atlas* right, all five *Sterna*
species nesting there in 1968–72. To protect it, a line of
posts was put up, but with no wire between them,
only a notice asking people not to pass the line. As far
as I know this 'psychological' approach proved successful, which should make the barbed wire school of
conservationists think. Aberlady, of course, is a prime
haunt at all seasons, and one of the spin-off pleasures of
visits to the Edinburgh Festival in recent years has been
visits to the reserve, whose bird life has now been well
documented.

To return to student days, 20 June 1931 saw my first visit to the Bass Rock in a party of ten. This was the period when my notes were getting laconic, but I did note the tree mallow and I can remember the trepidation with which we approached the sitting gannets in the 'east rookery' to become accustomed quite quickly to the drop and the blue sea far below. Next day, with the Davidsons, also migrants from Winchester where R. P. Davidson had been a master, we skimmed the cream of the East Lothian shore, from the famous links at Muirfield, via Tantallon Castle with its fulmars and a colony of house martins on the cliff below, to Tyningham spit with its small colony of little terns, the first I had seen. But all these high ornithological jinks brought their retribution: I failed in Chemistry and had to re-sit it in the autumn.

The 1932 season was a great contrast to 1931. I made six visits to Aberlady and there was much more exploration of places nearer Edinburgh, especially well wooded policies like Dalkeith Palace, to which Pa got an entrée, and Woodhouselee. There were only two visits to the Pentlands, one to Auchencorth's black-headed gull colony, and one to the Moorfoots, where at last I found a wheatear's nest with eggs. There was a arduous cycle ride back from Berwickshire after a night's camp with Tom Edwardson and three other foresters near Longformacus, where we had climbed to a solitary heron's nest, and I paid my first visit to Fast Castle and St Abbs Head. Pedalling home into a headwind, I was passed by the others triumphantly seated in a lorry. My own attempts at a lift involved helping unload a ton of seed potatoes on a farm and then left me at Musselburgh to negotiate the spring race-meeting traffic.

Jim Verney became my most regular companion this season, especially useful as he had charge of a three-seater bicycle on which generations of South

African students had toured Britain. This formidable vehicle had no free-wheeling mechanism and could attain tremendous speeds even, as we normally used it, with only two riders and our kit on the third seat. Jim and I took it by train – its dimensions baffled the ticket office – on May Day 1932 en route for a peregrine's eyrie which I had located after our spring forestry course at Dunkeld. We had one epic skid on loose stones down a steep, twisting pitch but survived. On our way back we stopped to search a likely wet field and Jim put his foot square on a snipe's nest. Granted his was a size 12 boot, the odds against such a mishap must still be considerable. On a follow-up visit to the Berwickshire coast, Geoff Rouse was handing jack-daws' eggs to Jim when he slipped and rolled down the steep bank below the cliff, knocking himself out in the process. Fortunately on this trip we had a car, Archie Macpherson's baby Austin, into which we eventually packed Jim's limp 6 feet 8 inches.

We also reached the Peebles-shire glens in 1932 and, on 8 May, cycling happily back after finding a kestrel's and a ring ouzel's nest, I saw what I thought at first was a house martin sitting on the roadside wall. I had just time to correct my identification to a cock pied flycatcher before he flew off: my first meeting with a bird which was to engross me for so many hours.

In fact, my next meeting was just about a year later in the Forest of Dean, where we were on field work for our final year forest working plan. After our field work we returned to Edinburgh for the traditional burning of midnight oil before handing in some 250 foolscap pages of handwritten text, figures and maps. Somehow I managed to satisfy the Professor (how did he read my writing?) and on 30 June joined the ranks of the graduate unemployed, in those days without a benevolent Manpower Services Commission to look after us.

8
Years of Movement

What with the final throes of my working plan, my twenty-first birthday and graduation, the summer of 1933 was fairly hectic. Even before I had handed in my plan, Jim Verney and I spent a twenty-hour day visiting the hills of Rannoch, where we had been given a tip by a gamekeeper friend that dotterel might nest. We saw an eagle, several broods of ptarmigan and a magnificent panorama of High Tops, but no dotterel. It was so hot that I bathed with pleasure in a lochan near Corrour station. Although I did not know about it until I read his diaries years later, about three weeks earlier Arthur Whitaker had made a similarly unsuccessful but more arduous trip from Sheffield to look for whooper swans a bit farther down the West Highland line. He walked through the night to a couple of hill lochs, fortified only by biscuits, and caught the 7.20 a.m. train from Crianlarich the following morning. I actually came of age when investigating the kittiwakes nesting on Granton breakwater; nests on human artefacts were considered by Misses Rintoul and Baxter to be 'of an extraordinary nature'. Now, since John Coulson's study of the window-ledge nests over the Tyne, we take them for granted.

Two days later reports of a 'mysterious grebe' got me up at 5 a.m. to chug out to Aberlady with Niall in the bull-nosed Morris that had been our working group's transport in the Forest of Dean. On the Marl Loch we could find nothing more exciting than a moorhen, and I returned for a sleep before setting out with Jim Verney and Alistair Drummond for Tents-muir, a place of almost fabulous repute and, on this occasion, fabulously difficult to reach. After careering sedately between a number of Fife stations, we at last got to Leuchars at 5.15 p.m. and set out on foot, guided at the end by a billowing cloud of white birds. These proved to be mainly black-headed gulls, but there were several 'clots' of what we had really come to see: my first nesting Sandwich terns. One group had been devastated by a photographer's canvas hide, left to flap in the wind, and the watcher reported a great deal of vandalism, not only a postwar phenomenon. Common terns nested scattered over the moor; on the shore as we started back we came on a few little terns and then had to run for our train: three and a half miles in twenty minutes, according to my diary.

A month later Alistair Drummond and I hired a boat one evening at a Firth of Forth village and rowed out to a small rocky island. Whether I had received a tip-off I cannot remember or had we simply heard that birds had been seen over it? As we approached over the calm water, we were surrounded by common terns, among which I was able to distinguish the white-looking breasts, black bills, long tail-streamers and harsh calls of my first roseate terns, at what was then, I think, their only breeding place in the Firth. There were probably three or four pairs: I identified one typically 'spiky' chick and an infertile egg which had pencilled markings, a good but not certain recognition feature. As I had found arctic terns' nests on a visit to Knapdale, this meant that I saw nests of all the British breeding sea terns in one season. We counted 136 nests of common tern: on 19 July they must have been repeat clutches after failure elsewhere. Next year, having no wish to emulate Sir Patrick Spens, we gave the Firth best on a singularly unpleasant midsummer day, but on 22 June 1935 Niall and I landed briefly, to find about 170 pairs of common terns (119 nests counted) and 175 nests of Sandwich terns. We watched four roseates back to single eggs, estimating their strength at at least ten pairs. A rock pipit's nest added variety.

Terns are notoriously fickle; on 13 June 1937 Margaret and I landed to find only two Sandwich tern nests, but 184 common terns. Identifying from egg type, we attributed twenty-five nests to roseate terns and had five sitting birds in view at once. We also found an eider's nest with six eggs. For most of the next ten years the island must have been out of bounds; when Niall and I landed on 9 July 1947 the profusion of bird life exceeded that on any previous visit; it was unwise to put a foot down without first looking carefully, and there were large groups of eggs evidently washed up from nests made below the tideline. We estimated the common terns at between three and four hundred pairs, the Sandwich terns at about fifty and the roseates at sixty to seventy-five pairs, of which we counted forty-nine nests with eggs or very small young; there were also two hatched-off eiders, a rock pipit's nest and a gull's nest with two small eggs but no attendant birds; could they have been kittiwakes which sometimes nest on low shores?

What interested me most were the deeply recessed sites used by the roseates as against the exposed nests of the common terns. The roseates also tended to concentrate, except in their last year of abundance, in a zone above the tideline where the thick vegetation began. In a short paper I wrote for *The North Western Naturalist* (September–December 1947: 174–7), I argued that the roseates chose these sites to avoid ecological competition on this densely populated little island, much as we found on Loch Sunart that lesser black-backed gulls preferred cover to the open sites of the herring gull. The largest roseate colony I have seen was on Rockabill in June 1949; of over two hundred nests, the majority were hidden in tree mallow and some were almost under stones. Also in Ireland, Raymond O'Connor has found nests 'buried in bluebells and grasses', and some Farne Island nests are certainly well hidden.

I have dwelt on the roseates because they led to a published communication, something rare in the years of movement following my graduation. All the indications were, in fact, that birdwatching, with the accent on birds-nesting, would remain for me a hobby as it had for my father, once I had found some sort of work that suited me. Gradually, by way of a tutoring job near Melrose, where I lived in luxury, played a few games for the famous local Rugby club, shot pigeons (one had ninety-one beech nuts in its crop), rabbits and, on the Tweed, a drake goldeneye which I sent to George Lodge, I found myself in January 1934 back at Oakley Hall to do some teaching in preparation for a post near Worcester in the summer. Things were very different, with my cousin Francis Letts and Bill Jackson as headmasters, from my days as a pupil; one of the staff, Roger Bickersteth, was a keen bird-ringer, using potter traps. One day he produced a pair of bramblings on his desk in triumph, but most of his captures were greenfinches, followed by dunnocks. The birds showed their individuality by their reaction to the traps. Some, caught once and ringed, were never seen again, but greenfinch FH 598 would be retrapped two or three times a day, its face becoming quite bare as it put up a token struggle every time it was released, sticking its bill through the wire mesh.

On a brilliant May Day I embarked on the first of many drives between Edinburgh and the south, at the wheel of Tony Legard's old Fiat. After driving through two unprepossessing characters who tried to stop me on Tweedsmuir, stalling in the middle of Wigan, and hitting an ancient cart, which disintegrated like a conjuring trick in crowded Shrewsbury, I eventually reached my destination on the outskirts of Worcester. The car had had enough too and most of my excursions were by public transport and foot. Principally these were to see the Steele Elliotts at Dowles Manor, which I regard as one of the 'houses in my life'. Although the hawfinches and stonechats had gone, the area round about, on the edge of Wyre Forest (now partly a National Nature Reserve), with the Dowles brook, holding both dippers and kingfishers, purling below the garden, was still very rich. On six visits that summer term I saw the nests of thirty-six species within half a mile of the house and at least seven more must have been nesting. But on 3 June Elliott took me down to a bed of osiers and nettles by the Severn, where I heard my first marsh warbler, giving a 'subdued, jazzy song, with some mimicry and some good phrases, but not at all sustained'. Quite a casual search revealed a new nest of green grass with the 'tell-tale binding round each nettle stem'. We walked away and soon saw a bird go to it. When I came back alone on 14 June there was a clutch of five characteristic eggs in it, but our estimate of six pairs at the first visit was probably excessive; after a hard, hot search, I only found one more occupied nest and a possible 'cock's nest'. Sedge warblers and whitethroats were also nesting. On 20 June 1937 Jon Painter and I found both of these again, with garden and reed warblers, but failed to identify any marsh warblers. The only other Gloucestershire nests I have seen were those studied by John Burton and photographed by Eric Hosking south of Gloucester in the 1950s.

One term's full-time teaching was enough for me; by October 1934 I was working as a 'student labourer' (we got paid less) for the Forestry Commission on Loch Ard Forest, on the borders of Perthshire and Stirlingshire, and staying in the village of Gartmore, famous as the home of 'Don Roberto', R. B. Cunningham-Grahame. The winter I spent there was one I have never regretted and though it did not lead to a job, it provided the data for my first paper, Notes on the Birds of Loch Ard Forest (*Scottish Naturalist*, Nov/Dec 1935: 151–9). Altogether, on the job and on our walks to and from the 'forest', as yet only boggy moorland which we were draining and planting, I noted sixty-two species, most of them on the farmland or in existing scrub and conifer woods, though the waders began to appear on the hill before my observations ceased in April. The leks of the blackgame started up in March, with up to sixteen cocks on the sward of a deserted croft, but red grouse, meadow pipits and stonechats were the only resident moorland birds all winter. The stonechats, robin-like, perched on our rutting spades at lunch-time: what did they find to eat in the peaty drains? Maddeningly I did not even record if they ate the crumbs of our pieces.

From Gartmore I went in April 1935 to Fort Augustus, where William Anderson, formerly forester at Glenhurich, was now in charge of the nursery. In my spare time I covered a lot of exciting country and sat above Loch Ness looking for the monster, then quite a novelty. Ornithological highlights were an occupied eagle's eyrie in a great Scots pine, and my first goosander's nest, which I found while relieving nature on the shore of the loch: the duck flew into a hole in the rock just above me. On the way back on foot I had a splendid view of a sitting peregrine on a wooded cliff. But I think finding three stonechats' nests in one evening gave me the greatest pleasure, as I have spent so many hours baffled by their disappearing tricks.

Much of the early summer was taken up with a surveying course which it was thought would strengthen my qualifications. We did the field work at Straiton a few miles south of Edinburgh in an area of waste land and scrub which was not without bird interest. On one June evening Niall and I not only found our first Lothian corn bunting's nest there, but eight song thrushes as against four blackbirds' nests. Assuming the nests of the last two species are equally easy to find, our Midlothian notes suggest that in the 1930s both were equally common, which is what S. E. Brock found in his sixteen square mile survey in West Lothian in 1913. Nationally, as Howard Ginn has shown, this was borne out by ringing totals up to the war (the nest record scheme only started in 1939). Then, apparently because the song thrush is more vulnerable to hard winters, the balance shifted in favour of the blackbird, which *Atlas* puts at seven million pairs, twice as numerous as the song thrush.

In July I spent a week looking at the fine forests round Grantown on Spey. Here I met the Marshall brothers. Willie, who lived at Nethy Bridge, was an outstanding field naturalist, a great friend of Bernard Tucker. His brother James showed me not only my first crested tits but two floral rarities, one-flowered wintergreen *Moneses uniflora* and twinflower *Linnaea borealis*, the diminutive relative of elder and honey-suckle. An eighty-four-mile ride on a hired bicycle took me to the Slavonian grebe colony, where I saw the striped young riding on their parent's back. Earlier in the season Niall and I, sometimes with Pa and frequently pressing car-owning friends into service, visited many old haunts south of Edinburgh with success. The Misses Rintoul and Baxter beat us by a year with a Peebles-shire breeding record for the great crested grebe at Portmore Loch, but we claimed a first for oystercatcher in the same county.

By the autumn it was clear that I would not get a job in British forestry, so I joined my father in the University gymnasium, where his instructors kindly nursed me along. Fortunately, whatever my shortcomings in agility, I was able to control a class, which stood me in good stead for the next thirteen years. There was not much birdwatching that winter, but I did complete a first year of monthly lists of birds identified, a ploy I have continued ever since.

In the spring term I made a brief return to prep school teaching, to fill a place in the Junior School at Loretto. I began to discover the winter bird life of the Lothian shore and during February and March made twenty-one counts in different zones at the mouth of the Musselburgh Esk; these ranged from grassy links through the steep bank at the high tide line to extensive mud and gravel which gave way to mussel beds where the river fanned out at the low tide. The counts were not sustained or detailed enough to merit publication, but I suppose they were good practice. I recorded forty-two species, of which rooks, house sparrows, herring and black-headed gulls, dunlin, redshank, mallard and goldeneye were the most numerous; the list included my first black-necked grebe, long-tailed ducks and reeve, not then considered as a winter visitor.

Margaret and I had some of our first walks along the coast, from Cramond to Queensferry and at Aberlady, where on 9 February – just in case anyone thinks of bird corpses on beaches as a modern phenomenon – our finds included red-throated diver, velvet scoter, shag, black-headed and herring gulls and redwing. Aberlady also produced a 'black' lark which Niall shot and we took to Dr A. C. Stephen at the Royal Scottish Museum. It proved to be an example of 'industrial melanism', not genetically inherited as by Bernard Kettlewell's peppered moths, but acquired from the small coal and dust which were washed up on the beach from the East Lothian coalfield.

A 'scatter' north at the beginning of April took me to Willie Marshall again in Strathspey; with him in one day I saw four Scottish crossbills' nests at all stages from building (which the female did over our heads as we ate our pieces in the pinewood) to young, and met Desmond Nethersole-Thompson, who was collecting material for his monograph, *Pine Crossbills*, which Poyser published in 1975; I recognize some of the incidents. Next day I played in the Inverness Rugby Sevens for Edinburgh Wanderers, losing the final to The Geits, an Edinburgh Academical team which included George Waterston. From Inverness Alec Crampton Smith and Murach Beaton took me to see the Boarstone, with its sparse, stirring carving; in fields near it were the most northerly stock doves I have seen in Britain. My farthest point reached was south-west Sutherland, where with Alastair Sutherland I saw not only the hills of the Coigach, with golden eagle and greenshank in attendance, but stark Canisp and Suilven for the first time. Also, rather to Alastair's dismay, I climbed a sample of trees in the rookery at Ullapool where he stayed.

On 10 April I took the (rail) road south to become an

expatriate Scot once more. The jolt was mitigated by an Easter weekend at Margaret's home in Moseley. We visited Dowles, as magical as ever, and a new locality to me, the Bittell reservoirs, still a handy mecca for Birmingham birdwatchers. Some of the events of the next three months, when I was based at Farnborough once more, are mentioned elsewhere. They included my first penetration of East Anglia's breckland, with Geoff Rouse, now a forest officer living at Brandon, and John Pringle, engaged in post-graduate research on insect physiology at Cambridge but as ready as ever for a day with the birds. I also joined John and his friends in a camp near Swanage in June, thus making contact again with one of the most exciting areas in England.

Finally, on 1 September, I drove to Cinderford in the Forest of Dean, which I had left as a student three years earlier, to my first proper job, responsible for physical education in the social service clubs catering mainly for the unemployed miners of this distressed area. For most of my eight and a half months there I stayed on a farm with John White, who was teaching biology at Lydney and riding motor cycles in the summer. When raven time came, he introduced me to my first Welsh haunt. Nearer home we climbed to the nests of the smaller crows with which the Forest abounds.

In May 1937 I joined what was then the Central Council for Recreative Physical Training, with head-quarters near Westminster Abbey. This meant visits all over the country, some of them giving off-the-cuff opportunities to watch birds. On one weekend, when I was doing a job in Chester, Tony Legard and I nearly drowned ourselves at Aberdaron, still the nearest I have got to Bardsey; on another, driving back from Edinburgh, I turned my Riley over near Carnforth and it was never the same again. This meant that Margaret and I had to travel the weel-kent rail and steamer route to Salen for our July holiday under the gentle chaperonage of Aunt Kitty and her friend Ethel Boughey, with whom we stayed for New Year 1938 in her flint-walled house at Brancaster.

The pattern of snatched birdwatching breaks continued in 1938. John White took me on 10 April to High Halstow heronry, at times the biggest in England and made famous by Capt C. W. R. Knight in *Aristocrats of the Air*. There were rooks' nests too and John did a daring climb to one in which an early kestrel was sitting up a slim elm. Next month I was at Halifax with Jane Solkhon (now Madders) as colleague. She became indoctrinated enough to find a merlin's nest on the moors, a second laying after persons unknown had substituted grouse's eggs (which I removed) in the first nest. The Yorkshire moors reminded me of the Moorfoots and Pentlands and searching them made a good preparation for a trip with Rodney Butler at the end of the month to the far north, by way of Aberlady, Lindores Loch, Glenfincastle and Strathspey. On this somewhat breathless tour we saw at least 112 species with nesting evidence of fifty, including my first crested tit, scoter, greenshank (hatched-off), fulmar, black-necked grebe, water rail and ptarmigan.

Margaret and I were to be married in September but an accident when riding meant a postponement and several trips to visit her in Cornwall, a new county to me. When I could not be with Margaret, I walked the coast and was rewarded by finding one of the last Cornish pairs of choughs. Our wedding eventually took place on 19 November at Moseley, with John Pringle as best man, and we left for a short honeymoon in Galloway, at Isle of Whithorn, where our bedroom looked out on the little harbour, full of waders at low tide. Margaret, however, spotted our 'best bird', a black redstart, which remains my only Scottish sighting, on the cliffs of Burrows Head.

We began our married life in a flat at Kew, and the Gardens, the riverside, with Richmond Park not so far away all showed us that London had plenty of birds. My peripatetic life with the CCRPT continued to let us see the country: one weekend, with Alistair Drummond and Mervyn Horder, we visited Peter Scott's proto-Slimbridge at Sutton Bridge by the Wash. Another one saw us walking in Dovedale, full of singing dippers. In a cold spell around Christmas we caught in Kew Gardens an exhausted skylark, its tail clogged with frozen snow which we thawed off in the flat before releasing it hopefully. Bramblings also visited the Gardens and we saw more in February 1939 when staying with Bernard Keeling and his mother at Cobblers Hill near Great Missenden. On 12 March John White and I climbed to the herons at High Halstow to see the first eggs of the year; a female hen harrier gave the day's list a touch of class. Our best local outing from Kew was on 6 May when we took a boat on the river and then walked up Richmond Hill to the Park. Our forty-three species that day included all three woodpeckers and a pair of hawfinches, apparently feeding on aphids among the young oak leaves.

Our next river trip was on 31 August, after returning from Margaret's traditional family holiday at Newquay with the news daily more ominous. We rowed up to Shepperton, seeing migrating sandpipers and resident kingfishers, and tied up for the night. Next day we got as far as Bell Weir above Staines before hearing of Germany's attack on Poland, sounding incongruous in that placid riverside, down which we now returned hurriedly, but noting house martins nesting on a houseboat, to the chaos of our first blackout.

We actually heard of the declaration of war when staying with the Keelings at Cobblers Hill. Thence we went to Edinburgh where I helped in the gym for six weeks until a role for the CCRPT was decided. This was, of course, the phase of 'phoney war' and there were no restrictions on walks at Aberlady which we enjoyed at weekends with John and Peggy Beaton, who had become our chief Edinburgh friends. On 25 September there was 'a plethora of bird life' of some thirty species, including kittiwakes and common and Sandwich terns, which two skuas were harrying without much success. Although we saw these birds on several occasions, we never came to a firm identification, which shows how difficult things were before the coming of field guides; the relevant volume of the *Handbook* did not appear for another two years. On 26 October I was called back to London: The CCRPT was decentralizing and I was to go to Wales and be based on Cardiff. We had a few days at our flat, which we had lived in less than a year, and final walks in the Gardens and by the river, before setting out by road on 8 November with my colleague Margaret Holmes.

9
Wales

My first penetration of Wales was with Tony Legard in August 1932 following an inauspicious day at Chepstow races. After driving as far as Crickhowell, we retreated and spent the night huddled in his Fiat up a lane on the slopes of Skirrid Fawr, reputedly the last nesting place of the chough in those parts. I awoke to find the car trundling backwards; 'We've been charged by a bull!' I cried, evidently in progress from dream to reality; I suppose one of us had kicked the hand-brake off. No birds were recorded that trip and my first notes were made on 11 October 1936 when I drove Aunt Kitty Brockman to Builth Wells and we saw a grey wagtail, a dipper and two kingfishers on the Wye.

By November 1939 I had identified just over a hundred species in Wales and found or seen the nests of thirty-five. I had also, due largely to a tour on behalf of the CCRPT in June and July, been in every county. While my list included buzzard, peregrine and raven (and their nests), I had seen only three species of duck and had made no record of mute swan or tawny owl.

But I had heard a corncrake call on the Dowrog Common in Pembrokeshire, found a red-backed shrike's nest in the Vale of Glamorgan and my first pied flycatcher's nest in Brecon in May 1937. (Ornithologically I continue to use the old county divisions.)

Early in December 1939 we set out on a fortnight's tour of the country to make or remake contacts for the CCRPT; we subtitled this 'Wales through a Windscreen-wiper', but in fact we enjoyed several fine days; on one of these, at Heancastle near Tenby, I saw my first Welsh black redstart. After drinking out of a hole in a tree stump near the shore, it flew up to a roof to give us excellent views; it showed pale wing patches so was probably a first winter male. There were also parties of common scoters in the bay, another new Welsh species for me. But birds were mainly titbits to be picked up en route, like the short-eared owl flapping over Anglesey's Malltraeth Marsh or ten cormorants flying over the Severn near Welshpool, at least fifty direct miles from the sea, but something quite well known in those parts. A red grouse and a 'hoodwink' enlivened the last day's run over the Breconshire moors.

Early in 1940 we took a flat overlooking the river Taff near Cardiff Bridge. We could feed gulls on the balcony and at the seasons of passage sandpipers called invisibly along the river, across which we looked into a spinney of apparently pristine woodland, full of small birds at times and with the wyvernous (but quite modern) towers of Cardiff Castle beyond. Just across the main road lay Sophia Gardens, a fair exchange for Kew; in them there was a chance of seeing a hawfinch, after first hearing the *tzik* call which local starlings tend to mimic with maddening skill. I write 'a chance' advisedly, for my diaries show only three actual sightings (30 March and 7 April 1940, 27 February 1941) during the one and a half years we were in Park View Court. What do hawfinches do with themselves? Nearly forty years later and in spite of Guy Mountfort's splendid New Naturalist monograph, I am little the wiser personally.

Cardiff's Civic Centre can be regarded as of a piece with the Castle and Sophia Gardens. Farther north lie Roath Park Lake and gardens which I got to know pretty well on early morning visits after stretcher-bearer and fire-watching duties. The lake in winter might always be good for some unusual duck, particularly the smew, which now seems to have become such a rarity. The wild gardens north of the lake, where the great Cardiff naturalists Geoffrey Ingram and H. Morrey Salmon had done some pioneer bird photography, were wild indeed during the war and attracted breeding chiffchaffs, blackcaps, spotted flycatchers, bullfinches and kingfishers. Almost the first sign of returned peace was a concerted attack by the parks staff which soon reduced the wilderness to uninteresting order.

I found my first Welsh redpoll's nest in an ornamental shrub near the lake in 1943. I think this may have been the day I was accosted by two policemen not unnaturally curious about my activities, an experience birdwatchers all over Britain were having in those days, and continue to have in countries less familiar with the hobby. In October 1975 Alasdair Maclean and I spent a good hour crouched by the River Eden, our glasses apparently trained on Leuchars RAF station across the river, and no one showed the slightest interest in us. Where else in the 'sensitive' world could this happen?

North of Roath Park are the Llanishen reservoirs which I got to know very well when, after four and a half years in rural Gwent, we came back to Cardiff at the end of 1945. Here I saw part of the great arctic tern migration of April 1947, here I made my first Wild-fowl Counts, and in a spinney alongside them found the first willow tit's nest recorded for Glamorgan. Reservoirs, by nature of their construction, are among the coldest birdwatching places I know and I am afraid Llanishen's wintry blasts blighted our David's enthusiasm for ornithology when he was sent out to trail round after me. I tried to interest him in the activities of the coots, the most numerous waterfowl, and his mournful 'What coots doin'?' passed into the family phraseology.

But David did not appear on the scene until October 1942, by which time we had explored much of the Cardiff area and, farther afield, visited Kenfig Pool, reputed by some to be the Lake of the Lady and Excalibur. Here on 26 May 1940 John White saw at least one duckling with a garganey duck, the only breeding record for Glamorgan, accepted by *British Birds* (vol. 34: 88, 1940) but omitted from *The Birds of Glamorgan* (1967). The dunes between the Pool and the sea, with their wet slacks and rare orchids, were then pretty well undisturbed, the haunt of redshank, oys-tercatcher and lapwing. After the war they became much exposed to human incursions and I trust that local nature reserve status may restore some of their former diversity. Kenfig Pool is one of the few waters where I have seen the three British swans at the same time.

By the spring of 1941 I had given up my car, but that did not stop us reaching Gower by bicycle for a couple of therapeutic week-ends at a time of constant air raids. We clambered to the end of Worms Head and made a count in late May of the great black-backed gull colony at what was apparently its peak. On the downs above Rhossili we saw Montagu's harriers and merlins and I found my first nightjar's nest, two deserted eggs among the growing bracken.

As a complete contrast was the Vale of Ewyas in the eastern Black Mountains, to which we were introduced by Hugh and Shifa Doncaster. This area has now become very well known to ornithologists and the 'improvement' of the once grassy track from Capel-y-ffin to Hay by Bwlch-yr-Efengyl (Gospel Pass) has opened it up to tourist traffic as well. When we knew it first there were three pairs of peregrines in the valley, peak predators of woodland and moorland communities that are still rich and well studied by the Gwent Ornithological Society.

At about the limit of a day trip was Llyn Safaddan (Llangorse Lake), the largest natural sheet of fresh water in South Wales, where great crested grebes and reed warblers bred in some numbers. The train that ran from Newport to Brecon was a great help in those carless days. By stopping at Talybont we could also visit the hillside heronry above Vaughan the Silurist's grave at Llansantffraed, or walk up Glyn Collwn to the reservoir. Here on 11 May 1946 I led a party from the Caerphilly School Field Club. I was in celebratory mood as our second son Robert had arrived two days before, and Dame Nature responded by producing my first black tern. But, while the goodies of the club and I were enjoying this bonus bird as it flapped over the head of the reservoir, the less high-minded members were, I discovered afterwards, busy digging out sand martins' nests from the bank of the feeder stream behind us.

In the summer of 1941 Margaret and I helped with a series of farm camps about seven miles north of Newport at Court Perrott, where 'the other' Peter Scott, the Quaker philanthropist who had initiated subsistence production schemes for the unemployed in parts of South Wales before the war, was now based with his wife Richenda. As a result of the camps and our mutual interests, the Scotts invited us to join them and help with various projects, from running a magazine to a detailed survey of the two parishes of Llandegfedd and Llandewi fach for the Wales Survey Board, one of Peter's many brainchildren. This move was, quite apart from the value of the work, an obvious economy if it could be integrated with our commitments in Cardiff, Caerphilly (where I was now teaching at the then Boys' Secondary School) and to various boys' and youth clubs in the valleys.

For two or three years of our time at Court Perrott I used to cycle early in the morning (7.40 to 8.20 BST, changing to Double Summer Time in April) nine miles into Newport station. To relieve the monotony I started to count the number of bird songs heard en route. Not having any mechanical devices to help me, I used to record the songs in my head thus: 'song thrush 2, blackbird 2, robin 3, wren 5' . . . 'song thrush 3, blackbird 2, robin 4, wren 6' . . . 'song thrush 3, blackbird 3, robin 4, wren 7' and so on, stopping at fixed points to jot the score down and start again with a clean mental slate. No one could claim perfect accuracy for such a rough and ready method, but it should at least allow a comparison to be made from day to day. I included every song I could hear from twenty-five species, though I had to put blackcap and garden warbler together, not having time to discriminate between this difficult pair.

The best records were kept from January to July 1943 and showed a peak of resident song on 24 February when my transit coincided with the dawn chorus, and a peak of all song on 21 May when the summer visitors were at full strength. Surprisingly the blackbird, which gives the body to most dawn choruses, scored well below the song thrush all along. The dominant voices at the early peak were wren (39), robin (25), and chaffinch (24), followed by song thrush (18), starling and dunnock (17). In May willow warbler (32) led wren (28), chaffinch (26), with robin on 13 and whitethroat and song thrush on 12. I corresponded with another and statistically better equipped enthusiast, P. R. Cox, for some time with a view to preparing a paper for publication. But other interests supervened and the data remain as a possible task for the leisure that old age is supposed to bring.

Apart from the song counts, my rides in and out of Newport were not without ornithological and sometimes other interest. I found nests of nightingale, a rarity in Wales, and yellow wagtail close to the road and on it a squashed water rail, a casualty still unique in my records. On reaching Newport station, usually short of time, I would weave through the crowd to my parking place, but once found myself heading as if mesmerized for a statuesque lady. Finally I embraced her round the waist while my bicycle clattered to the ground between us. 'There's only one place', she said, handing me off majestically, 'for people like you, and that's jail.' Less embarrassingly, I was waiting for the Caerphilly train when the announcer went on the air, whereat a railman standing in front of me turned to his mates: 'There 'e goes again, Mr Baritone Bloody College Jones.'

I had been a continuous subscriber to the journal *British Birds*, which then ran the ringing scheme, since 1929, and took up ringing again at the end of 1941 when we were established at Court Perrott. I also counted the only accessible heronry for the national census begun in 1928. This was at Pwllhead Wood near Llanmartin, where I did some of my last high climbs up its formidable oaks, now long felled. In 1943 I joined the British Trust for Ornithology as a result of meeting James Fisher, then its dynamic hon. secretary. I was already involved in the woodpigeon enquiry run by M. K. Colquhoun, and James, who was organizing the national census of rookeries, persuaded me to become local organizer which enabled me, on a special petrol allowance, to explore Gwent and east Glamorgan during the spring of 1945.

In June James announced that he and Edwin Cohen were coming down on the 23rd to certify kites' nests for the reward scheme then operated by the Royal Society for the Protection of Birds: would I like to join them and, if so, could I book them a double room for the previous night at a nearby guesthouse. Unfortunately I did not realize that the double room involved a double bed, but James and Edwin were still on speaking terms when they arrived at Court Perrott about 9.15 a.m. and we set out to pick up Miss Dorothy Raikes, who lived near Llangorse Lake and had organized kite protection for many years. Guided by her (the country was still without signposts due to the war) we eventually reached a farm in a valley characterized by its hanging oakwoods, the chosen breeding habitat of *y barcud*. These woods were also notable for the four indicator species of highland scrub: tree pipit, wood warbler, redstart and pied flycatcher.

Passing a cock pied flycatcher feeding fledged young, the farmer led us only about a hundred steep yards uphill from the road and pointed to a nest a little farther ahead. It was in the main fork of an oak some thirty feet up and looked rather smaller than a buzzard's nest. Even from below we could see a reddish-brown bird on it, which we took for an adult. But, climbing above, we saw that it was one of two large young, lying flat on opposite sides of the nest. We were surprised to find how near the adult's their plumage

was. The sun was shining on their rich, glossy backs
and wing-coverts, and, as I wrote to my parents afterwards, 'to be looking at close range on young kites in
the nest, in this wild place and with a chorus of interesting small birds all round, was a birdwatcher's dream
come true'.

But Miss Raikes said we might have to wait two or
three hours for a visit from an old bird and we had
'much to do'. This first involved James in an attempt to
certify a second nest on the same farm. He returned to
say he had seen an empty nest and disturbed a probable
young bird near it, but to check, Edwin and I were to
go through the wood again while James and Miss
Raikes spotted from the road. We found the nest, in a
tree which there had been a very recent attempt to
climb. I went up and decided that it was a crow's nest
and that no bird had fledged from it. Edwin and I got
back on to the road higher up and waited for the others
. . . and waited. Edwin bathed in the river and we then
amused ourselves finding a grey wagtail's nest with
young. Deciding that James and Miss Raikes had gone
to another site, we sauntered on up the road, seeing
ravens and buzzards and hearing a ring ousel, until the
car came up from behind us, having waited patiently
for us at the point where we entered the wood.

We were now, as cricketers say, well behind the
clock and Miss Raikes was overdue at another farm. So
it was agreed that Edwin and I should walk to Nan-
tymwyn, whence we could telephone Henry Elton,
with whom we had promised to have tea at Llansantffraed, a mere fifty miles away. It was now 4.30
p.m. Dr Elton was mildly ironic when I spoke to him,
but at least we did not lack a wonderful tea at Nan-
tymwyn of Welsh cakes and strawberries in an entirely
empty house, a sort of fairy-tale meal. Our hostess left
a note to say she was pitching hay, which might have

turned the food to ashes in softer mouths. She was, in fact, Mrs Vaughan who with her husband Captain Vaughan RN was to do so much for the kites and the cause of rural Wales in general in the post-war years.

Our second reunion with James and Miss Raikes took place as Edwin was wading the river, which I had crossed by a delirious bridge of narrow rusty rails, to ring his first ever brood of wood warblers. We went on together to a very famous site from which no young kites had fledged for twenty years. The nest was only twenty-five feet up a straight oak and contained a pierced egg on a lining of sodden wool with a little grass. The feathers of a young crow and half the lower jaw of a lamb were in the nest. It was now 8 p.m. and beginning to rain, but James said we must try to clinch the second site. This time we found another nest, to which I climbed under some protest in a heavy shower. It was obviously a fledged crow's nest and I threw it down for James to verify, hitting him on the head with it. We were explaining all this to the farmer when I caught sight of a huge wingspan over the house. We rushed round and there was the kite at last, 'primaries very frayed, but the forked tail as clear as though carved from wood. It looked far lankier than a buzzard, with the wing-beat of a large gull, slow and measured, each move evident ahead, as when it went up to perch on the skyline.' By now it was nearly 10 p.m. so there was nothing for it but to eat another meal, this time largely of home-baked bread and farm butter, and hope that Miss Raikes would be able to pay another visit of verification. We got her home at 12.30 a.m., just seven and a half hours late. 'This', said Edwin, 'is a record even for James.'

Among James Fisher's multifarious activities – as he liked to call them – was membership of the editorial board of Collins's New Naturalist series of books, which made their appearance at the end of the war like a rain of manna on a public starved of good reading in natural history. Coincidentally there was great interest in the possibility of National Parks, and the board decided that books about the most favoured regions would be appropriate as 'New Naturalists'.

So I was very much flattered when James asked me to write the natural history section of the proposed book on Snowdonia. Richenda Scott agreed to cover human history and Dr F. J. North, keeper of geology at the National Museum of Wales, completed the team. Some field work was essential for Richenda's and my sections and I paid four visits to North Wales in 1946. The second of these, from 24 to 29 May, was in company with Margaret's brother Carl Gibson-Hill.

Carl had been a keen naturalist as a boy, but parental pressure induced him to read medicine. After qualifying and marrying Ann Halliday, he went as medical officer first to Christmas Island in the Indian Ocean and then to the Cocos Keelings, where he had leisure to resurrect his boyhood interest, especially in birds, and add to it his great skill with the camera. His superbly illustrated articles on tropical sea birds appeared in *The Field* in the early years of the war, but when Japan invaded Malaya he was called to Singapore, just in time to be interned at Changi. He came back to Britain, characteristically via South Georgia, early in 1946, still full of pent-up energy and determined to do for British sea birds what he had done on his far-off islands.

He and Ann could scarcely have chosen a less propitious summer to make a grand tour of our sea bird haunts. But they accomplished it, and the results were *British Sea Birds* (Witherby, 1947) and *Birds of the Coast* (Witherby, 1949), which was revised by Robin Prytherch, also as illustrator, my son Robert and myself as *A guide to the birds of the coast* (Constable, 1976).

On this May trip Carl was alone with me and our first objective was Ystymllyn near Criccieth, then a wonderful mixture of marshy habitats with dry islands of whins and grass and surrounding woodland, both oak and conifer. Today a massive drainage scheme has converted it into featureless rush-grown fields, of little use to wild life or farming. But in 1946 it held Caernarfonshire's only pair of great crested grebes, breeding mallard, teal and shoveller, possibly garganey, and a sizeable colony of black-headed gulls, which Carl wanted to photograph.

The alarm clock borrowed from our landlady went off at 4.15, so we were out on the marsh before 5 to put up Carl's hide. What with the wind and the lack of firm ground for pegs we had a tricky time but were reassured to see the gulls return to their nests as soon as we regained terra firma. We came back after breakfast and I cut a mass of reeds which sank at once under Carl's feet, but there was nothing for it but to leave him there. After three hours he emerged, having stood nearly up to his knees in water (not very good for post-internment rheumatics), most of the time clutching the hide round the slit facing the nests. Still, he was delighted at the way the birds had come back and hoped he had got a good series, which proved to be the case.

Early next morning I visited a hillside quarry where both choughs and peregrines were nesting. I had excellent views of the choughs from an old shack; when one parent flew in to the clamorous young in their crevice nest, the other stayed just in sight. Twice I saw faecal sacs carried away from the quarry, but I picked up an eggshell below the nest. The peregrine still had eggs and I ringed the young on my June visit after a descent I do not remember with pride; but a quarry of loose shale was a poor exchange for the hard Highland rocks on which John Pringle and I had done our raven climbs.

In an afternoon of deteriorating weather Carl and I drove on to Anglesey and Llanddwyn Island near Newborough. We hoped to find a tern colony, but Mrs Jones the watcher was profuse in her apologies for the lateness of the birds, a few of which, common or arctic, we saw over offshore skerries. Among them was my first pair of Welsh roseate terns. To compensate, Mrs Jones showed us a nest of young rock pipits. 'I call them mountain larks', she said as if it increased their rarity. Two days later we returned to the area and located a ternery on the spit of Abermenai; in June Carl photographed his little tern there.

Our other objective on this trip was at the north end of Menai: Puffin Island which I had visited briefly with Margaret in 1939. According to Carl the morning of 27 May typified the British spring: 'intermittent drizzle lashed into periodic fury by a half gale'. However, Huw Goronwy Jones was willing to take us over from Beaumaris in his sixteen-footer and we duly made Puffin's one stony beach, up which we carried a tiny dinghy. Carl's bird here was the great black-backed gull, which likes prominent sites. The first nest we tried was so exposed that we could not put the hide up, so we transferred to the lee slope where another bird sat amid a carpet of bluebells. I made a quick survey of the island before releasing Carl, who had been quite successful, and we were just deciding where to put the hide in the cormorant colony when Huw reappeared waving frantically. As we made for the beach, a lesser black-back came off its nest deep in the alexanders, an abundant legacy of the island's monks, but could not rise, so I threw the hide bag over it and ringed it; it flew perfectly from my hand, but there was no time to exploit this technique.

Quite a hectic operation ensued, getting us and the gear out in the dinghy to Huw's boat. This was followed by a comprehensive wetting as the boat cut into the waves and their contents dropped on us. At Beaumaris they said the lifeboat had been told to stand by for us, the only time I have had that honour. In spite of his detestation of our climate Carl stayed on to make another and more successful attack on the cormorants. On my way east with Jack Hollins, who had organized our comfortable base camp with the Verneys at Rhianva, we stopped by Llyn Ogwen where, following up a nine-year-old tip, I found my first Welsh sandpiper's nest on the shore quite close to the road.

10
Serious Censuses

When I began visiting Court Perrott in the spring of
1941, I had the ambitious plan of a breeding bird census
over the farm's whole 250 acres, carried out on five
searches between March and June. This was because
the only comparable study I could find was made over
nearly 300 acres of farmland near Oxford by
W. M. M. Chapman and members. of the Oxford
Ornithological Society in the 1930s. In 1942 I cut my
area down to 100 acres (about forty hectares) about as
much as a single observer can tackle in open country; in
woodland his area should be much smaller if he is to
achieve any sort of accuracy.

How the Court Perrott censuses became the germ of
a Ph.D. thesis I cannot now recall; but clearly a breeding season study made a great appeal to a birds nester
from boyhood and related to those stirrings I had felt at
seeing Max Nicholson's Greenland maps. I discovered
that there was already a fairly profuse literature,
mainly Finnish and American, bearing on the assessment of breeding populations in the North Temperate

Zone, and that there were two main methods, the strip or transect count, favoured in Finland for getting relative numbers over large areas of uniform habitat, and the plot or block with definite boundaries, capable of being worked over regularly to give an accurate census.

But the 'breeding population' is a fiction in the sense that birds do not have identical breeding seasons and some may have finished nesting before others begin; indeed late breeders like the hobby use the hatched-off nests of crows. So an assessment of breeding population must take place throughout the season, the emphasis on species changing all the time. I took as my mentor on methods S. C. Kendeigh, whose paper 'The Measurement of Bird Populations' appeared in 1944 in No. 14 of the U.S. series *Ecological Monographs*. Kendeigh and the Finnish pioneer ecologist Pontus Palmgren recommended six visits to areas of reasonable size as sufficient to discover between 96 and 100 per cent of the breeding birds. It was A. B. Williams in 1936 who hit on the idea of using a separate field map for each visit and then combining the data on them at the end of the season.

This, of course, is the method used by the British Trust for Ornithology's Common Bird Census, which acts as a monitoring system for all types of habitat. Since it is not usually possible to find all or even a high proportion of nests on a plot, the occurrence of a singing male in the same spot on several visits, the behaviour of parents and other indications of breeding are all taken into account. The risk has to be faced that a consistently singing male is not unmated, and Kendeigh suggested that for some species as many as 9 per cent of songsters may be loners.

Chapman believed in assessing the 'summer population' rather than the breeding population. This includes birds that are feeding but not breeding on the area and could therefore add enormously to the numbers and biomass if flocks of rooks, jackdaws and woodpigeons are involved. The difficulties of making an accurate assessment of the summer population are much the same as I encountered when trying to make counts of the winter population.

In 1943 and 1944 I spent about 75 hours each season on the Court Perrott 100 acres which consisted of arable and pasture fields, a 'dingle' with the remains of an orchard, a steep 'ferny bank', and the course of the little river Soar, the whole garnished with substantial hedges. I also included the farmhouse 'complex' with its buildings, small garden and shelter belt of conifers. In these years I reckoned I had found the nests of 89.5 and 90.3 per cent of the pairs of birds present. Most were found by 'cold' searching, simply looking in likely places and spotting them; others, pre-eminently tree pipit and willow warbler, usually yielded to 'hot' searching, when the sitting bird is flushed after location of the pair. 'Watching back', the most sophisticated technique, is unfortunately time-consuming but played its part, especially when birds were carrying food.

I spent less time on the plot in 1945–7 and found a lower proportion of nests, but managed to justify to myself, and evidently to the gentlemen who read my thesis, that the accuracy of the census did not suffer. As it may have at least historical interest, I am showing the full Court Perrott series (1942–7), the species arranged in the 'Voous order', on the use of which for Holarctic birds there seems to be general agreement. The column next to the birds' names relates to the visits or periods in which I concentrated on each species, from 1 (second half March) to 6 (first half June). Nests found outside these 'specific' visits were not rejected, unless, like the one lapwing's nest in 1945, it was unusually late. One of the difficulties in defining a census plot neatly is to know where to fix its boundaries. Hedges, streams and ditches are not satisfactory ecologically because they may hold the nests of birds whose territories extend along and around them. But sometimes I had to use them and they account for the odd .5s in the table.

I compared each year's totals with the lowest mean monthly temperature of the previous winter and to these Dr D. G. Tucker applied the only statistical test in the whole thesis, an odd thought today when hardly a sentence of reasoning is advanced without mathematical backing. He found that correlation between the winter temperature and the population of resident species the following spring was 99.9 per cent reliable, which he considered 'a remarkable result'; correlation with species was 99.0 per cent reliable. There was no correlation between temperature and the number of breeding summer visitors. The effect of the previous winter differs considerably between species. The catastrophic drop in wrens in 1945 followed a winter apparently far less severe than 1946–7 and was accompanied by decreases in robins and song thrushes but not of blackbirds. Sometimes, of course, a quite short severe spell can kill small birds but not larger ones and is hardly noticed by man. Chaffinches also fell in 1945, recovered remarkably in 1946 – the tall hawthorn hedges were optimum nesting habitat for them – and shared in the general decline of 1947, when the total of breeding residents was under half that of the peak season 1943. My eye falls on the high total of magpies in 1945: could this have been due to plentiful carrion?

Serious Censuses

The Court Perrott 100 acre Censuses, 1942–7

		1942	1943	1944	1945	1946	1947
Lowest mean monthly temp. of previous winter in °C		1.4	5.8	4.4	1.2	3.0	−1.7
Month		2/42	1/43	2/44	1/45	1/46	2/47

Species	Specific Visits	Pairs of birds					
RESIDENTS:							
Kestrel	3–5	—	1	1	—	—	—
Grey Partridge	3–5	1	1	1	2	2	1
Pheasant	2–4	—	—	1	—	—	1
Moorhen	2–4	3.5	4.5	3	4	2.5	4
Lapwing	2–4	—	—	—	(1)	—	1
Stock Dove	3–5	—	—	—	—	0.5	—
Woodpigeon	3–5	5	8	5	3.5	8	4.5
Little Owl	3–5	1	2	1	1	2	—
Tawny Owl	1–3	—	—	0.5	—	—	0.5
Kingfisher	2–4	1	1	1	1	0.5	—
Green Woodpecker	3–5	1	1	1	0.5	—	—
Skylark	2–4	4	5	4	4	3	3
Wren	2–4	10.5	12	11.5	1.5	2	—
Dunnock	2–4	10	11	16.5	12.5	12	5
Robin	1–3	6.5	8.5	12	6	6	1
Blackbird	1–3	14	22	18	18.5	13	5
Song Thrush	1–3	2	4.5	3	0.5	1	1
Mistle Thrush	1–3	2	2.5	1	1	0.5	—
Long-tailed Tit	1–3	0.5	1.5	0.5	—	—	—
Marsh Tit	2–4	2	1	1	2	2	—
Willow Tit	2–4	—	1	—	1	1	—
Coal Tit	2–4	0.5	—	1	—	—	—
Blue Tit	2–4	4	4	5	3	6	2
Great Tit	2–4	4.5	5.5	2.5	2.5	2	1
Jay	3–5	1	—	—	—	1	1
Magpie	1–3	3	4.5	5.5	7.5	5.5	4
Carrion Crow	1–3	2	2	2	2	1	2
Starling	2–4	6.5	5	2	1.5	2.5	2.5
House Sparrow	3–5	17	21.5	21	15	18	17.5
Tree Sparrow	2–4	—	1	2	4	3	1
Chaffinch	2–4	11.5	33.5	29.5	22	32	19.5
Greenfinch	3–5	3	4	4.5	4	2	2
Goldfinch	3–5	—	1	2	2	2	—

The Court Perrott 100 acre Censuses, 1942–7 (contd.)

		1942	1943	1944	1945	1946	1947
Lowest mean monthly temp. of previous winter in °C		1.4	5.8	4.4	1.2	3.0	−1.7
Month		2/42	1/43	2/44	1/45	1/46	2/47
Species	*Specific Visits*	*Pairs of birds*					
RESIDENTS:							
Linnet	3–5	1	1	1	—	—	—
Bullfinch	3–5	2	2.5	1	2	1	2
Yellowhammer	3–5	6	6	7	6	7	6
	TOTALS	126	179	168	130.5	139	87.5
SUMMER VISITORS:							
Turtle Dove	4–6	1	—	1	—	—	—
Cuckoo	4–6	1	1	1	—	—	—
Swallow	4–6	1	2	3	1	1	1
House Martin	4–6	9	3	9	6	3	6
Tree Pipit	4–6	4	4	2	1	2	2
Yellow Wagtail	4–6	—	1	—	—	—	—
Lesser Whitethroat	4–6	0.5	—	0.5	0.5	—	—
Whitethroat	4–6	9	9.5	10.5	12.5	10	9
Garden Warbler	4–6	1	1	—	—	—	—
Blackcap	4–6	1	1	1	—	1.5	—
Willow Warbler	4–6	10	9	9	10	6.5	9
Chiffchaff	3–5	—	—	—	1.5	—	0.5
Spotted Flycatcher	4–6	1	1	2	1	—	0.5
	TOTALS	38.5	32.5	39	33.5	24	28
TOTALS ALL SPECIES		170.5	211.5	207	164	163	115.5
Species nesting each year		39	40	42	35 (+1)	34	30

During 1942–7, when I got to know the county well, I believe that almost exactly a hundred species, several of them confined to the highlands in the north-west, were breeding regularly in Gwent; is it remarkable that forty-nine of them nested or attempted to nest in at least one year on the Court Perrott plot? Given variety of cover, with plenty of 'edge effect', water, and access to feeding areas, high densities both of species and of individual pairs seem to follow. The Hordley censuses (pp. 264–9) showed this 'oasis effect' even more strikingly and I suspect that many ornithologists could produce pet areas with similar totals. In the USA Gilbert H. Grosvenor found fifty-nine nests with eggs or young on one acre of his Maryland farm in mid-June 1915, but forty-two of them were in nestboxes.

Once I had more or less perfected a census method for a reasonably large area, the next question was to what problem it should be applied, and Professor Ritchie (see p. 45) suggested that the effect of industrialization on a bird population had not been studied, and there was I on the edge of an industrial area where farming was still carried on amidst the collieries. The final title of the thesis was therefore 'A comparison of bird populations upon "industrial" and "rural" farmland in South Wales'; (a shortened version was published in the *Reports and Transactions of the Cardiff Naturalists' Society*, vol. 81, 1950–2).

It was decided that the field work should take place over two years and that I could not work more than two pairs of census plots at the same time. So I set out to find four 'industrial' farms with suitable 'rural' controls. Ideally, of course, I should have laid a grid on the map and fixed my plots by random selection. But that was simply not possible in the fragmented area like South Wales and in the end I had to pick as best I could.

I retained Court Perrott as a rural control (Ar), only a few miles west of 'Ai', a farm close to the polluted Afon Lwyd and almost cut in half by a factory. 'Bi' was on a steep slope near Abertridwr, north of Caerphilly; 'Br' was of similar aspect on the south side of Caerphilly Mountain. 'Ci' was north of Bargoed, close to a colliery and found for me by Emlyn Evans, as was its control in a valley that, apart from a railway line, had escaped serious industrial effects. 'Dr', which included the historic farmhouse of Plas Machen, was by the Rhymni downstream of 'Di', just within the coalfield.

All the farmers were most helpful, though birdwatching was still something of a mystery to most people; as I approached one farm past a row of small houses, I sensed a message being passed from one to another and a faint ripple of lace curtains along the terrace. But what I could not have foreseen was the prolonged hard spell of early 1947 which seriously affected my data for the second breeding season, quite apart from the winter counts, and showed how vulnerable are studies based on only one or two years.

The breeding season field work I found enjoyable. The winter counts, whatever the weather, were much more of a slog as they really needed a party walking in line to be effective. At times I had help from members of the Caerphilly School Field Club, some of them good observers, but others less reliable. During the 1947 cold spell the work became only too easy on the high level C plots as the birds either disappeared or congregated round the farm buildings, except for scavenging crows and magpies looking for dead sheep. Red squirrels were driven by hunger to run about on the snow and my footprints remained frozen and inviolate between one visit (I tried to do a count every fortnight) and the next. One day, crossing the mountain ridge between the plots, my eyes began to water in the wind and the drops froze. I think that was the day I met a gang trying to raise a fallen metal power pylon. As their vehicle hoisted it, a ram – one horn encircling a cable – was lifted high in the air, then slid down sickeningly to earth.

It was during my census work that I finally ceased to collect eggs. One of the pleasant features of 'my' farms was that they all had tree pipits on them and on 'Cr' I found a remarkably obvious nest of white fescue stems in which lay the six most beautiful eggs, deep plummy purple, on which human eyes have ever rested. Like the drunkard with his bottle I sat on the bank for several minutes and reflected. If I continued to take eggs, I could never enjoy the full confidence of other ornithologists, and all that I was dimly foreseeing might follow from my thesis would be jeopardized. At last I got up and walked away. On my next visit all six eggs had hatched.

At the end of my field work and the pretty agonizing process of writing it up – and 'writing up' included the preparation of thirty-two coloured maps – I came to no earth-shattering conclusions. General observations, both mine and other people's, combined to suggest, as might be expected, that industrialization had impoverished the bird life of the South Wales coalfield, but as the process began so long ago a certain stabilization had set in and the status of many common birds was probably the same in the 1940s as it had been fifty years earlier. It would be interesting to assess the position now, in the light of a further thirty or more years' general tidying up of the landscape.

As regards farmland, the habitat chosen for my study, my counts suggested that winter populations were much the same on the industrial 'i' and rural 'r' plots, fewer rooks on 'i' being balanced in numbers but not in biomass by more starlings and house sparrows.

The winter populations were practically identical in species. The breeding population, however, was richer both in species and numbers on 'r' than on 'i'. But the difference in numbers was largely due to a concentration of birds round the farmhouse on rural farms; in the industrial area, starlings and sparrows tended to nest on buildings surrounding the farmland. This could, of course, be regarded as an effect of urbanization rather than of industry.

I could find no evidence of greater predation on the 'i' plots, though in general their vegetative cover was poorer. On the other hand some species may have fared better in 'i' than on 'r' in severe weather, due to food provided by man, again an urban rather than an industrial effect.

Since these contributions to solving the problem set me were so tentative I had to fall back on the methods used for something more definite if negative: 'It is extremely difficult to establish valid controls to specific blocks of farmland'; and 'An accurate method of counting winter bird populations on large areas has not yet been devised'. But I concluded that reasonably accurate breeding censuses could be carried out on 100 acre plots of farmland by a single observer on the six visit basis. That this is the method used by the BTO seems a reasonable endorsement, although I do not think my thesis influenced its choice. Indeed the only flicker its publication aroused was in the USA where Robert A. Norris gave it an excellent review in *The Auk*, some five years after the Cardiff Naturalists generously put it into print.

11
The Great Seal Flight

During the cold spell of early 1947, between 8 January and 25 March, I caught in small traps and ringed 187 birds of twelve species in the little garden of the Cardiff house to which we moved from Court Perrott at the end of 1945. It is now well known that large numbers of birds may pass through suburban gardens, but to me then it seemed surprising that we should host ninety different blue tits. We also saw the territorial behaviour of the robin break down under the stress of the cold, catching five birds at the same site in thirty-three minutes one February morning. Our only mildly exciting recovery was a starling, trapped in a blizzard on 4 March and found two days later at Bishopston in Gower about forty miles west, an obvious hard weather migrant. We caught two willow tits, the bird I had put on the Gwent list six years earlier, and I carried a large rotten stump into the garden, hoping that they would stay and excavate it. No such luck but, during the three seasons (1946–8) we lived in Derwen Road, chaffinch, blue tit (in a nestbox), blackbird and dunnock nested on our sixth of an acre, and robins attempted to nest in an open-fronted box; great tits (in a vertical drain pipe) and song thrushes nested next door.

Altogether thirty-nine species perched on the house or in the garden, including sparrowhawk, tawny owl, cuckoo, black-headed and common gulls (during the 1947 'spell'), and redpolls which came in autumn to attack the seeds on our two rows of birch trees. We saw or heard another thirty-nine species from or over our minuscule property but the nearness of the Llanishen reservoirs helped, giving us five waders and the arctic terns in April 1947. With the help of Leighton Reynolds, a talented member of the Caerphilly School Field Club, I also made a list for the garden of fifty higher plants and ferns, the most surprising being a helleborine, which forced its way through the thin cement leading to the garage.

Derwen Road was the by no means uninteresting base from which I visited my study areas and, when the long cold spell ended, made trips farther afield, with the newly formed and very enthusiastic ornithological section of the Cardiff Naturalists' Society, with the Caerphilly club and the Fochriw Youth Centre. One of the oddest exploits was to take a young raven for the Zoological Society of London. Before the 1954 Bird Protection Act there was no legal way in which birds could be taken for scientific or educational purposes, so Emlyn Evans , his brother Gwynne and I had to risk a visit to a nest in the Brecon Beacons, remove a well-grown young one and send it by train to London, where it arrived safely and I saw it for many years afterwards.

By now I had become a member of the British Ornithologists' Union and in June 1947 Margaret and I attended the unofficial international congress organized in Edinburgh by the Union and the Scottish Ornithologists' Club. Here was a chance to meet or at least put a face to names I had known for many years. It was also the first time I saw ornithologists in the mass on an excursion, when we surged over Tentsmuir, which had suffered somewhat from the depredations of hungry foreign soldiers during the war. The Sandwich tern colony we had visited so briefly in 1933 'vanished' in 1940, but we saw a few birds, as well as arctic, common and little terns, all nesting. Eiders and shelduck were everywhere on the moor and the dunes; at one pool with feather-littered banks I was delighted to hear a French colleague exclaim: 'Ah, la place de toilette des tadornes!'

There was also, in July, a visit with Niall to the Bass Rock and Craigleith off North Berwick at the invitation of the Midlothian Ornithological Club, who had founded the Isle of May Bird Observatory before the war and done so much to organize scientific ornithology in Scotland. I ringed a few young gannets and a young puffin which I found in a hole by the path leading up the Rock. Since gannets and the Bass are literally synonymous (*Sula bassana*) it is surprising that their presence there is not mentioned before Fordun's *Scotichronicon* (1447), but Bryan Nelson's splendid monograph (*The Gannet*, Poyser, 1978), which came to hand as I was writing this chapter, suggests they may have been there 'before man existed'.

The congress was marked by various celebrations. After one party, at Luffness near Aberlady, I decided to walk back to Edinburgh. I said goodbye to a heron by the Peffer Burn at 11.40 p.m. and the song thrushes and robins ceased singing as I passed through Aberlady village a few minutes later. Bats, moths and roding woodcock – once two flew along together above the road – saw me through the wooded Wemyss estate and

I heard what may have been a young long-eared owl. Redshanks, curlews, oystercatchers and gulls called over the shore approaching Longniddry, then there was silence from 1.30 to 3.30 a.m. until I met a tawny owl on a light standard in Milton Road West. Coots called from Duddingston Loch as I made my way up Arthur's Seat to a snatch of skylark song near the summit at 4.10. At 4.25 the blackbirds began singing from the whins by the Salisbury Craigs and the town birds took up the chorus from them all the way to George Square, where at least four serenaded me. The only other time I have walked through a June night was in 1932, from Dunkeld to Blairgowrie and back, with corncrakes as my constant vocal companions.

In the autumn of 1947, when I was getting down to writing up my thesis and also battling with my section of the New Naturalist *Snowdonia* (published in 1949 and never reprinted), James Fisher came up with another of his irresistible invitations. Through ACARF, which I think stood for Advisory Committee for Airborne Research Facilities, he had in June laid on a flight to Rockall, on which, some years later, he actually landed when it was claimed for Britain. The present proposal was even more ambitious, an aerial count of calves or pups at most of the known British stations of the grey seal, of which over half the world population breeds round the coasts of Britain and Ireland. For the first three weeks or so of their lives the calves or pups have a white pelage which could make them conspicuous from the air. Although some colonies were known to breed in caves, it was hoped to cover these by ground observers. The only large colony omitted from the programme was on the Farne Islands, which was counted regularly by the National Trust's local committee.

My total flying experience had been a five bob flip

144

many years previously, so apprehension as well as
excitement moved me as I took the train from Cardiff
for what seemed an interminable journey to Pembroke
Dock. Here I spent two night at the RAF station while
others of the party gradually assembled. The most
distant members were coming up with the Sunderland
flying boat from Calshot. A visit to Orielton, the
famous duck decoy, and to Pembroke Castle, with
Ronald Lockley, who knew them both so well, as our
guide, passed the time of waiting most enjoyably. In
the Wogan Cavern of the Castle we heard the lesser
horseshoe bats and trod in their copious droppings; the
more visually acute claimed to have seen them. As we
were walking up a minor road nearby, Keith Piercy
suddenly pounced and lifted a large brown rat out of
the hedgerow by its tail, a feat equivalent to Dunky's
picking dogfish out of the sea (see p. 68).

At 9.20 on the fine morning of 28 September the
aircraft took off from Milford Haven and we were
soon over what are now called the Priseli islands:
Skokholm, where the bird observatory staff waved to
us (Ronald Lockley, its founder, was, of course, with
us), Skomer, where we saw our first four seal calves,
and Grassholm, still covered with gannets, shining
white and a secondary target for our observations.

During the flight James usually sat between the co-
pilots, able to talk to us by the intercom, Stephen
Potter sat in the astrodome, thinking literary thoughts,
while Eric Hosking our photographer was by the port
rear hatch, and the rest of us occupied the saloon,
armed with notebooks and sometimes all rushing to
one side in our excitement, somewhat to the captain's
dismay, though his reproofs were studiedly mild.

We made two circuits of Ramsey, where Jack
Davies, one of our party, was studying the seals and
knew there had been fifty-two calves the previous day.

None of us now saw more than three and they, it emerged later, may have been bleached driftwood. So our census, in the words of James Fisher's log, 'was hopeless and as a survey it was indifferent and inaccurate'. But there was no time then for regret as we flew north over Cardigan Bay, past Holyhead's South Stack, over the Calf of Man and on to the Scar Rocks, a small gannet colony at the mouth of Solway Firth. Here we made three circuits and got a reasonable estimate of the birds. Ailsa Craig's larger colony was in view and we had to hang on to Eric Hosking's coat tails as he leaned out of the hatch to photograph it.

Forty choppy minutes later we had crossed southern Scotland and I was surveying the Bass Rock once more. But the turbulence had somewhat upset our equilibrium and the flight up the east coast to be waterborne at Alness on the Cromarty Firth was, in today's jargon, somewhat low key. Here, with Ben Wyvis, already snow-capped, as our backcloth, we spent the night and were joined by Frank Fraser Darling, so that, with Ronald Lockley, we had Britain's two most noted island naturalists aboard.

Next morning we were airborne just before 8 a.m. and soon moving up the ironbound coast of Caithness to round Duncansby Head and circle the Pentland Skerries, where we saw our first seals of the day. Thence onward a maze of islands, first Orkney and next Shetland, streamed past below with James happily intoning the crisp Nordic names the vikings gave them. One was Copinsay, now a memorial nature reserve to James himself and over which appropriately his favourite birds the fulmars were flying. Over North Ronaldshay he warned us of the local seaweed-eating sheep, easy to confuse with seals. Passing Fair Isle Eric took his classic picture of this renowned bird island; then came the Mainland of Shetland and rock doves in the Broch of Mousa.

A circuit of Noss showed a lower percentage of gannets on its fierce face than at Ailsa Craig. After that the names took charge: Rumble, Out Skerries, Vongs, Lunna Ness, Samphrey. About 11 a.m. we were over Fetlar, famous as the snowy owl's nesting place, and somewhere hereabouts I heard over the intercom: 'Sir, we have eighteen bodies aboard and only ten parachutes.' 'At this height,' came the reply, 'we might as well have none', and indeed the thrill of the flight was to be travelling most of the time only a couple of hundred feet above the white-flecked sea.

Soon we rounded Muckle Flugga, Britain's northernmost point, and the names took over again: Ramna Stacks, the Ossas, the Drougs, Vee Skerries, where Brian Roberts reported five seal calves. After Fitful Head we flew out to Foula, seeing a blue phase fulmar and the corn still uncut, then back to Orkney and a circuit of Eynhallow, the sacred island where many years later I helped ring young fulmars. From Marwick Head and the Kitchener Memorial we headed west for those mysterious islets Sule Skerry and Stack – another gannetry – and then to North Rona, the largest grey seal colony of all, where Frank Darling had spent a season and counted 1500 calves. Our aerial figure was 410 plus.

From the air the island, rubbed brown by the adult seals' bodies, looked like a huge decaying joint on which the white calves were maggots. A cohort of great black-backed gulls waited for their pickings, anything from afterbirths to dead calves. Nature was certainly in the raw. A few minutes more brought us to Sula Sgeir, still visited by the Men of Ness in Lewis for an annual crop of young gannets, or 'gugas'; by now most of the birds had gone. On the Flannan Isles we saw a few gannets (though breeding was not recorded there until 1969) but no seals.

Seventeen minutes later we were over St Kilda, to most of us the most dramatic moment of the whole trip. So it was aeronautically: we climbed to 2,000 feet over the big hills of Hirta, hit an air pocket and swooped down over Village Bay so fast that, as Max Nicholson put it during the evening's re-cap session, 'I was more concerned to know whether the tail was still attached to the 'plane than whether there were seals in the water.'

The ceaseless weaving network of fulmars over the sea round these remote islands remains my other vivid memory. Yet to the crew, as their comments over the inter-com showed, it was just another routine flight. After this high moment, the flight back round the north of Scotland in sunshine was a pleasant anti-climax, seeing how the farming pattern changed from the crofts of Sutherland to the orthodox fields of Caithness and even more fertile Easter Ross. We were back at Alness by 5.30 p.m.

On our last day we retraced our path to Cape Wrath, then flew down the west coast past lovely Sandwood Bay and Handa to the Summer Isles Frank Darling knew so well, and out to the Shiants, whence it was only a hop to the Outer Isles and the important seal colonies of Gasker, Shillay and Haskeir, where I counted 20 to 25 calves. From Benbecula we turned back to the Inner Hebrides, passed between Coll and Tiree and made our various counts and estimates of the seals on the Treshnish Isles to the west of Mull. As I had landed on the largest, Lunga, earlier that summer, I found the aerial view particularly interesting. Oronsay was our last counting point and just over two hours later, with a glimpse of Ulster's Copeland Islands en route, we were waterborne at Pembroke Dock, whence it took me about five hours to get home.

What had we proved? That you cannot, by the amateur methods we used, count or even estimate grey seal calves from the air. But we had gained an unforgettable impression of cliffbound Britain and her islands, and I had met for the first time men who have been my friends ever since. They included Max Nicholson, who had already exerted an influence on my ornithological life and who was now chairman of the British Trust for Ornithology, rapidly expanding in the post-war birdwatching boom. Next summer I met Max, Edwin Cohen, who had succeeded Richard Fitter as hon. secretary, and Philip Brown, the hon. treasurer, in a Soho restaurant. They invited me to become the BTO's first full-time secretary (made possible by a generous covenant from Edwin) and on 1 October 1948 I started work in Oxford.

12
Ornithological Functionary

I was not a complete stranger to Oxford in 1948. Staying with Neil Wylie on Boar's Hill before the war, I had seen the local hawfinches and had walked on Port Meadow, one of the most birdwatched areas in Europe. More recently I had sought advice about my thesis from Charles Elton, the director of the Bureau of Animal Population (BAP) and founding father of the science of animal ecology, and from Wilfrid (W. B.) Alexander, the first director of the Edward Grey Institute of Field Ornithology (EGI) and one of Britain's only two pre-war professionals. Compendious of memory (he really could take a book off the shelf and open it at the page he wanted) and master of the throwing sentence, he greeted me: 'H'm, I expected someone very much older', a reference to a namesake who had contributed notes to the *Scottish Naturalist*. James Fisher and Edwin Cohen had been housed in the University Museum with their National Rook Investigation and I had perambulated Addison's Walk with James discussing it.

But to work permanently in Oxford was another matter. In Cardiff I had latterly been a fairly big fish in a fairly small pool. Now I was a new boy again. I had become used to the Welsh courtesy of daily greetings as a matter of course; now I found that people who knew me perfectly well would pass by without a word unless they had something of import to say. Fortunately John White had joined the staff of St Edward's School in 1946 and he and his wife Barbara (whom he had met during the war at 'Livags') were now living at Steeple Aston, some twelve miles north of Oxford, and most kindly housed me until we could find a place of our own.

My one-room office, which I shared with my secretary Rosemary Wilkinson, was in the EGI, temporarily housed with the BAP in a wartime hospital in the grounds of St Hugh's College. David Lack had succeeded 'WBA' as director in 1945 and had attracted round him a remarkable group of enthusiasts. Peter Hartley, Robert Hinde, David Snow and John Gibb were all engaged in different aspects of a massive study of titmice in Wytham Woods, thanks to Charles Elton and the BAP the best inventoried two square miles in the natural world. Monica Betts (now Turner) as an entomologist studied the food of titmice, much of her work being done in the Forest of Dean. Reg Moreau was one of David Lack's great captures. Already an expert on African birds, he became editor of the BOU's journal *The Ibis* and brought it triumphantly into the mid-twentieth century. Later he became a distinguished President of the Union and found time to write a gem of a book, *The Departed Village* (O.U.P., 1969), about Berrick Salome where he lived for many years with his wife Winnie, a green-fingered gardener who was also an excellent ornithologist. David Lack's secretary was Elizabeth Silva, who became his wife and collaborated with him in many important papers.

Finally, there was 'W.B.A.', who, after retiring as director, had been persuaded by David Lack to stay on part-time at the EGI to look after the library which he had personally built up and which bears his name. Years afterwards I told him that I had systematically picked his brains during my first months in Oxford and he did not take this at all amiss. He loved imparting information, laced with anecdotes and hedged with caveats. Once David Lack and I were pressing some incontrovertible point on him; eventually he conceded: 'That is, to a very considerable extent, true'. One of my BTO jobs was to act as secretary to the Bird Observatories Committee of which he was chairman. We used to have one 'central' meeting a year and one at a bird observatory. When we were planning a visit to Spurn Point, his description of a journey there by public transport verged on the horrific. 'And even when you have got to Hull,' he would say with relish, 'your troubles are by no means at an end.' I was only one of many recipients of wisdom from his great storehouse: he was ready to help the freshest of undergraduates at any time and, as I wrote after his death in 1965, 'he directly influenced almost everyone of the generation which has given the study of birds its present high standing'.

The other leading ornithologist when I arrived in Oxford was Bernard (B. W.) Tucker, whose immortality is ensured as one of the authors of *The Handbook of British Birds* (1938–41), in which his sections on 'field characters and general habits' are masterpieces of concise lucidity. He succeeded Harry Witherby as editor of *British Birds*, for which it was said with some truth that his office was the chest of drawers in his dressing room. He wrote innumerable letters in meticulous longhand and guided the journal expertly through the first postwar years of expanding interest.

Bernard's conversation was an idiosyncratic mixture of long words and Bunteresque slang; of one unreliable correspondent he complained: 'He keeps sending me accounts of perfectly bilging birds', while at David Lack's first student conference, when Gwen Davies of the RSPB and I were also introduced, he described us as 'a parade of ornithological functionaries'. He continued to the end of a life tragically cut short by cancer to combine a highly trained scientific brain with an infectious and boyish enthusiasm for seeing birds. Only two or three months before his death he was taken to see pectoral and Baird's sandpipers at Perry Oaks sewage farm. Asked afterwards how he felt, he replied: 'Terrible, but it was worth it'.

Very soon after I had arrived in Oxford, we held a meeting there of Regional Representatives, who had recently been appointed as the BTO's membership was increasing so rapidly. The biggest intake was from the application form which James Fisher had managed to get included at the end of his tremendously successful Penguin *Watching Birds*, first published in 1943. In contrast to the small group of professionals at the EGI, I now met the amateurs, many of whom had kept ornithology going during the war. One decision of this meeting was that I should get around the country as much as possible, speak at meetings and generally show the BTO's flag and encourage people to contribute to its various enquiries.

I do not intent to describe in detail what the Trust did, or does in its greatly expanded modern form, especially as I hope that a history of its first fifty years may appear to mark its jubilee in 1983. But it was founded on the basis of the co-operative enquiry, the germ of which may be seen in Gilbert White's circle of correspondents and which was developed as long ago as 1865 by the Anglo-Irish naturalist A. G. More, who enquired into the current status of British birds and whose questionnaires are preserved at the EGI. The BTO took over from *British Birds* the national ringing scheme, operated from the Natural History Museum by Miss E. P. Leach, and the annual census of heronries, organized and reported on for many years by W. B. Alexander. The Nest Records Scheme was actually started under BTO auspices in 1939 by Julian Huxley and James Fisher; it is, of course, another permanent enquiry. As well as these continuing studies, there are trust-aïded investigations which, at least in my day, were thought up by individual members and submitted as proposals to the research or scientific advisory committee. If approved, they received the full backing of the BTO's organization; my own enquiry into the status of the pied flycatcher in 1952 is an example, and it was followed up by a repeat in 1962. In addition the BTO could run an enquiry of limited duration on its own, like the mute swan census of 1955–6 which I organized as part of my duties, whereas the pied flycatcher enquiry was a 'private' effort. There were also Requests for Information by members which had to be approved by the research committee, were then given publicity by the BTO and might lead to a trust-aided investigation.

In 1948 the BTO communicated with its members through a periodic Bulletin which it fell to me to edit. The annual report on the ringing scheme continued to appear for many years in *British Birds*, whose subscribers, as well as the BTO members, were entitled to take part. It soon became clear that something more substantial than a bulletin was needed if reports on other enquiries were not to be held up. But it was not until March 1954 that *Bird Study* was launched with 'Mick'

(H. N.) Southern of the Bureau of Animal Population as editor. When the first number appeared, we held a celebratory lunch with the printers, the Holywell Press, at the Trout Inn by the river at Godstow, with the peacocks screaming outside.

I could not have had a more dynamic chairman to train me than Max Nicholson. Periodically in the early years I would stay the night at his house in Chelsea and spend the evening listening to ideas, suggestions and admonitions sparking off him and trying desperately to keep coherent notes for future action. I am afraid not everything put forward so brilliantly at these sessions bore fruit, but they were certainly an experience, and I was not surprised that, when Max became director-general of the then Nature Conservancy in 1952, it began to hum with life, or that in a short time the first of many contracts came the way of the BTO.

My first major flag-wagging was at the beginning of December 1948 when I spoke on six out of seven days to societies in the north and Midlands of England. The tour began with a meeting of the influential Natural History Society of Northumberland, Durham and Newcastle upon Tyne (now the NHS of Northumbria), at which W. B. Alexander was the main speaker on bird observatories and I talked for a few minutes about the BTO. WBA was not the man to miss the chance of a little bird-watching and in the morning we had a look at the Gosforth Park sanctuary with Grace Hickling and Guy Robinson, seeing a good show of waterfowl, including a long-tailed duck. I then went on alone to Barrow, Bolton, Accrington, Leicester and Shrewsbury, saying my piece at regular meetings, at a club social which included recitations and at an all-day Sunday gathering of several societies, with tables of exhibits. The Lancashire occasions enabled me to spend two nights at Frandley in

Cheshire with Violet and A. W. Boyd (James Fisher's Uncle Arnold), the first of several refreshing interludes there over the years.

Arnold Boyd, who suceeded Max Nicholson briefly as chairman of the BTO, needs no eulogies from me. His New Naturalist book *A Country Parish* and his *Country Diary of a Cheshire Man* (a collection of his short articles from *The Guardian*) put him in the league of Gilbert White. But to know him was a unique experience. His knowledge ranged so widely, with natural history, Cheshire lore and English literature as his specialities, that I could not help feeling almost illiterate in his company, though that was the last effect he wished to have on anyone.

On this first visit he showed me something of the Cheshire countryside round Frandley, which was a farm as well as a most comfortable house with a trim garden. We had a look at several meres and their water-fowl and he pointed out to me the evergreen bog rosemary *Andromeda* growing at Oakmere. Two years later I arrived with a stinking cold and was put to bed after a good hot bath, to be awoken in the middle of the night by what appeared to be a stampede. Some of the young cattle had broken into the treasured garden and there was nothing for it but to get up and join in the corralling exercise under a frosty moon. That same full moon was a factor in assembling the record flock of about 15,000 lapwings which we saw next day on Witton Flashes.

AWB usually had some surprise for his visitor. On 26 October 1956 he took me to see G. H. Clegg, who showed us a hoopoe in his garden at Poole Hall not far from Crewe; indeed its plumage looked distinctly 'industrial'. We watched it probing rapidly over the close-cut lawn; suddenly it would stop, dig more deeply and usually come up with what looked like a pupa. Then it would raise its head, throw up the prey within the gape of its mandibles and swallow it. It made about half a dozen captures while we watched. We also saw a male great spotted woodpecker fly to a calling female in a sycamore. She greeted him with open bill and we heard low chattering. Both pecked at twigs before flying off together. Woodpeckers are generally solitary outside the breeding season, but almost exactly twenty-two years later, while writing this book, I watched from our windows two come together in a dead elm and fly off following one another. They were briefly joined in the same tree by a green woodpecker, which added to the complexity of the observation. On 23 November 1957 I was introduced by AWB to Rostherne Mere, the most famous water in Cheshire, which had recently become a national nature reserve. Our count of thirty-nine species included a red-throated diver, thousands of mallard and hundreds of teal. Six years later Margaret and I attended the opening by James Fisher of the Arnold Boyd Memorial Hide looking over the mere.

My one triumph on these visits was on 17 January 1953 when, with W. B. Alexander, we were looking at scrub land in Forge Pool Valley. I spotted what initially I thought was a magpie, but it proved to be the first great grey shrike our host had ever seen in Cheshire. Named 'George', what was evidently the same bird returned for several winters to the area. In May of that year I drove AWB down to see the nest-boxes in the Forest of Dean. On the way we had a look at the treacherous Wybunbury Moss, another national nature reserve. 'Uncle Arnold', never one to hang back, managed to sink up to his waist in the sphagnum before I could pull him out, and we proceeded south with his trousers flapping from the bonnet of the car.

Equally enjoyable were visits nominally in the

course of duty to Edwin and Jean Cohen. Former neighbours of the Boyds, they had moved to Sway in the New Forest, where Edwin had saturated their garden and woods with nestboxes of all types (he and I collaborated in the BTO's first field guide on the subject), at the same time carrying out a massive ringing campaign at his bird tables. Hundreds of titmice were colour-ringed and their returns to the feeders assiduously recorded. This operation was eventually filmed for BBC television, including the house mice which scavenged on the ground below.

Like so many of the ornithologists I have known, Edwin Cohen was a one-off. His predilection for fast open cars, and his devotion to wearing shorts in almost all seasons when well over seventy marked him out even among birdwatchers. I last saw him on 7 May 1970, years after I had left the BTO staff, when Michael Rowntree drove Mary Radford and me down from Oxford to look for firecrests, whose presence as breeding birds in the New Forest had recently been revealed. Although we failed to find them, Edwin spared no pains and even produced what must have been a honey buzzard, though I was nosing after grey wagtails and missed it. We finally repaired to a traditional tea on the terrace at Hazelhurst, surrounded by song and by ringed birds and ready for anything that might turn up. First came a hen kestrel and then a cock sparrowhawk, fiercely attended by a mistle thrush. The hawk soared round above us, giving splendid views, before deciding that the thrush was getting a bore and sliding away over the oak trees.

Although he gave me a lift home after the initial meeting of Regional Representatives in Oxford, my first vivid memory of Tony (C. A.) Norris dates from February 1951 when I took David Snow and John McMeeking (then an undergraduate, now President of the BTO) to join a party from the West Midland Bird Club who were catching starlings in bat-fowling nets at a big roost near Shipston on Stour. It was wet and we staggered about in the mud, illuminated from time to time by torchlight flashes; and it was obvious that Tony enjoyed it all enormously. Five years later Ronald Lockley's brother in law, John Buxton, introduced mist nets to Britain and let me have a couple. On 30 June I drove over to Clent and gave one to Tony. We tried it out in his garden and, though we only caught two cock bullfinches, two swallows and a hen blackbird, it was obvious that a revolution in catching birds for ringing was upon us.

By this time Tony had become treasurer of the BTO and we worked together with complete understanding for several years as a fairly rapid expansion set in. The first contract from the Nature Conservancy was in 1953 for two years' survey of proposed national nature reserves. The BTO council therefore appointed John Burton as assistant secretary, leaving me free to visit a number of the reserves and keep a general eye on the survey, which showed that the woodpigeon was the most abundant bird on almost all the woodland areas; I hope the Conservancy felt they got their money's worth. It was also decided to make as complete as possible a heron census in 1954 and John Burton took over organization of this from W. B. Alexander.

Also in 1954 Miss Leach retired as honorary organizer of the ringing scheme and, with more help from the Nature Conservancy, the BTO was able to appoint Robert Spencer as her full-time successor, continuing to work from the Bird Room at South Kensington. In quite a short time, as ringing began its mushroom growth, he was justifiably asking for more staff. Finally in 1958 the BTO negotiated another contract for a migration research officer and Kenneth Williamson, who had made such a success as first warden of the Fair Isle Bird Observatory, joined us in the tiny offices in King Edward Street, Oxford, where we had moved in 1951.

During my years with the BTO the annual programme came to include joint meetings with local societies up and down the country, peripatetic annual conferences of Regional Representatives, and the Bird Observatories Conference which Bob Spencer took over. We also ran, in the gaps between International Ornithological Congresses, two summer conferences in 1952 and 1956 based near Seahouses in Northumberland where Eric and Dorothy Ennion had established at Monks House a private field studies centre looking straight out to the Farne Islands. In April 1955 John Burton organized the Trust's first overseas event, a weekend conference at Amsterdam in collaboration with our Dutch colleagues. Everyone who came remembers sitting in a coach beside a canal, watching a hen marsh harrier trying to drown a singularly resistant coot, something more or less paralleled at a Scottish Ornithologists' Club conference outing in October 1960, when the only rough-legged buzzard I have yet seen took a moorhen from the Dunbar Tyne.

The BTO Council was also kind enough to pay for me to attend the International Congresses at Basle in June 1954 and Helsinki in 1958. Margaret was able to come to both and at Basle her brother Carl, who became successively curator of zoology and director of the Raffles Museum at Singapore, joined us. So great was the interest at that time in the pied flycatcher that a special session was devoted to it the day before the main congress opened and I had the honour of giving the first paper; in view of my international audience I tried to speak very deliberately. Margaret came in late and said to me afterwards: 'I thought you were reading it in German.'

Quite early in my time with the BTO I wrote a piece for the RSPB magazine, then called *Bird Notes*, which to some extent sums up the lighter side of my experiences and which follows as the next chapter. How far I carried out the suggestion in its last paragraph is a matter of opinion but, when I left the Trust at the end of February 1959, I had certainly spoken in some dozens of places from Inverness to Truro and from Enniskillen to Norwich and had enjoyed some excellent birdwatching with my kind hosts all over the country.

13
Birdsmanship
(with acknowledgments to the Master Potter)

An interest in birds is to-day almost *de rigueur* in the more cultured parts of these islands, and the success of S. Potter's courses in Lifemanship and Gamesmanship have led me to try to put together for the benefit of my fellow birdwatchers (hereafter: birdsmen) some hints which they may find of use when attempting to establish their dominance in the ornithological pecking order, in the field, in the meeting-room and (where we shall begin) in the hurly-burly of a social gathering.

1. The Birdsman in Society One of three questions is inevitably asked of the birdsman following the stock introduction by his hostess: 'Oh, Mabel, I do want you to meet Mr Er; he's a great authority on birds.'

    (a) 'Oh, how interesting, do tell me, is this a good place for birds?'

Provided the questioner is not outstandingly pretty, and it is not desired to prolong the conversation for other reasons, the correct answer here is a flat, 'No place is bad for birds, you know'. Unless Mabel is a real trier, there will be no come-back to this and an escape can quickly be made.

(b) 'Oh, how interesting, do tell me, do you know Peter Scott?' Answer: 'Well, I saw him when I was at the New Grounds the other day.' This is what C. E. Montague called paying the truth the homage of equivocation, since it does not stress the fact that you were one of a coach party from your local natural history society and that all you saw of the Director was the top of his head as he talked to two admirals and a bishop at the far end of the Rushy Pen.

From this it should be easy to lead on to an account of your own observations on wildfowl, which should play out time successfully.

(c) 'Oh, how interesting, do let me tell you about my robin!' This is superficially the easiest of the three to meet, since it initially requires from you only a listening role, but as the inevitable anecdote (the bird is sometimes a blackbird, occasionally a chaffinch or 'a little brown bird, definitely not a sparrow' and it always does one of three things: taps on the window, builds two nests on top of each other, or seems *really* to recognize her) winds to its end, you realize that some fitting comment is needed.

By far the best is: 'Most interesting: of course, there's something just like it in the Dutch literature.' The beauty of this is that your questioner probably does not know the specialized meaning of 'literature', and will credit you with uncanny omniscience; in any case the fact that many Dutch papers have English summaries or are abstracted in *The Ibis* will almost certainly be unknown to her.

2. The Birdsman in the Field But birdsmanship is

not all social cut and thrust; sooner or later the birdsman must come into the open and show his mettle,
probably at a field outing of his local society. Here the
preliminary build-up is of great importance, so we will
consider first:

(a) Equipment: It is essential that the successful birdsman should be the *worst-dressed* man in the party. The
remains of (preferably) two ancient plus-four suits
form an admirable base, on which should be superim-
posed as many bits of leather as possible. The more
unusual their location, e.g. the small of the back, the
seat of the plus-fours, the more deadly their effect, and
the whole should be topped by a tweed cap (only
advanced students should attempt a 'deer-stalker') on
which birds have paid numerous tributes (a couple of
nights in a chicken-house should do the trick). Just
because most birdwatchers now wear wellingtons, the
birdsman should sport an enormous pair of boots lib-
erally larded with a revolting preservative and brought
to notice if necessary by some such comment: 'Go
anywhere in these y'know; wellingtons are no good in
brambles.' An old Wodehousian gambit may also be
used by experienced performers: 'Useful for snakes'.

Now we come to the vital question of optical aids,
and the birdsman may have to show considerable skill
if he is to take a trick here. Three usual situations
present themselves.

(1) You have an old and battered pair and your chief
potential rival has a large, new pair of binoculars.
Attack is the best defence in this situation, with the
opening line: 'Nice little toy you've got there; they're
the latest fashion, I believe, but can you *see* with them?'
Then, for you have picked the moment carefully, you
flick your ancient pair to your eyes and say: 'Gosh, that
juvenile foxed me for a second; I thought it was a

female. Oh, sorry, didn't you get on to them in time?'
Your rival, who is still unlimbering his pair, is thus
caught at a disadvantage and not only feels that he is
guilty of ostentation in the eyes of the rest of the party,
but that he has probably wasted £120.

Your advantage can be rammed home later in the
day if he lags behind at any point, by suggesting that
the weight of the glasses is holding him back.

(2) Reversed position to (1): You have the new pair
and your rival has an old pair. This needs greater
aplomb to carry off, and the recommended line is to
wave them about merrily, saying, 'Well, there's my
wife's winter coat, *and* our summer holiday, but I
simply had to have them – one owes it to the birds, if
you see what I mean'. Carry on in this vein, prattling
ingenuously about their illumination, and periodically
offer to lend them to your rival just as he has focused
on some object of interest.

(3) You both have large pairs. There is nothing for
it now but to go into a technical huddle, making much
play with exit pupil diameters, and await your chance
to gain advantage in another opening altogether.

The same general rules guide the birdsman in dealing with telescopes. If he doesn't use one, he should say
loftily, 'After all, they're not much good for passerines,' thus implying that he has only come on this
particular wader-watching expedition as light recrea-
tion, and then, as soon as his rival has got ensconced
with his telescope, stage a diversion some way off to
look at a meadow pipit.

But if he is a telescope man, then the utmost must be
made of thumb-sticks, straps and other gadgets, and
the whole party must be held up while he converts
himself into a sort of cocoon on the ground for at least a
quarter of an hour. This is especially effective if the
wind is cold and the rival is at all lightly clad.

Note: Extra points may be gained by using the abbreviations 'glasses', 'binos', 'binocs' or 'scope'; cf. 'photogs' instead of the vulgar 'photos'.

(b) Identification: The first task of the birdsman in the field is to show his superior skill in bird recognition, and while his opportunities will to some extent depend on the co-operation of the birds themselves, it is possible to engineer certain favourable situations in advance.

The rival should be trapped early on into offering to show the party a particular species, e.g. a curlew sandpiper. Then, when his attention is held elsewhere, remark casually but briskly: 'There's your curlew – with that pack of dunlin. Oh, sorry, I'm afraid they're out of sight now.' This is a development of the Binocular Play (1) already described, but note the use of 'your' to convey that you have had to find his bird for him. If by any chance he doesn't know the birdsmannish omission of the 'sandpiper', he will be even further outplayed; in fact this species is the ideal birdsman's bird.

In the case of a not readily identifiable bird that stays put, the birdsman must combine patience and a sense of timing to an unusual degree, for, after a prolonged and silent inspection, he *must* be the first to ask, 'Well, what do you think?' which gives him the chance of trapping an unwary diagnosis from his rival. Should this agree with his own private opinion, he jumps in with: 'Of course, but the superciliary stripe [or absence of superciliary stripe] was a bit unexpected, wasn't it?'

If he disagrees, then he must use an enigmatic smile, directed to the most receptive member of the party, and make some more entries in his field note-book. This stalling enables him to come out on top whether his rival's identification is confirmed by others, in which case he must convey that he knew all the time but was just giving the rest a chance; or whether it isn't, which puts him at an obvious advantage, clinched by such moral remarks as 'I never think it's safe to diagnose at this time of year unless one can see the wing-pattern'. The phrase *At this time of year* should be noted, as it indicates easy familiarity with all phases of the bird's plumage.

(c) Tally-hunting: The principles underlying previous advice also rule in this important aspect of field birdsmanship: find out your potential rival's line, and play the opposite for all you're worth.

Thus, if he is an acknowledged tally-hunter, you must use the scientific gambit, 'After all, it's only the common birds that really count, isn't it?' and continually hold up the party by calling their attention to robins or dunnocks sitting in huddled attitudes on the vegetation. If after five minutes' observation the robin gives a perfunctory peck at its plumage, you murmur, 'Ah, an intention movement!' make profuse notes, and add, to the air in general, 'I must write to Tinbergen about this'. A slight hesitation before the Tinbergen should make it clear that among your real associates you would say 'Niko'.

On the other hand, if your rival is a serious ornithologist you follow the line already suggested in Binocular Play (2), crying, 'I'm frankly pot-hunting to-day; leave the sparrows alone for once, old chap, and come and see some real birds! Tally-ho! Yoicks!' By incessant remarks you should manage to scare away any of the commoner species at which he may wish to look, and if you can keep up your flow, and have the luck to see one or two scarce birds, you should manage to convince the party that your rival is an introverted spoil-sport living in an ivory tower.

(d) Field Investigations: The birdsman should not let himself in for any real field studies until he has worked his passage in Identifications and Tally-hunting. By then he should know what he is up to, and can take part in, for example, a winter census of titmice in rather rough woodland, with good prospects of enhancing his reputation in return for the minimum expenditure of energy. Indeed, his goal should be never to take his hands out of his pockets either to use his glasses (strung apparently purposefully round his neck) or to make notes. This will be more easily achieved if the observers on either side of him are reasonably painstaking, by playing on their anxieties with such leads as 'You got that blue tit, I hope? It was definitely off my line'; or 'Long-tails coming over: one, two, three, four – oh, awfully sorry, I'm poaching: they're yours now'. Difficult country can be avoided by a deft change of direction. 'Sorry, I'm off my line; that big bramble-bush is yours now, I think. Nearly always a willow tit in it.' At the end of the drive, the birdsman saunters up with a rueful smile, 'You people have all the luck; I only got one great tit. By the way, you did get that marsh tit I heard calling just at the end, didn't you?' It is also a good plan to insinuate, by well-timed aposiopeses, that everyone else is going too fast and probably missing birds.

3. The Birdsman at Meetings The greatest test of the birdsman comes when he takes part in an ornithological discussion. Silence and a billowing pipe between them make a useful build-up and literal smoke-screen, out of which, when the speaker makes any assertion not backed by a mass of evidence, should be jerked in a tone indicating apparent sympathy over-ridden by devotion to truth (admittedly not very easy) and with equal emphasis on each monosyllable: 'Do we know that?'

This line, for which we are indebted to Mammalsman D. Chitty, is guaranteed to throw all but the toughest out of their stride at the first application, and may even bring their contribution to an early and humiliating end.

In the event of a convincing reply, however, the birdsman must make a quick decision. If he feels that his opponent really knows his subject, he can still sign off without losing face by saying: 'Exactly, thanks very much, but I wasn't quite sure if everyone (inclusive-exclusive wave of the pipe-stem round the gathering) here knew of Blobsch's work on substratal stimuli.' But if he decides a counterbluff is being attempted, then he should simply nod and try the line again at the next opportunity. If a third use of the gambit is successfully met, there is nothing for it but to have trouble with the pipe until interest is focused elsewhere.

Should the birdsman ever be trapped for prestige reasons into speaking himself, he must – short of actually mastering his subject – rely on two things: first, immediate acknowledgment of his indebtedness to the work of his most likely critics; and secondly, a rigid refusal to come to any conclusions whatever. The work should always be in progress, as indicated by such a parry and riposte to a questioner: 'That's just what I'd like to know; perhaps by this time next year, if all goes well, we'll have some more data to help us.'

In this way the adept birdsman may succeed in dining out for two or three years as the guest of ornithological societies up and down the country before equipping himself with a new, and perpetually unfinished, problem.

14
Birdwatcher on the air

My first script for radio was written when I was still at
school. It was part of a programme for Scottish youth
organizations and was read from the Edinburgh studio
by my father's friend, George Troup, because I refused
to sacrifice a day or two of my treasured Easter holiday. I did, however, listen to it, probably on a crystal
set. Two more short talks which I gave myself com-
prised my pre-war output and it was not until 1946,
when I was introduced to the drama producer, Lor-
raine Davies, that I found a piece of the mantle of
Romany descending on me. We did a series of studio
programmes from Cardiff with two children, the format which Romany had used so successfully before
and during the war until his untimely death.

   We worked very much on the lines of radio drama:
tightly scripted and thoroughly, even fiercely,
rehearsed; it was not unknown for my girl 'feed' to
burst into tears. The only time we went outdoors was
to be photographed against a tree in Cathays Park for
the *Radio Times*, and we had absolutely no natural

sound effects. When I wanted to introduce the call note of the wood warbler, there was nothing for it but to imitate it myself on to a disc, which was played in at the appropriate moment. I hope no wood warblers overheard it.

Of course, there were excellent bird recordings before the war and Witherby produced five discs of Ludwig Koch's recordings with explanatory books by Max Nicholson. But I did have a little to do with Ludwig Koch's involvement with the BBC after the war.

Kenneth Ashton, who had started up the ornithological section of the Cardiff Naturalists' Society, returned excitedly from a weekend course at one of the adult colleges that sprang up in those hopeful post-war years. He had met Ludwig and his wife Nellie and found them very disheartened and in financial straits; he suggested that we should write to Max Nicholson, as Chairman of the British Trust for Ornithology, and urge that something be done to bring Ludwig back on to the radio and the ornithological scene. Max responded warmly and in due course Ludwig's whole collection of recordings was bought by the BBC and he was given a three-year contract to make and broadcast wildlife recordings. An advisory panel was set up of which Julian Huxley, whose Brains Trust contributions had put biology on everyman's map, was a member and so was I when I became secretary of the BTO in 1948, but I do not remember that Ludwig ever took our advice. He did, however, become firmly established as a radio nature personality.

His appointment did not stop other people in the regions taking recording cars into the country and trying their luck or skill. Indeed, a chiffchaff's song which an enterprising engineer captured with me in a rookery on the outskirts of Cardiff is still in the BBC's library of recordings. The wood itself has long been engulfed in a housing estate. Around the same time, in

May 1947, I was lowered by Emlyn and Gwynne Evans with a microphone round my neck to ring a brood of young ravens in a not very terrifying crag on the northern edge of the coalfield. The birds contributed their quota of sound and the first time I ever heard my voice (all our studio programmes went out live and were not repeated) was in the playback on that bare mountainside; like most other people, I was absolutely horrified by this brassy stranger.

Meanwhile Bristol, where Desmond Hawkins was a producer, began to establish itself as the centre of natural history broadcasting with programmes like 'The Naturalist' and later 'Birds in Britain'. 'Nature Parliament', on which I sometimes sat as a substitute for the regulars (I even took the chair once when Uncle Mac was not available) continued to go out from London, and other regions made their own nature programmes. The format remained very much that of the live studio show, carefully rehearsed. Ludwig Koch often took part and, if a junior was standing in for Desmond Hawkins, was not above various 'leetle chokes' at his expense, though the final performance was always exemplary.

The coming of tape revolutionized the sound broadcasting of nature, just as video-tape has revolutionized television on location. Ludwig Koch clung to his cumbrous and complicated disc outfit for a long time but even he was eventually converted. Now we could go out and about and record *ad lib* and, though some engineers could perform miracles at editing discs, tape editing is infinitely easier. Tape also led to the demise of live programmes, but this mattered much less than might be supposed, as it is usually the first 'take' which goes on the air, cleared of a few 'fluffs' by the editor's razor.

After some ten years of performing, mostly from Bristol, I went there from the British Trust for Ornithology in April 1959 for three years as the senior producer of

172

the Natural History Unit, following a six weeks' training course in London. Actually the first programme I produced was in Wrocław (Breslau) in Poland with a monoglot Polish studio manager in June 1959. Our host, Professor Szarski, acted as interpreter and Stanley Cramp recorded a talk about our trip (see p. 221).

The most complicated sound programme I undertook was on the island of Rum in 1961, with Kenneth Williamson as 'anchor man'. Born with two left hands where machines of any kind are concerned, I was continually afraid that our tape recorders would go wrong, and there were several agonizing conversations with engineers in Bristol over Rum's radio-telephone in which they tried to explain to me what was, technically speaking, what. We carried the heavy but reliable EMI L2 recorder up to the peaks where the Manx shearwaters nest and recorded their nocturnal chorus, but we took a small portable machine to the ancient site of a white-tailed eagle's eyrie, whence Ken recaptured the scene as the sitting bird must have seen it. Perhaps, if the present experimental re-introduction succeeds, sea eagles will once again nest in that remote and vertiginous site.

I forget how many tapes we took back to Bristol but I reckoned that we spent some forty hours of editing time to make the final forty-minute programme: a word picture of the synthetic community established by the Nature Conservancy on its largest owned reserve, now one of my brother Niall's responsibilities, and of the research being undertaken. I made a strong and successful plea for the programme to be added to the BBC's archives for its historical interest.

My first involvement with television was due to James Fisher. It was in a children's programme, live from Alexandra Palace, where I attempted to show a charming young lady how to put together a nest box expertly prefabricated by my Woodstock neighbour,

Denis Jordon. A year or two later, in 1955 when I was organizing the census of mute swans for the BTO, I took part with Peter Scott and Fred Lexster, the Swan-keeper of Abbotsbury, in one of the programmes which later attained fame as the 'Look' series.

We did a preliminary rehearsal in a pub near Lime Grove, in a back room reached somewhat off-puttingly through a door marked 'Ladies'. On the programme we appealed for information about nests and received some hundreds of replies, several referring to sites which were not reported by the birdwatching network, who found it difficult to take half-tame swans seriously. Both tele-vision and radio have shown that good public support can be enlisted for enquiries of this kind.

In April 1958 I began to introduce from Bristol a television programme for young people produced by Winwood Reade, herself a fine naturalist. It was called *Out of Doors* and its memory has been submerged under the fame of its most popular successor *Animal Magic*, for which I can claim a part share in devising the title and in choosing its anchor man, Johnny Morris. I realize now that *Out of Doors* was too educational and I was never as composed in front of the cameras as in the invisible world of sound radio. I introduced some twenty editions, until after I was actually at Bristol, and then Ian Mercer took over and breathed new life into it with the help of Leslie Jackman, one of our discoveries. Eric Simms kindly persisted with me in a series of schools programmes on trees, for which we did much of the filming in Blenheim Park, close to our home, but television front man was not my forte.

My main tasks in Bristol were to keep an eye on the general output of the Natural History Unit, especially on accuracy – no nightingale songs in an August set-ting – to produce some programmes and to look after others in their final stages. Pre-eminent among these more or less package deals were the *On Safari* series of Armand and Michaela Denis, and the underwater exploits of Hans and Lotte Hass. Hass's programmes were edited in Bristol by Paul Khan, but he used to come to London and record his commentaries in a commercial studio while I sat by to make suggestions. He was such a perfectionist that there was very little I had to do: he spotted his own mistakes so quickly. One phrase of his that sticks in my mind is 'these curious prawns', which seemed to epitomize his type of commentary just as 'Keine Grotte ohne Lotte' summed up his fair partner's contribution. At the age of forty Hans Hass wisely came to the surface: by his courage and technique he had made a tremendous breakthrough, just as Heinz Sielmann did with his woodpecker film, which was the sensation of the Ornithological Congress at Basle in 1954.

But to Armand and Michaela must belong the credit for putting the conservation of wild life, with special emphasis on the 'big game' of East Africa, as an issue to millions of viewers. Many of Armand's team of photographers have become great names in television, so his influence continues to spread. He and Michaela attended the conference at Arusha in Tanzania which saw the launching of the World Wildlife Fund in 1961, and shot some film for use by Chris Parsons and me in our programme *L for Lion*, which was the first of its kind, I think, wholly devoted to the rationale of conservation. Peter Scott introduced it and we interviewed Julian Huxley at the Nature Conservancy – 'razor-sharp', said our cameraman – and Frank Fraser Darling in his Berkshire garden. We also filmed toy animals in a famous London store where my daughter Ròna was part of the background and was asked by a shopper if she were Hayley Mills.

We made a less successful attempt to put geology on television. Chris Parsons (now head of the NHU) again directed the filming, while Emlyn Evans was the expert interviewed by Tom Salmon. Our theme was how geology influences human use of the landscape, in this case the development of Torquay as a resort. To set the scene we 'vox-popped' the crowd on the beach and it was my job to go ahead of the camera and get people's agreement. Naturally a young lady in a silver bathing dress caught my eye, but her escort said apologetically: 'We'd rather not, old man, if you don't mind; the firm doesn't know I'm here'. In spite of these embellishments and the wonders of Kent's Cavern, the high-ups did not think well of our efforts; so I was very pleased when years later BBC Wales returned to the geological charge with Emlyn Evans as their adviser.

I do not regret my three years based at Bristol. The BBC is the kindest of employers and made it possible for me, on the flimsiest film-hunting pretext, to take up invitations to visit Poland and the USA. I also had the excitement of producing a few programmes live, with a staff of forty nominally at my command; but a director needs to be younger than I was when I started and I also lacked the technical curiosity which makes a good producer. Time and again only the experience and *savoir faire* of Pam Everett my secretary saved me from disaster. One black she could not prevent followed our successful feeding in of a live item from a rookery to the original *Tonight* programme. What else can you do, we were asked, so I suggested a heronry. Eventually all was ready, including a microphone inserted by a nest, and we did some precautionary filming, which went quite well. But the evening itself was studded with crises and I suddenly realized that I could not go from the camera on the nest to telecine, as the actions would not match; I had to go to my other camera, which was trained on Macdonald Hastings the commentator, on the hill above the heronry. Unfortunately at that moment he was bent double looking into his monitor and *Tonight*'s millions got an unrivalled view of his posterior. We were not asked to do another live item.

Quite early on in my three-year stint we decided not to move from Oxfordshire, where by now Margaret had an interesting and important part-time job, and this really meant that I would not work more than one contract. When John Cripps asked me to become part-time natural history adviser to *The Countryman*, for which I had been writing odd articles for some years, and which was edited from Burford, only sixteen miles from home, I accepted with alacrity.

But I have continued to broadcast on sound radio and to do occasional items on television. Some of the most enjoyable outings have been for Radio Oxford, which started up in 1971, with Ken Jackson as producer and his children Jo and Dougie (my godson) as the enquiring young: a return to the Romany format but with all the freedom of tape. For three years we roved the Oxfordshire countryside on our Nature Trail and then I handed over to W. D. Campbell, a situation not without some confusion south of the Border, where Campbell is not such a common name.

Looking back on over thirty years of television and radio, however, I think the most exciting item in which I have taken part was by the Hayle estuary in Cornwall, when Franklin Coombs and I had to identify birds as they came up on the screen from several cameras, which Winwood Reade had managed to commandeer for a few hours on their way back from a major assignment. This was in black and white, of course, which made our task all the more tricky. I have often wondered why the idea has not been tried again because it ensured maximum 'viewer participation'. Perhaps I overestimate the percentage of viewers even today who can tell black-tailed from bar-tailed godwits.

15
Nagshead

My first memory of the Forest of Dean is of a mild orgy in July 1932 when, innocent Caledonian forestry students, we were introduced to the local cider at about 4d a pint. When we should have been listening to the sylvicultural top brass assembled to edify us, we lay on the grass in the pub's orchard, then staggered off into the woods behind our mentors. Is it significant that the only plant I recall from that day is deadly nightshade?

Our second year visit was followed by our working plan in May and June 1933 (see p. 103) and then, under quite different auspices, I returned for eight months in 1936–7 (see p. 113). Owing to John White's continuing to teach at Lydney until the war and our getting to know Neil Wylie, one of the Forestry Commission's District Officers and a very good birdwatcher, I kept turning up in the Forest over the next five years. Then came a gap in petrol-less times until 18–20 May 1946 when I spent a wet weekend at a youth hostel with the Cardiff University Youth Course for which I was then responsible and whose members I felt should be given a taste of nature, something I tried with more persistence years later when chairman of the Council for Nature's Youth Committee.

One excursion we made through the dripping woodlands was to Nagshead Enclosure near Parkend, where in 1942 J. M. B. Brown had put up eighty-four nestboxes in a bid to attract insectivorous birds which might prove beneficial to the adjacent forest nursery. By 1946 J. M. D. Mackenzie, a retired overseas forester and keen ornithologist, was employed part-time by the Commission to inspect its scattered nestbox schemes and he kindly showed us round the area, which was of oak *Quercus robur*, planted in 1814 as a strategic reserve for the wooden walls of Old England.

When J. M. B. Brown looked at the boxes in 1942 he found to his surprise that fifteen were occupied by pied flycatchers. We now believe, largely on the experience of Harry Hook of Parkend, that there must have been a small population in the Forest perhaps for years but, as the area was ignored except by egg collectors after woodlarks' and grasshopper warblers' eggs in the open habitats, it is not surprising the flycatcher escaped notice. By 1946 'piedie flies' had taken 37 of the 91 boxes, more than any other species. Their ticking calls and simple song, which I verbalize *chee chee chee chay cher*, could be heard all round us, competing with the trills and nightingale *pius* of the wood warblers, one of which was nesting in creeping honeysuckle just below Box No. 3.

Next year, his last with the Commission, J. M. D. Mackenzie suggested to Miss Leach that there was an excellent opportunity to ring young birds in the Nagshead boxes and as I was then, in Cardiff, the nearest ringer, she invited me to have a go. I was able to make two visits in June 1947, when Neil Wylie, who had returned to the Dean as Deputy Surveyor after the war, and I ringed 144 young flycatchers and 11 young redstarts and, with some trepidation, two hen flycatchers and a redstart which we caught in the boxes. In 1948 David Lack asked me to supervise the inspection of all the boxes and record their contents, as part of his work on the great tit. Other areas, in Surrey and Norfolk, were also in the scheme which was based on his main study area in Wytham Woods (see p. 151). The help of the Forester Training School at Parkend was enlisted and, as its principal was my Edinburgh contemporary Tom Edwardson, who was succeeded by the equally co-operative John Goodwin, there were no difficulties. The number of boxes was increased to 144 and eventually to 275 over 60 acres in 1952, and four first-year students from the school carried out routine inspections weekly during the breeding season, while I paid between five and fourteen visits according to my commitments.

David Lack did not want the Nagshead titmice ringed, so I was free to concentrate on the pied flycatchers and redstarts. On 5 June 1948 Derek Lewis, a former Caerphilly pupil, picked B 6121 out of Box No. 41. She was one of the two hen flycatchers ringed in 1947. By this time I had begun to realize from reading about the work of Lars von Haartman in Finland that we were dealing with an ideal guinea pig among birds and that, provided we used the care expected of all ringers, we could catch adults in the boxes freely.

What was the area like in which I was to spend so many hours during the next seventeen years? In 1948 I could stand by Harry Hook's house on the old tips where he showed me a woodlark's nest and look over Parkend to a rolling hillside covered with old oak, grey-brown in mid-winter, almost yellow as the leaves opened in May, dark green in high summer, then bright brown in autumn. In the nestbox area the great trees were widely spaced (about 63 to the acre). Among them were a few Scots pines, beeches, syca-mores, sweet chestnuts, birches and two huge Nor-way spruces, in one of which ravens twice nested. My climb to ring the four young on 23 April 1960 was on the thirty-sixth anniversary of Pa's successful climb to the heron's nest at Rudha an Daimh and my last really big one.

The wide spacing of the canopy trees allowed an understorey to develop; this included dense clumps of holly and, well as I got to know the area and with numbers painted on all the trees carrying boxes, I quite often got temporarily lost in summer when the bracken was high. In winter, however, it was a case of 'ruined choirs', especially in the lower 15 acres which remained open to grazing, after the top 45 acres had been fenced off in the 1947–8 winter and acquired quite a heavy bramble layer. The flora of the whole area, overlying the cheerless pennant sandstone, lacks var-iety but in spring, as the wood fills with bird song, there are sheets of bluebells, supported by red cam-pion, stitchwort and yellow archangel. The star of the cast, from my point of view, appears any time after the middle of April: a black and white morsel flitting from perch to perch or landing briefly on a nestbox from which he might later display. In the hand the pied pattern is not so marked: there are grey feathers, par-ticularly on the rump, and brown feathers left over from the winter plumage which resembles the hen's. (In parts of the range the cock's summer plumage is brown and we had odd brown birds breeding at Nags-head.)

The peak of the piedie fly's song is soon over; the hens, who arrive a few days after the cocks, are wooed and won and get down to building, laying and incubating.

The cock, though he will sometimes build the rudi-
ments of a nest while waiting for a mate, plays a
minimal part in the hard work except when the brood
is being fed. Even then some cocks do very little and
others none at all. This may be because they have
another mate ('successive polygamy' occurs regularly)
or are beginning to moult.

All very annoying when we were trying to catch the
cocks, something that can only be done when they are
entering the box regularly. We also preferred to catch
the hens at this stage. Our original device was an
automatic shutter of wire prongs devised by John Gibb
for his titmice, on the lines of the shutter used by
pigeon-fanciers to retain birds in the loft. But some
cocks, though practically no hens, refused to face the
wires. So Harold Jenkins of Coventry made me several
types of non-automatic shutter, the base of which
could be pinned like the automatic model inside the
box above the entrance hole. A pawl in the base held
the shutter up until released by a trace running under
the lid of the box, just as a fisherman strikes when a fish
takes his lure. This was the most exciting part of the
action, lying among the bracken and the bluebells –
and the flies – waiting for the bird to return. All sorts of
minor disasters could follow, from striking too soon
to the whole gadget falling off and, even when the bird
was trapped, there was the problem of extracting it,
which we did by covering the whole box in a sleeve
with an elastic wrist into which a hand was inserted.
There was still the lid of the box to cope with and all
this took place at the top of a ladder because the human
predator had to be checked by siting the box at least ten
feet up the tree.

The original object of our ringing was to get distant
recoveries which would throw light on the migration
routes of the pied flycatcher and redstart. Our first

foreign recovery was of a 1948 young flycatcher from Biarritz in November, and others continued to trickle in, confirming the south-westerly trend of autumn migration. But one of my last, a cock, first ringed in 1961, was reported near Genoa on 31 March 1964 on a return route hitherto only suspected. It was soon obvious, however, that the recoveries of birds back at Nagshead were going to be of major interest, as a contribution to their vital statistics. Recovery percentages of ringed adults were, of course, far higher than for birds ringed as pulli (young), which have all the rigours of a first migration to face and may also return, as recent ringing has shown, to other areas. The returns of adult birds to Nagshead bore out the view that, once a small bird has survived a winter, its expectation of life remains much the same, as it is far below the possible life-span. The 52 hens ringed in 1950 provided a classic example; 26 were recovered in 1951, 10 in 1952, five in 1953, two in 1954 and none in 1955, showing a continuing annual mortality of about 50 per cent. The longest lived hen in my day was E 31279. Ringed as pullus in 1957, she laid a clutch of six eggs in 1958, about 7 in each of the next four seasons, and her final appearance in 1963, thus also illustrating that clutch-size rises and declines with age.

Another hen I remember was K 1505 in Box 172 in 1958, C/7 in each of the next four seasons, and C/5 on and John Markham, who had been the photographer for the Snowdonia book (see p. 127) and was spending most of the season in the Dean, got a fine series of photographs of her and her mate. She returned to a neighbouring box the next year, when we thought her plumage was less black. Then there was the ringed bird whom I took from a box to show to a visiting natural history society. When I released her, she fell to the ground. Covering up as best I could, I put her back in the box. On my next visit, I was not surprised to find the eggs deserted; but some weeks later she was back in the same box, incubating another clutch of eggs. Did she suffer some temporary shock when I handled her? If so, she was exceptionally temperamental for a piedie fly. Another hen was found dead in her box after ringing, one foot caught in wool (which is not a common nest material). To my relief it was the unringed leg that had become entangled, because there are always people ready to tilt at ringing casualties.

My oddest ringing story from the Forest of Dean has nothing to do with pied flycatchers, but with the Deputy Surveyor, the Forestry Commission's chief officer, who lived in those days at Whitemead Park quite near Nagshead. John Q. Williamson, another Edinburgh contemporary of mine, who had succeeded Neil Wylie, saw a white pigeon on the roof of an outbuilding. The bird was caught and found to be carrying a Norwegian ring. John Q. wrote to the address on it and in due course received a long reply in English, containing the injunction: 'Take care of your web-footed friend'; it emerged that the ring had originally been put on a young common gull in Norway. How it found its way on to the pigeon's leg is a nice exercise for the imagination, but the incident does make me wonder sometimes about records of longevity based on ringed birds.

By the end of the 1964 season, when I handed over my immediate responsibility to Peter Evans, then at the EGI, with John Niles as the man on the spot, we had ringed 7,713 pied flycatchers and recovered about 290 cocks and 400 hens. As the ringing had to be carried out in the short period when the vast majority of the broods became 'ripe', I relied on the special help of past Parkend students, who came back and spent an intensive week in Nagshead. As well as John Niles, Peter

Lewis, Eric Roberts, Peter Wormell, G. T. Hamblin and the late Pat Banks rendered splendid help and Robert Creed, now a distinguished biologist, worked the 1954 season on a Nature Conservancy grant. Both the Conservancy and the Forestry Commission helped with expenses, and the BTO and the BBC generously allowed me time for my visits.

What did all this effort achieve apart from the large number of recoveries? We learned that pied flycatchers could have second layings after a successful first brood, but only in very early seasons like 1948 and 1949 and in very small numbers. We learned a little about competition between species for nestboxes, even involving fights to the death; we also had a few cases of mixed broods being successfully reared. I discovered that surviving adults seldom returned to the same box in succeeding years, but that cocks returned significantly closer than hens. But the best use of my data was made by David Lack, who devoted most of chapter 6 of his *Population Studies of Birds* (O.U.P., 1966) to a consideration of them. His interest relieved me of the immediate necessity of producing more than a general 'thank you' paper on the whole scheme, which appeared in the journal *Forestry* for January 1968. But there is a lot more that could be done, on problems like the inheritance of clutch size, since we did enough ringing to enable family trees to be compiled. At the moment the data, on specially overprinted nest record cards, are deposited with the British Trust for Ornithology.

By chance I was responsible for starting off another ringed pied flycatcher population, this time from scratch. As part of the BTO's survey of the bird life of nature reserves, Max Nicholson thought it would be interesting to find out whether small hole-nesting birds showed different height preferences. So we mounted a statistically planned experiment with fifty boxes in an oak area of Yarner Wood on the edge of Dartmoor. In 1955, the first year of the scheme, pied flycatchers, hitherto hardly known to nest in South Devon, bred in one of the boxes, and there were six broods in 1959, after I had handed over management and ringing to Ray Smith. The experiment on height preferences proved quite inconclusive.

The Yarner Wood boxes can be said to have extended the breeding range of the pied flycatcher; elsewhere large-scale nestbox schemes, as in Herefordshire, have filled in gaps, or have greatly augmented known populations, as in some of the Welsh reserves of the RSPB. These schemes have led to a great deal more ringing of pied flycatchers nationally and to recoveries of birds between British schemes, something virtually unknown when I started ringing in the Dean. There is now a Pied Flycatcher Group, of which I am an inactive member, but which promotes studies of this fascinating little bird.

Peter Evans's research at Nagshead ended after the 1967 season and for a number of years Steve Cooper (who with John Niles produced an excellent booklet on the birds of the Dean) continued ringing and keeping an eye on the area. Jack Lee also ran another smaller area at Blakeney Hill, where we tried boxes low on the trees to cut down inspection time. Vandalism by human beings was negligible, but there was a rogue great spotted woodpecker which did quite a lot of damage and even laid an egg in one of the boxes. I continued to visit the Forest, where there is always something to be seen, but I was worried about the future of Nagshead which, from the commercial forestry point of view, was over-ripe for clear felling and replanting with conifers, as had already happened during the 1960s to much of the surrounding old oak. At last, after prolonged negotiations with the Forestry

Commission, who made one heavy felling as their pound of flesh, the RSPB were able to announce in 1974 agreement for a reserve of 378 acres, based on the nestbox area, but including the remaining adjacent oakwoods down to the Cannop brook, where kingfishers and dippers still fly and, when allowed to, nest; also many acres of conifers, ranging down in height to what could in places be called grass heath and therefore attractive to whinchats, stonechats and grasshopper warblers.

I am delighted that the heartland of the Dean as I have known it is now reasonably safe and, although the breeding population of pied flycatchers has been declining in recent years, perhaps because the canopy is now so open and the undergrowth so thick, under a series of enthusiastic RSPB summer wardens the number of nestboxes has been increased over the whole reserve and the ringing programme is under way again.

My own visits in the 1970s have a sort of ritual quality. I like to peep into one or two flycatcher nests, nearly always of oak leaves and fibres, with a fine lining for the six or seven pale blue eggs; to have lunch at the edge of the newly leaved oaks, listening to the songs within the wood and to the tree pipits singing over the old nursery, where the warden has his headquarters; then to have a look at localities elsewhere in the Forest. Recently the Spruce Drive near Speech House has been the attraction, with parties of crossbills in May 1977, and a siskin disappearing into the top of an immense spruce in June 1978. In July 1975 Steve Cooper showed John White and me a nightjar's nest found, as usual, when weeding young trees. It took me back to June 1951 when nightjar was on the menu for a visit by the Oxford Ornithological Society. We could then also offer red-backed shrike (last nest 1963) and woodlark, which disappeared after the 1963 cold spell. In May 1974 Steve Cooper and Eric Bignall guided us on a Living World programme, which included a raven's nest and an off-the-record incident when a tawny owl knocked Eric down its nest tree, this again harking back to one that attacked me when in the nestbox area.

Early on in the study of the Nagshead birds, I decided to have a look at the pied flycatcher's British status and distribution. This was accepted as a Trust-aided investigation by the BTO for 1952, and on 24 May I started out on a three-week tour as the guest of a dozen hospitable ornithologists, concentrating on the less well-known parts of the species's range and hoping, now that I had a clear idea of its habitat preferences, to find some new localities myself. By the end of my tour on 17 June I had seen pied flycatchers nesting, mostly in boxes, in two areas in Yorkshire; in Northumberland where I explored that wonderland for wild life, the Hulne Park at Alnwick; in Berwickshire, where I watched Henry Douglas-Home conducting his end of the annual bird song contest on radio between Scotland and England; in Dumfriesshire where fifteen pairs of piedie flies nested unmolested in low boxes in the policies of Lann Hall; in Perthshire where I ringed a brood in a box put up by the indefatigable J. M. D. Mackenzie on Drummond Hill; and finally in Midlothian, very much a marginal seat.

My frequent roadside whistle-stops revealed cock birds at two places near the Teviot in Roxburghshire, and one at Inverbeg by Loch Lomond, probably the second record for Dunbartonshire, where pied flycatchers now breed regularly. I also saw former sites in several other counties, including Argyll: the bird that laid at Salen (see p. 45) in 1951 did not return. As a by-product to my concentration on suitable habitat with associated species, I was able to fill in nest record cards for four tree pipits, six wood warblers and a number of redstarts, both in nestboxes and natural sites. Altogether I saw the nests of sixty species and enjoyed northern Britain at its very best, epitomized by the star-like flowers of chickweed wintergreen *Trientalis europaea*, of whose delicate charms I do not seem previously to have been aware. Then, after inspecting a wooded glen near the A74 in Lanarkshire, I decided that I had done enough and drove more or less straight home, arriving with the dawn chorus of blackbirds in rural Oxfordshire.

Although I have not watched pied flycatchers seriously outside Britain, I have seen them in Ireland (on passage on Howth Head), Sark, Sweden, Finland, Switzerland, Austria, Poland and France, where in August 1978 I found one silent in a wooded creek in Morbihan, an observation that gave me pleasure out of proportion to its mild unexpectedness.

16
Hordley

At first sight the prospect of finding somewhere to live suited both to our tastes and pocket seemed a bleak one in October 1948. But I had only been in Oxford two days when I met Miss Mabel Fitzgerald, who had occupied the flat below us in Edinburgh, and was now living in Oxford. She told me of a friend who wanted to give up a tenancy on the Blenheim estate, and a couple of days later, on a perfect autumn evening, I cycled out to see and fall for Hordley, a sixteenth-century farmhouse situated in the parish of Wootton and by the little river Glyme, famous for crayfish and as the source of Blenheim Lake.

The house is built of Cotswold stone with a Stonesfield slate roof round a courtyard in the middle of which we placed the bird bath given us by W. B. Alexander. This heirloom, as I now regard it, is distinctly fragile and it took the determination, strength and skill of my brother Niall and his son Ronald to achieve its removal to our new garden, where I can see it as I write.

When we arrived at Hordley, the courtyard walls were covered with Virginia creeper, but this had to be removed as a danger to the roof, so some good nesting sites were lost. But starlings bred under the slates, a spotted flycatcher built from time to time in a pear tree against the wall (making its last late effort as we were moving in July 1975), blackbird and dunnock in the winter jasmine, robin and blue tit in holes in the wall. Winter and summer house sparrows occupied a nest-box which eventually disintegrated with age. Its first occupants were tree sparrows, but they were dispossessed, leaving four eggs behind them. Jackdaws filled up several chimneys and for several of our earlier years we had a pair of barn owls in one. They were such unobtrusive neighbours that we usually did not discern their presence until they began daylight hunting for their brood. A barn owl sailing in against a blue sky, with a vole dangling from one foot, is a sight to cherish. But the owls did not come back in 1962, after a winter whose killing effect has been overshadowed by early 1963.

My list of birds landing in the courtyard or on the roof reached twenty-seven species, ranging from pheasant and green woodpecker (on a chimney stack) to a flock of long-tailed tits and a skylark in hard weather. The most remarkable incident was a fight to the death between two robins close to the bird bath and which I watched from a window on the morning of 18 November 1972. In the last letter he ever wrote to me, David Lack commented: 'How extraordinary. Hardly anyone, I never, has seen one robin kill another.' The full, somewhat gruesome details are in *British Birds*, vol 67, pp. 121–2 (1974).

Another unusual but inconclusive fight took place between two cock pheasants in the crown of the monkeypuzzle which stood on the east lawn and was, we were told, the only one on the Blenheim estates. The sun shone on the metallic plumage of the birds and on the metallic foliage, but the details of the battle could not be seen. My list of monkeypuzzle birds made up in variety for its lack of numbers: great spotted woodpecker, kingfisher, tawny owl, juvenile cuckoo, treecreeper, goldcrest and wood warbler all put in an appearance. Starlings and several mistle thrushes roosted in it at times; and mistle thrush, song thrush, chaffinch and collared dove all nested or tried to nest in it. In 1958 there was quite an invasion of house sparrows building their untidy domes on the spreading boughs. A pair regularly used a nestbox on the trunk, after blue tits had tried once or twice.

Our tenancy at Hordley was some 2¾ acres but my farmer neighbour John Smith allowed me unrestricted access to his land and, after trial runs in 1949 and 1950, I tried to keep as accurate a check as possible on the birds breeding on 8 acres which formed a sort of oasis in the agricultural landscape. In fact, about 4 acres of this consisted of two small paddocks with few nest sites. The rest (house, and garden, 1 acre; old orchard, ½ acre; separate walled garden, ½ acre; riverside tree belt, about 1½ acres) held the bulk of the birds. Inevitably the area saw a number of changes during the twenty-five years of study.

As well as the creeper in the courtyard, we cleaned ivy off the east face of the house, forcing a number of sparrows elsewhere. The riverside shrubbery below the west side of the house was gradually tidied up, but a grassy bank close to it provided compensating cover as brambles, hawthorns, elm sucker shoots and young ashes have carried out the botanical succession; and elder bushes sprang up everywhere. The walled garden was cultivated, allowed to go wild, partially worked again and then reverted once more to what was largely a riot of nettles, but where plum saplings and old fruit trees attracted a few nesting birds. The orchard behind the house lost three big walnut trees – one a regular jackdaw site – early on and became very much a bird sanctuary with thickly ivied fruit trees for early blackbirds and song thrushes.

On the steep riverside bank below the orchard two big elms fell before they could be attacked by disease. One in April 1973 took with it a traditional and occupied stock dove site.

The greatest change hardly affected the census series as it took place in August 1951: the virtual demolition of two old thatched barns standing close to the walled garden. Here the barn owls sometimes nested, with blackbirds, robins, wrens, tits and several pairs of jackdaws. But the chief interest was the colony of stock doves, some twenty pairs strong, whose long breeding season I tried to record in 1949–51 by regular visits to the nest sites deep in the rotting thatch. Most of the doves, like woodpigeons, started to breed late, after the jackdaws had finished, and reached a peak of activity in August. Indeed the night before the roof of the larger barn was removed, I sadly took all the eggs, including one 'clutch' of six, all apparently fertile and incubated. Several times I found clutches of three eggs, some of which I believe were genuinely the product of one bird, but no pair ever succeeded in rearing three young. After the loss of the thatch I provided large nestboxes in the adjacent walled garden, and for several years some stock doves and one pair of jackdaws did occupy them. But the barn obviously exerted a great attraction and the doves tried to nest in the ventilation holes of the gables that were still standing, exposed to a through draught and to predators. So the colony dropped away and I did not score more than four pairs over the whole area in any season after 1955.

Oxfordshire's first collared dove was seen at Hordley on 18 December 1962 just before the cold spell started. Birds occurred more or less regularly thereafter but it was not until 1970 that I could find any evidence of nesting and I did not see eggs until 1972, which made *Streptopelia decaocto* the forty-eighth proved breeding species for the study area. But not more than 33 species were recorded as breeding in any year and only 23 were proved to breed in 1962.

In the most intensive census years (1956–75 inclusive), 14 species were proved to breed every season: moorhen, woodpigeon, dunnock, swallow, robin, blackbird, song thrush, mistle thrush, blue tit, jackdaw, starling, house sparrow, chaffinch and greenfinch. At the other extreme of numbers, kestrel (1951), willow tit (1966), coal tit (1974) and nuthatch (1957) only bred once, great spotted woodpeckers twice (1963, 1975) and pied wagtail three times (1958, 1960, 1975). Kestrels nested in other years just outside the area, and species which I suspected but never proved breeding were little owl, treecreeper, marsh tit and carrion crow. A single coot built a platform in what is called Pool Orchard in 1971 and again in 1975, not laying until 1976. Pool Orchard, a rectangular sheet of shallow water with a central tongue of land, right alongside the Glyme, may well have been a pre-Reformation fish pond. During our time at Hordley its cover of willows and general tangle made it a good imitation of the Everglades (so those who have been there assured me) and favoured by many birds, both breeding and transient. The mute swans made a nest like an eyrie with fallen sticks rather than water weeds, while for the last eight years of the series (and three years since) long-tailed tits have built an early nest in the fork of some slender ivied sapling along the central tongue.

The aftermath of the winter of 1963 produced a rookery of eight nests in the tall elms above the river; next year they were down to three and in 1965 there was a solitary but apparently successful nest. The woodpeckers nested in 1963 after a pair had kept themselves going on the fat we put out; rooks also visited our lawn for scraps: could this have influenced their colonization? The coal tits in 1974 came after Mike Webber of the EGI had been putting out nuts and trapping tits in the garden only a few yards from where they nested. Normally we hardly ever saw them. The goldcrests which nested more or less regularly for the last seven years probably reflected a general increase after a long run of mild winters, while a small influx of linnets in 1954 was due to something quite local: the late trimming of hedges in the vicinity.

Summer visitors formed a very small proportion of the birds nesting in the area; the spotted flycatcher, with five pairs in 1973, was the top scorer in any year. Swallows began to nest in 1953 (though there were 'fossil' nests in the attics) and varied from one to three pairs; turtle doves were fairly steady at one or two pairs, while for the last five seasons there was a cuckoo which laid robin-like eggs in dunnocks' nests (I found two in 1973). The warblers fluctuated; over the whole period seven species nested, but only blackcap, chiffchaff and willow warbler with any regularity. The last garden warbler's nest was found in 1959, the last sedge warbler in 1966, while whitethroats followed the national trend and disappeared after 1968. In compensation, the lesser whitethroat nested in most years after 1963, once only a few feet from the house. In 1954 I proved as well as circumstantial evidence can (that is, without ringing the birds) that garden warbler and whitethroat raised second broods on the area. In 1966, there was a bigamous cock chiffchaff with nests in each of his song territories, over a hundred yards apart.

The total number of pairs present is much harder to assess than the number of species. They should really be called 'breeding units' because polygamous pheasants, red-legged partridges with the hen laying a second clutch for her mate (as must have happened in 1965), bigamous wrens and perhaps communally nesting dunnocks were all involved. In the best years I estimated 170 'pairs' or about 20 to the acre (50 to the hectare) with a trough of under 100 in 1956. Nearly a third of the total were jackdaws, starlings and house sparrows, with song thrushes and blackbirds accounting for a quarter. Details are given in the Appendix, which I have tried to make as intelligible as possible.

Unlike the Court Perrott censuses (see Chapter 10), I had at Hordley almost unlimited searching time and a very small area to cover. I use the first person singular, but some nests were found by members of the family, even accidentally, and visitors. David Snow gave great help in 1960 when I was in the USA for most of May and part of June, while Pat Williams and Trevor Young made a valuable contribution, particularly in the last two seasons. Yet I seldom felt that I had found all the nests of any but the scarcest or the most conspicuous species. Song thrush and blackbird nests may be easy to find but I had not realized how many have to be built before one is successful and how many, in fact, are apparently never laid in. As, in a 'good' year, there might be up to 15 pairs of song thrushes and between 20 and 25 pairs of blackbirds, it was not easy to decide which nests belonged to which pairs, even after entering them all on large scale maps.

Exceptionally there were tantalizing indications of continuity or succession. The song thrush that raised a brood of six in 1972, the only one I have ever seen, must have been the same bird that laid C/6 10 yards away in 1973 and lost them. But the bird in the original site in 1974 only laid C/4. Sometimes egg type gave a clue to identity. Should I have concentrated on a few species only? The temptation to make a total census is strong, and I succumbed to it.

The most difficult species of all – and I can well understand why the BTO omits it from the Common Bird Census – is the house sparrow. For the first five years of the Hordley study I recorded ridiculously low numbers, from open nests and nestboxes; then in 1956 they began to climb as I realized that the majority built in little holes in the many stone walls, and my totals from 1957 to 1970 were between 20 and 30 pairs. The best means of finding the nests was by hearing the calling young: waiting for a parent to return can be remarkably time-consuming. In 1971 and 1972 my score dropped to 11+ (the plus sign being usually an admission of failure), in 1973 I roused myself and actually found 18 nest-sites, but only 8 in 1974 and 1975. Had there really been a steep decrease in the local population or was it due to my being less energetic and less observant? Unfortunately a million sparrows look very much the same as two million; only a special study can reveal the truth and, as the house sparrow is economically one of our most important birds, there seems to be a case for taking a closer look at its population.

As with the Court Perrott censuses, there was the general problem of checking accuracy. One method I tried was based on the view that all cock song-birds holding territories take part in the 'dawn chorus'. During the season 1963–8 I tried to check this, with gradually decreasing energy, by making rounds of the Hordley census area and counting songs, and then comparing the highest figure for each species in any count with the final score in my census.

The first year, of course, was immediately after a classic cold spell. I made five dawn counts between 17 April and 24 May but the populations were so low that only for the blackbirds were the results of interest: I counted 11 singing cocks on 5 May, when 11 nests had eggs or young, and four had recently fledged, giving a census total of 15 pairs.

I made 10 counts in 1964 and give the maxima for the common residents followed by their census scores: wren: 3, 4; mistle thrush: 1, 1; song thrush: 5, 9; blackbird: 15, 20; robin: 7?, 7; dunnock, 2, 9; chaffinch: 3, 6. The following seasons confirmed the indication in 1964 that not all 'eligible' song thrushes and black-birds, probably all robins, but only a low proportion of dunnocks take part in the chorus. Wrens were characteristically puzzling; sometimes I recorded many more songs than there were subsequent occupied nests, which seems all wrong for a frequently bigamous species; sometimes the totals agreed as in 1963 and 1968. Great tit and blue tit corresponded pretty well; about half the chaffinches sang, but possibly I was too early for this rather late riser. Summer visitors were always in such small numbers on the area that I could only say, 'Yes, the blackcap (or chiffchaff) is still there.' All I can honestly write in summary of this somewhat subjective survey is that the dawn chorus does not provide a reliable census method, though, as with the blackbirds in 1963, it may indicate the total of birds at a certain stage in their cycle.

The Hordley dawn chorus featured in a Living World programme on Radio 4. Apparently it was considered a success, because a television producer became interested and sent a camera team in the middle of the night to film it. Fortunately we had that year a singularly extrovert cock swallow who perched on the garage door and burbled away happily among the floodlights. This scarcely representative species was, as far as I know, the only one filmed and I never saw the item on the screen.

The Court Perrott censuses showed that, over five seasons, half the species nesting in the surrounding county bred on 100 acres. At Hordley this was repeated on a very much smaller area over a longer period. Oxfordshire, like Gwent, and a number of other inland counties, has about a hundred regular breeding species. In several seasons about a third of the regulars nested: in some ways the area was the counterpart of a sea loch island, providing a variety of cover; and certainly a good deal of the food-collection by jackdaws, starlings and thrushes took place in the fields around. The wet field across the Glyme would be dotted at times with foraging blackbirds and song thrushes. Flying insects were provided abundantly on the spot as Margaret, who suffers greatly from their bites but is a keen gardener, could certainly testify.

What might be called my 'fun list' of birds seen or heard at, over or from Hordley was some 110 species out of an 'old' (pre-reorganization) Oxfordshire total of about 250. As this includes a number of ancient records, my total is surprisingly high. Of course, I counted whimbrel and oystercatcher heard from my bed, also a quail; but its liquid *wet-my-lips* coming in at the window had me downstairs and running barefoot up the lane to clinch it. David Lack had heard one over his house on Boars Hill, and now I was equal. Birds of prey included peregrine, merlin, hobby and an osprey making for Blenheim Lake with a ragtag of corvids pursuing it. I claimed a nightingale singing upstream on the edge of Wootton village, a dipper sang from the Glyme below the house, and on 30 April and 1 May 1953 a cock pied flycatcher perched on a wire stretched across the river. I brought W. B. Alexander to see it, his first for Oxfordshire. This elicited a 'perfectly splendid', the highest praise I ever earned from him. Through George Stonebridge, our gamekeeper neighbour and a first-rate observer, I was able also to show WBA Oxfordshire long-eared owls in winter. They were present for some months and I was surprised to find how many well-known ornithologists were anxious to see them.

George Stonebridge's most remarkable feat was to find a hatched-off quail's nest after a large field of clover near Hordley had been cut. When the bird was calling, I could hear it more than a quarter of a mile away over the clatter of farm machinery. Wootton parish's 4000 acres are quite good quail country, something I can safely reveal as this is surely a self-protecting bird. I have only seen one locally, in early October after it had lost its legs in a cutting machine; it was beautifully fat, obviously just about to migrate. Quail habitat is likely to be corn bunting habitat too, but I have only seen four nests in the parish in thirty years, because most of them are in the crops, where Trevor Young found one in 1978 when pulling false oats; he estimated there were half a dozen more in the same field. The yellow wagtail is another crop nester locally, as Trevor and Pat also proved in 1978.

Wootton parish, although primarily an agricultural plateau on the upper oolite, has the steep-sided Glyme valley running through it and in its south-western quarter a belt of woodland with a good deal of old oak over a deadly bracken-bramble ground layer. Here John Stonebridge, worthy son of George, has found four woodcocks' nests in a season. In the village itself there is the beautiful garden of Wootton Place, where its owner, Elizabeth Clutterbuck, tells me hawfinches used to nest regularly and where Nick Davies did the field work for his study of spotted flycatchers' food and feeding habits. When I told him the house (the old rectory) was alongside the churchyard, he said, 'Good, flycatchers often perch on tombstones and leave droppings on them'.

The parish's list of regular breeding species is about seventy-two, with several on the edge: tufted duck, snipe (once regular), green woodpecker, nightingale (nested 1977), wood warbler (nested 1976). In my time we have (probably) lost redstart, certainly tree pipit, which in 1949 was quite regular. I found four nests in the next few years. Now I have to go four miles to be tantalized by it, though it sometimes breeds in Blenheim Park, where I have ringed young in a nest close to the main entrance, with litter and loving couples in the vicinity. Wootton has recently gained Canada goose (a pair arrived in the floods of early 1975 and stayed to nest on the island in an artificial pool), collared dove, of course, and in 1978 reed warbler (Trevor and Pat again) in the parish's new nature reserve, a welcome sign of the times.

17
Walks, Counts and Lists

When birdwatchers go out for a walk, though nowadays such activities are often motorized, they fairly inevitably make a list with notes of what they see. I began making such walk-lists from an early age but it was not until the 1940s that they took on a repetitive form and therefore might in time acquire some comparative value. But there was, and is, often a strong recreational, even festive aspect, inspired by the Audubon Christmas counts in the USA, which are now of considerable antiquity.

Between 1944 and 1953 we spent several days each Christmas with Margaret's parents in Moseley, and I carried out a Boxing Day walk, sometimes alone, usually with Hugh Doncaster, then living in Birmingham; once, in 1951, we were joined by Horace Alexander and Duncan Wood, who upheld the journal *British Birds* during Bernard Tucker's last illness. This was my first meeting, I think, with 'HGA', like 'WBA' a legend in his lifetime; his *Seventy Years of Birdwatching* (Poyser, 1974) is the best account of the development in the first half of the twentieth century of amateur scientific ornithology, with the Alexander brothers (the third ornithological one, Christopher, was killed in 1917) in the van.

Horace's birdwatching has been world-wide and he would as easily knock up a century of species round Delhi on New Year's Day as we recorded our half-century on the outskirts of Birmingham, and enjoy both occasions equally. Assisted by a car, we covered quite a large area, including the Barnt Green or Bittell reservoirs, our usual beat, the wooded Lickey Hills, where we lunched, assorted farmland, a swampy marsh near the 'new Austin works' and finally Bartley reservoir. The full score was fifty-five species, the highest of the series, though how much was due to Horace and how much to our wider range I cannot say. A covey of ten partridges (we usually met one: would we today?), some twenty-five tree sparrows, but only a single rook to put against at least sixty crows were features of the day.

On the first walk of all, Hugh and I saw a little grebe make a crash landing ahead of us on the roadside between two of the Bittell reservoirs. It failed to rise again, was just missed by a car and then flopped on for about a hundred yards before collapsing. When we picked it up, its feet were slightly cut. We put it down near the water; it sat for about a minute then managed to take off and fly back to the four companions it had originally left. It fluffed itself out after landing and was soon indistinguishable from them. We also flushed a jack snipe and found one in the same spot exactly two years later, quite characteristic of this cryptic little bird which I have yet to see before it has seen me and taken off, sometimes almost at my feet. We often saw a sparrowhawk, and could count on six or seven kinds of duck, with the resident flock of Canada geese. In

1949 we watched a water rail catch what looked like a small stickleback transversely in its bill, shake it, flick it through 90° and then swallow it. Two or three times we identified a willow tit, while goldfinches, siskins, and redpolls were 'nice' birds to be found feeding in the alders.

These pleasant annual events ended when the Doncasters moved out to live in a nature reserve of their own at Alfrick Pound near Worcester. But in 1952 I had 'doubled up' by going out on 27 December with Tony Norris and his father-in-law, Lord Hurcomb, on a motor tour of some of the Staffordshire reservoirs. The now famous Blithfield was in the early stages of filling, and wrapped in fog when we arrived. Walking down to the stream we saw the reflection of a flying bird in the water and said 'water rail', which is on a par with the hoopoe John White and I identified from its shadow across a French road in 1962. At Belvide we saw a peregrine which circled a dying black-headed gull on the bank before flying on. At Gailey there were up to seventeen cormorants roosting, mainly on the pine trees of the heronry island with their distinctly Japanese silhouette against the sunset. In recent years Gailey has been a frequent stop when driving along the M6. Once a friend of Ròna's had fallen asleep in the car; when she woke up, she found herself apparently deserted in remote countryside. Eventually she located me inspecting the heronry and Ròna selecting a decorative spray of some kind from the hedge.

Our 1952 total was 55 species; in 1954 I joined Tony and Lord Hurcomb again and we did even better, with 65 species and a rough estimate of between 10,000 and 15,000 individual birds. There were 11 species of duck and the day brought my Staffordshire list up to the century.

After 1954 our Christmas visits to Birmingham

became shorter. In 1955 there was no Boxing Day walk at all; but in 1956 our then neighbour Grant Lee and I did a 'fifty species walk' from Hordley to Blenheim Park, round the upper lake and back again on a morning of light wet snow, which gave way to sunshine. I suppose a curlew was our 'best bird', being unusual in Oxfordshire in winter, but fifteen little grebes and no great crested on the lake is very different from the present position; so is 'only five' wigeon: today we should be happy to see one, but would be surprised not to see gadwall. A single black-headed gull over Woodstock was the harbinger of another notable change.

Next Boxing Day Grant and I did a new walk which has been our route on sixteen further outings. We go north from Hordley mostly along green lanes, then by a minor road to the Cherwell valley at Rousham, strike the Oxford canal at Lower Heyford and walk down the towpath to the Rock of Gibraltar at Enslow. Our tally of species has ranged from 43 to 54, except for the special walk we did on 19 February 1963 to see the effect of the prolonged cold weather: the tally was then only 28 species with an estimate of 600 individual birds, to which starlings, sparrows and a flock of chaffinches contributed about half. Of course, estimates of individuals on such walks are simply inspired guesswork, but it is of some interest that we have only once since arrived at an estimate of more than half the figure (7780) for our first walk in 1957, when we met huge flocks of lapwings, woodpigeons, starlings and greenfinches. The species total for all the walks is seventy-one, which includes most of the birds reasonably to be expected in Oxfordshire in mid-winter and one very unexpected one, a drake red-breasted merganser in 1972, the first record for the Banbury area for many years and a vivid reminder of Loch Sunart. One slightly curious feature of the lists is that only twenty-three species appear in all of them (excluding the 'cold spell walk' which eliminated six of these), even mallard and great tit being missed on single walks.

These Cherwell valley walks, in which Pamela Lee regularly and sometimes some of our children join, are also an opportunity for a good talk, often wandering far from ornithology, and this social aspect of bird-watching and field natural history generally is surely one of its great appeals. This is also to the fore in the walks in Blenheim Park which, as the somewhat inactive President of both, I have led members of the Banbury Ornithological Society most autumns since 1956 and the West Oxfordshire Field Club since 1970. Blenheim is, however, ideally suited for this sort of birdwatching. Along the canal towpath the first two or three people may see the kingfisher or the water rail and that is that. At Blenheim the birds are more or less habituated to humanity and the party can walk on a broad front or straggle happily and still see most of what is about. The total of species now recorded is 77, the difference from the Cherwell valley total being accounted for by waterfowl, 13 against 7, which are what most people come to Blenheim to see. The years reflect the build-up of gulls, the switch, already mentioned, between great crested and little grebes, which have not favoured the lake in big numbers since the 1963 spell, and the increase in pochard and tufted ducks. Good mast years are marked by high totals of chaffinches, bramblings and titmice and only in the years 1961–6 did we record tree sparrows during their period of rapid but apparently temporary increase. After the walks most of the party have tea at our house where we recap the afternoon and hazard estimates of numbers.

As enjoyable as the club walks but with a more scientific object are the monthly winter wildfowl counts, in which I first took part when in Cardiff. Soon after coming to Oxfordshire I found myself a local organizer, a job only finally relinquished to Roland Wilcock in 1978–9. I also took on the actual counts at Eynsham Park Lake and its two subsidiary waters, which has led to a long friendship with Michael Mason and his family. Eynsham Park, with its fine conifers, birches and rhododendrons, looks more like lowland Scotland than Oxfordshire and the spin-off from the duck counts, on which George Webb was my companion for a number of recent years, is the variety of birds, not to speak of the early spring flowers, that may be met on the estate, which is kept as a sanctuary. I have been lucky enough to see ospreys by the lake twice, the first in 1956 when a juvenile was about for most of September. Early on the 9th I found it on the riparian lime tree which seemed its favourite perch, whence, after ten minutes of snake-like twisting of its neck, it turned through a right angle and launched itself on a diagonal dive of some thirty yards, brushing by a terrified woodpigeon. It was submerged only momentarily, but thrashed on the surface for several seconds before, flapping wildly, it rose with a fish of about half a pound, held unevenly crosswise in its talons. This was the first osprey dive I had seen. That afternoon we watched it again and son David saw it make a spiral dive with wings half-closed. On 27 September 1969 another juvenile was at Eynsham Park and Mike Mason saw it dive seven times for one small fish. When we joined him, we saw it fly with a small fish, which it took to a low perch and pecked at delicately for about a quarter of an hour. This unfortunate or ill-adapted bird later flew into wires near the Thames and broke a wing.

I have only once seen the volatile black tern at Eynsham Park during a duck count. Two appeared on 12 September 1971 but by the time I had found Mike and we had walked to the lake they had vanished and there was only a kingfisher as consolation prize. In 1959 a pair of crossbills almost certainly nested in Scots pines near the lake, and hawfinches used to be almost regular fare – Niall and I once saw twelve over Freeland Pool – but have vanished in recent years. All three woodpeckers are the main side attraction now.

My annual visit to Clifton Hampden Bridge over the Thames dates from 1951 after W. B. Alexander, from his launch *Loterna*, had counted 436 more or less complete house martins' nests under five of its six brick arches. The graph shows the extraordinary fluctuations of the colony, for which I can offer no convincing explanation. In the case of terns, it is believed that a vanguard arrives at the colony site ahead of the main body. If house martins do this too and if, one year, the vanguard perished in a climatic freak, then it seems possible that the rest would go elsewhere to a site where birds had already arrived. John Brucker, who discussed the position of the house martin in the Oxford district in the Report of the Oxford Ornithological Society for 1975, does not favour this view and suggests that, in an exclusive population weakened by inbreeding, disease might be the cause of the declines shown by the graph. But neither of us has any hard evidence to support either theory.

Up to 1956 the count was made annually, usually in July, from *Loterna*. I write 'from' advisedly, as Carl Gibson-Hill took a photograph of WBA stripped to the waist and wading under the bridge to get at the arch nearest the old Berkshire bank, where the mud was deep. After WBA left Oxford, I carried on, often with

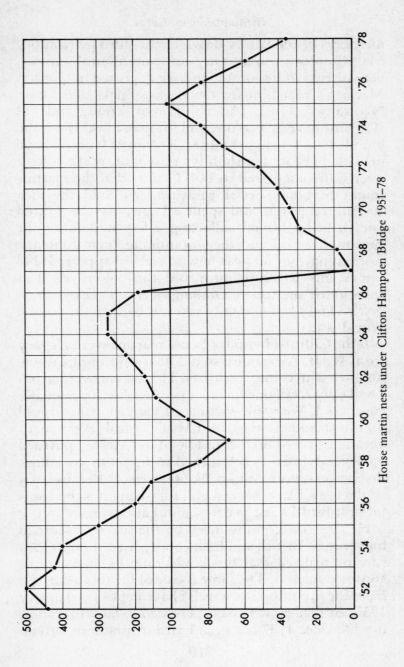

House martin nests under Clifton Hampden Bridge 1951–78

members of the family down to the third generation. Mary Radford was also my companion until within a year or two of her death, and we appeared in Gordon Maclean's first film for the Berks, Bucks and Oxon Naturalists' Trust. Latterly Trevor Young and Pat Williams have helped me, and for many years now the kind ladies of Bridge House, the Misses Gower, have provided a boat. The slightly unusual site of the colony over water suggested to Bob George that the martins might harbour special parasites. We sold the idea to Animal Magic and spent a happy day in a hired launch being filmed collecting a few nests after the breeding season and then examining their contents: fascinating, but no fleas new to science appeared. No one seems to know how old the colony is; it is mentioned in Robert Gibbings's *Sweet Thames Run Softly* (1940) but that only takes us back to the second world war.

If the Clifton Hampden house martins were a legacy from W. B. Alexander, so did he communicate to me his interest in county bird lists. This was proverbial but I will only retail one incident because I was personally concerned. We were waiting on the pier at Liverpool for our steamer to the Isle of Man in April 1950 when a heron lumbered up the middle of the Mersey pursued by several gulls. WBA turned to me: 'Do you think that heron is nearer this bank of the river? Because, if it is, the great black-backed gull following it is the commonest bird I have yet to see in Lancashire.'

He assessed 'commonness' by the species's score in his series of British and Irish county lists, though I am sure he realized that this could only be an index of conspicuousness. The same is true of the totals derived from the monthly lists which I have kept since January 1935. As readers who have persisted so far will realize, my life since 1937 has been based in southern Britain and, since 1948, specifically in rural Oxfordshire, so the bias in the lists is strongly southern inland farmland. My records are normally of sightings, but unmistakeable calls, as of tawny owl, cuckoo or quail, score as well. A 'full house' means a sight or sound record in every month of a year. When I began to keep my lists there was a national bird ringing scheme, but the nest records scheme had not yet been launched and the Common Birds Census was still many years away. Supported by numerous trained observers, it is now a far more accurate indicator of changes in bird status than my lists. What then, apart from the satisfaction of having maintained them for over four decades and for the memories they reawaken, is the point of them? Well, the CBC does not cover all species and, in the absence of other parameters, the lists do show certain broad trends which are not entirely due to changes in my birdwatching habits.

The Canada goose is an example of increase. For the first two decades its score was only 8 out of 240 months; then it began to climb, slowly at first but with a jump from 3 months in 1968 to 9 in 1969, to score its first full house in 1974. To make a record now for many months in the year, I have only to lie in bed with my ears flapping, as we hear the local gaggle go over, or in spring to look out of the dining room window to see the pair nesting on my neighbour's pool by the Glyme.

Just as striking are the records for two natural colonists. I saw my first little ringed plover and found its nest when showing the Reading gravel pits to Theed Pearse on 15 May 1950. Since then I have only missed noting 'LRPs' in three years and recently they have been scoring four or five months each year. I broke my rule about not going far in search of rarities to see my first British collared doves near Cromer in 1956, when they had just bred successfully. Their next appearance was in 1960, and from 1962 the totals rose rapidly, to reach a full house every year since 1968. No one who has been kept awake early in the morning by the *Türkentaube*'s mournful cooing or eldritch scream will doubt that my lists reflect a true situation.

What of birds that have notably declined? Three of these are summer visitors, for which the possible annual total is inevitably fairly low. Apart from a gap of three years when we were in Wales, the red-backed shrike scored in one to three months up to 1958, latterly mainly on the strength of the small group in the Forest of Dean. These finally disappeared after 1963 and my only two records since have been on visits to East Anglia, though I was one day behind a transient in Oxfordshire in 1976. I began my lists just as the wryneck was beginning to fade out in the south: on 28 April 1936 I noted 'several' in East Anglia, and heard two more there in May 1938, since when a single bird in Leigh Woods near Bristol in 1960 is my only score, apart from recently dead birds found in two Oxfordshire villages. Emlyn Evans and I have looked and listened in vain at one of the 'new' localities in Strathspey.

The nightjar has not such a disastrous record as the wryneck, but is now distinctly local. I have noted it in twenty-five years, usually in a single summer month. It illustrates the problem of scoring summer visitors. Although Robert Hudson's excellent BTO field guide 15, *Early and Late Dates for Summer Migrants*, shows that almost every species has been recorded in every month of the year, only three have scored eight months in a year in my lists: chiffchaff, swallow and house martin. Should eight then be regarded as their full house? The shorter-stay swift, noisy and easily seen, scores four or five months consistently and the cuckoo, calling from April sometimes to early July with sight records of juveniles up to August, does about as well.

Latest of the common passerine summer visitors is the spotted flycatcher, dull in plumage but conspicuous in action and scoring five months a year pretty regularly. The chiffchaff is well ahead of the other warblers, followed by willow warbler and whitethroat. Blackcap has a long lead over garden warbler and sedge easily beats reed warbler, partly because of its wider distribution. Whitethroats showed a sharp decrease after 1968 but have recovered since 1974.

Winter visitors rather defy analysis because a bird with this status in Oxfordshire may breed freely elsewhere. Even redwing and fieldfare, the traditional 'winter thrushes', now nest in small numbers, mainly in Scotland, and my redwing list includes a June score in 1964, the first breeding record for West Sutherland. But the brambling, the chaffinch's northern counterpart, has scored anything from two to six months during our Oxfordshire years, perhaps reflecting good beech mast in Blenheim Park or a failure of food on the Continent. These variable winter birds slide into the irruption category. Not living on the east coast, I can seldom reflect the waxwing's invasions (its total score is only four), but the crossbill seems to show evidence of its temporary occupation from 1956 to 1963, with a peak of seven months in 1959.

Because of their fatal involvement with poisonous residues, birds of prey have been much in the news. My sparrowhawk records show the expected trough, dipping from an average of 5.8 months per year in 1951–5 to 3.6 months in 1961–5 and recovering splendidly to 11.2 in 1974–8. Actually I saw no sparrowhawks at all in Oxfordshire during the middle quinquennium, which points up yet another bias, introduced by trips away from the home area. But what birdwatcher can resist the occasional one?

The bold peregrine scored up to five months a year during our Welsh period; when we came east, the records became fewer, with a run of nine blanks until 1974 when a November visit to the New Grounds with Michael Rowntree discovered one slowly reducing a crippled teal on the mud of the Severn. I am too seldom in the merlin's moorland habitat for its figures to have any significance, but we are broadly in hobby country and have had no blank years since 1967, a sign that this most glamorous of the small falcons is doing well. The kestrel has only dropped one month since we came to Oxfordshire: nothing here to indicate fluctuations. My buzzard totals are puzzling, peaking at eight months in 1959, about five years after myxomatosis hit the rabbit, its favourite food in Britain.

Among owls, the tawny keeps pretty steady, only twice dropping as low as eight months; the little owl's figures suggest a slight decline since 1963, but it scored a full house in 1975 and 1977. The barn owl introduces a new factor. After six full houses, it dropped to six months in 1962 and to a single month in 1963 and has not been higher than seven months in any year since, in spite of twice being my first bird on New Year's Day. The drop can, of course, be attributed initially to severe weather. The first 'killer' to show in the lists was 1939–40. This notably affected both long-tailed tits and stonechats, the stonechat dropping right out in 1947 and only in 1975–7 getting back to the scores of the 1930s. Other sufferers in 1947 were goldcrest, heron and mistle thrush, otherwise nearly a 'top ten' bird. But early 1963 had the biggest effect: I did not see a lapwing in January or February, the only months missed in 44 years. Linnet and pied wagtail also dropped two months each, while long-tailed tit, gold-crest, green woodpecker and woodlark all went down, and I have only twice recorded woodlarks since. Two riparian birds, kingfisher and grey wagtail, were hard hit but made excellent recoveries.

An interim report of the first thirteen years of the Common Birds Census listed pied wagtail, red-legged and grey partridges and lapwing as farmland birds which had been slow to recover their 1962 index. My lists are not nearly sensitive enough to show this, but I have tried to keep counts since 1962 of the lapwings breeding in roadside fields on my sixteen-mile route from Hordley to Burford. This is based on birds seen sitting, but includes some estimates where no nests are seen. From an initial low figure of 7 pairs, the total rose to between 29 and 34 pairs in 1969 and then declined to between 11 and 15 in 1977 and about 14 pairs in 1978. But the situation has been complicated in 1977 and 1978 by the discovery by farmworker friends of a group of late nests which I should never have found for myself. Presumably, for comparative purposes, they should be excluded.

Primarily, of course, my monthly lists have been fun to keep. They include only 259 species, which should absolve me from any charge of 'tally-hunting'. The totals range from 26 species in October 1935 to 147 in June 1969, when I started off in Shetland with a red-footed falcon and a crane, both by courtesy of Bobby Tulloch. Thirty-five have appeared in 90 per cent or more months. For those who would like to compare them with their own records, here they are, with the *Atlas* estimate of their breeding population in pairs in 1968–72.

528 (100%)	Woodpigeon (3 to 5 m)	523	Black-headed Gull (300,000)
	Dunnock (5 m+)	522	Skylark (2 to 4 m)
	Robin (5 m)		
	Song Thrush (3½ m)		Mistle Thrush (3 to 600,000)
	Blackbird (7 m+)	521	Greenfinch (1 or 2 m)
	Blue Tit (5 m+)	520	Mallard (150,000)
	Rook (1½ m)		
	Starling (4 to 7 m)	519	Kestrel (100,000)
	House Sparrow (3½ to 7 m)	515	Yellowhammer (1 m)
	Chaffinch (7 m)	509	Bullfinch (600,000)
527	Jackdaw (½ m)		
526	Moorhen (300,000)	504	Coot (100,000)
		501	Linnet (800,000 to 1.6 m)
	Lapwing (200,000)		
	Great Tit (3 m+)	498	Pheasant (1 m)
		494	Herring Gull (300,000+)
	Crow (1 m)	491	Goldfinch (300,000)
525	Wren (10 m)		
524	Mute Swan (5 to 6,000)	486	Heron (6,500+)
		480	Stock Dove (100,000+)
	Pied Wagtail (½ m)		
	Magpie (250,000+)	478	Meadow Pipit (3 m+)

Notes
1. m = millions of pairs.
2. Species with the same score are listed in 'Voous order'.

18
Birdwatcher Abroad

When I set out to write this book, I envisaged an extended look at my birdwatching exploits outside the British Isles. But the voice of reason, embodied as so often in that of my wife, began to say: 'Everybody's been to East Africa and the Camargue and the Naardermeer and Myvätn and, if not, they've read articles and seen pictures and films of them until they're dizzy'; and so I found myself concentrating on that boyhood world which, whether I was in Argyll or Hampshire, now seems so remote, and have left myself only a chapter for foreign parts.

About all I can remember ornithologically of my first visit abroad, to Dinard early in 1922, is the robins, which I was surprised to see because I somehow thought (and I have since found out I am not alone in this) that, like the language and the letterboxes, the birds and the natural scene would be absolutely different across the Channel.

Eleven years later, as part of our forestry final year, we did a tour which included the dune forests of the

Landes Mimizan, where Geoff Rouse and I cycled on cement *pistes* and saw our first hoopoes, and the great broadleaved forest of Tronçais and Dreuille, where I learned that the oaks were right out of my league as regards climbing to the nests of buzzard, red kite and what I believe must have been booted eagles (Peterson, Mountfort and Hollom were still twenty-one years away). My list for the area was only about 55 species but, when John White and I had an *al fresco* breakfast in Dreuille on our way back from the Camargue in April 1962, we found both grey-headed and middle spotted woodpeckers there, species of whose existence I was not aware in 1933, nor of the short-toed treecreeper and Bonelli's warbler which we also recorded, together with my friend the pied flycatcher.

Chronologically my next visit to France after student days was Margaret's and my second honeymoon (our Galloway week had been a bit brief) at New Year 1939 when we stayed at Beaulieu near Nice and I added several common Riviera birds to my French list: my notes made at the time show how difficult it was to identify them in pre-field-guide days. But the first two volumes of *The Handbook of British Birds* were published in 1938 so, when I got home, I could clinch firecrest, Sardinian warbler and rock bunting, all on the British list. Ironically the one Sardinian warbler and three of the six rock bunting records were purged as 'Hastings rarities', but the warbler has been readmitted on the strength of new records.

By 1961, when we had a family camping holiday mainly in Morbihan, the French avifauna no longer held any terrors but some surprises, for example a little ringed plover incubating three eggs in the shingle of the Loire at Saumur on 13 August. Not entirely irrelevantly I was equally surprised to find three young blackcaps in a nest at Fiesole near Florence on 25

August 1977: do we know everything about European breeding seasons? We visited Morbihan again in August 1978, had great difficulty in recognizing our old camp site and could not find the Dartford warblers on the heaths or hear the nightjars, for which we were perhaps just too late. At dusk I stalked up to an ideal churring tree, a lone pine, and found a tawny owl perched in it. But, as in 1961, there were cirl buntings, crested tits in the maritime pines and kingfishers in the bays. I also saw a common tern fishing from the mast of a moored dinghy.

John White provided the Ford Thames van for our Camargue trip so we had no tent-pitching problems. Between 18 and 30 April we scored 170 species, the last being a great spotted woodpecker in the pines at Le Touquet, our airport. My European list jumped up considerably and I came back full of the warm south, as inhaled intoxicatingly at a derelict lavender garden near Aubenas, recommended by R. J. Raines, where we saw our first spectacled warblers. The legend of birdless France has been truly laid in recent years by the discovery of more and more delectable new places. Next to France, I have paid more visits to Holland, where Karel Voous and Johann van Marle gave me a 'big day' in Flevoland on 31 October 1974, showing me everything from thousands of wintering greylags to a trickle of swallows heading south.

I have nodded at all the Scandinavian countries, Finland at the International Ornithological Congress of 1958 and Iceland in June 1972 for the British Ornithologists' Union's first overseas conference, in collaboration with our Icelandic colleagues and for which I arranged the scientific programme. On our day trip to the south-west I was fortunately placed, while everyone else was photographing or admiring Gullfoss, to see a pair of merlins fly into the cliff. The hen sat plump on her eggs as the cameras were turned on her, and by the end of the week I believe she had braved two more large parties. Our day at Myvätn was gloriously fine, and fine for the black flies too; but in Reykjavik we had our share of rain which made the birches on the way from our hostel to the lecture room smell as wonderfully as the lavender at Aubenas. There was a redwing's nest by the path and I found a redpoll which knew what was expected of it in the far north and laid seven eggs.

My birdwatching elsewhere in Europe has usually been in August, dictated by family considerations. My first visit to Switzerland, in 1930, when I joined the Pringles at Merligen, was notable for our catching in a fortnight as many kinds of butterfly as there are in Britain; but we did see a wallcreeper my first evening. Next door, so to speak, in Austria, I found Salzburg's forest surroundings quite rewarding in August 1973 and saw turnstones on migration by the Danube in Vienna. Our cultural visit to Florence in 1977 was enlivened for me by fantailed warblers (also calling in Brittany in 1978), by a passage of black terns along the Arno and by a trip with Sergio Frugis to see the Italian World Wildlife Fund reserve at Bolgheri with its herons and waders.

Our visit to Malta in 1966 was dominated by the kindness of the Maltese ornithologists, who have a close link with the Banbury Ornithological Society, and by schnorkelling, which I indulged in at ten different places round the coast. But I did see, while hoping for waders at Salina, the local sportsmen in full panoply, with dog and cartridge belts, ready for anything from a swallow to a honey buzzard. The species list for a fortnight was twenty, but I got splendid views of Malta's national bird, the blue rock thrush. We fared a bit better in Portugal in 1972 when staying with Harry,

Coralia and Penny Forster; on our last day, from the Tagus Ferry, I recognized a Mediterranean among all the black-headed gulls. In Lisbon's botanic garden I abstracted two used warbler nests, hoping to identify them at leisure. Hiding them under my shirt gave me, I realized in retrospect, a somewhat hermaphrodite appearance.

I still include the Channel Isles with continental Europe. My first brent geese were black dots out on the mud of Jersey way back in 1932; then in September 1953 W. B. Alexander and I flew over for a Bird Observatories Conference and our hosts laid on everything they could, including a juvenile woodchat shrike, which they caught, an aquatic warbler and a Napoleon weaver leading a flock of sparrows. Full of these sights, my eyes lit on a shiny black bird apparently with a red bill and my knees gave under me until the binoculars revealed it as a jackdaw in trouble with a tomato skin. On Sark in 1970 I had the honour of adding the redshank to the island's list so carefully compiled by Frank Rountree, but we were too early for any spectacular migrants. On the way back we had to spend some hours in Guernsey, so Ròna and I took a bus to the north side of the island and I found myself almost standing on the latest and most conspicuous stonechat's nest I have ever found.

Finally in Europe, there is the visit Stanley Cramp, Leighton Reynolds and I paid to Poland in June 1959, which was the first by British ornithologists to an east European country since the war. In 1957, at the suggestion of Professor K. W. Szarski of Wrocław University, I had looked after a young zoologist, Stefan Peters, in England for a month during which, incidentally, he had his first sight of the sea and ate his first banana. So, two years later, three of us paid a return visit for a fortnight, based on Wrocław, with a weekend in the Krakow area under the guidance of Zygmunt Bocheński who took us down the Dunajec by canoe and up the Tatra by cable car and on foot.

Stanley Cramp needs no introduction to today's ornithologists; senior editor of *The Birds of the Western Palearctic* and President of the BOU, he has also played a leading part in the promotion of wildlife conservation. Leighton Reynolds was one of my Caerphilly School Field Club 'finds' as an amateur botanist. A classics don at Brasenose and a fluent Russian speaker, he was also our interpreter to those Poles who would admit to understanding Russian. Both are to a high degree unflappable, ideal companions for a venture into *terra incognita*.

After spotting a harrier hunting over Hamburg airport, we met our first hitch in Berlin: we needed a visa to travel by train through East Germany. This meant the night of 16 June in the divided city and allowed a visit to the West Berlin zoo and a walk into the as yet unwalled east sector. Our visas were forthcoming all right next morning and eleven hours from the Ostbahnhof we were met in Wrocław by a worried Professor Szarski with whom we had been unable to communicate. I made notes from the train on the vegetation and animal life, which ranged from hornets via red-backed shrikes to roedeer. Our host housed us in a villa in a garden suburb full of fruitful cherry trees, a great contrast to the bomb-blasted areas in the centre of the city which we saw next day. But shrikes were nesting in the peaceful botanic garden and edible frogs called from its ponds; Stanley watched a great spotted woodpecker rifling a litter basket. In the evening we dined in the cultured atmosphere of the Szarskis' flat.

On the morning of 19 June, which was fine and hot, we were ready for our visit to the Milicz area of former Silesia, where the Polish Government had set up one of the largest bird sanctuaries in Europe, some 28,000 acres of shallow reed-fringed fish ponds and 22,000 acres of surrounding woodland: alder carr, deciduous forest and conifers. The ponds, artificial in origin, are devoted to the cultivation of carp, with some pike, tench and bream, for consumption in neighbouring countries. Professor Szarski's then students, Josef Witkowski, Andrzej Dyrcz and Adam Mrugiasiewicz have written up the bird life in detail since (*British Birds* vol. 55: 245–72 (1962)) so I can confine myself to a selection of personal impressions, which began on our drive in the University car from Wrocław to the fisheries village of Radziasz by way of Trzebnica with its superb baroque church and Zmigrod, where we lunched by the dusty square, through open country-side in which we counted at least thirty red-backed shrikes, mostly on roadside wires, as well as two storks' nests in the villages.

We reached the fishermaster's hut at 12.30 p.m. and were at once aware of the bedlam of a colony of black-headed gulls, some 700 pairs on an island in the nearest pond. This continued all twenty-four hours, periodically lashed into frenzy by a passing predator, usually a marsh harrier or black kite, and was fortified at night by the chorus of fire-bellied toads *Bombina*, of which we never caught sight. In a daze of sunshine, butterflies, dragonflies and birds, we followed the students along the path between the ponds to the punts in which Josef and Andrzej propelled us, jumping out to push when the water became too shallow.

Apart from the species new to me – ferruginous duck, penduline tit, Savi's and great reed warblers, belting away their *chiro chiro chiro*, the large colony of black-necked grebes, nesting apparently under the wings of the gulls was of great interest, reminding me of the lapwing/redshank and little tern/ringed plover associations in Britain. Then, in the distance, I saw what I took to be a solitary fisherman. Fisherman yes, but no human one: a white-tailed eagle resting on a post. We landed on its boggy island and the mate came off the huge stick nest, in the bottom of which tree sparrows were nesting. Josef had already climbed the seventy-foot pine to ring the young. Below it, also ringed, was a young cuckoo in a shrike's nest in a small hornbeam. Altogether the day's score was seventy species.

Next morning Josef & Co led us to the forest in brilliant sunshine. On the way we saw another example of protective symbiosis: a barred warbler with a juvenile in the same clump of sallows and lilacs as a family of red-backed shrikes. Hoopoes and white storks foraged in the cut hayfields and we saw out first crane. But the day's highlight was the black stork's nest with five young only 25 feet up an oak; the parent let us get within 25 yards before flying off. Near it I had my first good look at a cock Savi's warbler reeling his head off on an alder twig.

Nests of honey buzzard and black kite followed, each the host for a small colony of tree sparrows (how do they find these remote sites?) and we gazed into the empyrean at half a dozen black storks soaring with birds of prey, which included a pair of goshawks. About this time my interest in things avian began to wane and I tottered back to the hut in the first stages of a violent internal upset which prostrated me for about sixteen hours. Had I taken the advice of the fishermaster, an enormous ex-Guardsman, and drunk his invariable remedy of Schnapps, I might have recovered sooner. Our bedroom was near the loo, which was also the home of the fishermaster's chickens, and between spasms I wondered vaguely what happened to Britons passing away beyond the Iron Curtain. Stanley and Leighton, both confirmed smokers, were quite unaffected, which I felt was slightly unfair to a lifelong abstainer. But their solicitude was exemplary.

The following morning I was weak but somewhat restored. Leaving the others to go on a stork-ringing expedition, I spent the day slowly patrolling the tree-lined path between the two nearest ponds. As so often when not trying to see the maximum in the minimum time, I had a successful convalescence; my score of fifty species included an immature white-tailed eagle being attacked by a female marsh harrier. I found the nests of hoopoe, icterine warbler and, something I had dreamed of ever since Pa brought one from France, of golden oriole. This was in a small oak and I was just able to hoist myself up to see the three white, black-spotted eggs in their famous 'basket'. The cock came with his mate to the next tree and gave me fine views of his elusive beauty before flying off silently while she went on to the nest. The hoopoes were feeding young in the sawn-off stump of a big tree quite close to the hut. They entered by a vertical hole where the centre wood had rotted. When Josef returned, he lost no time in digging out the brood of six from underneath the roots to ring them. Although their feathers were still partly in sheath, they were able to erect their tiny crests in protest.

Our last day in the area began with an early bus ride to Milicz and a narrow-gauge train to Grabownica, where there was another group of ponds, then back to Milicz with its fine, pleasantly unkempt park. We spent three hours by a most exciting pond; in its dense sedge patches, pochard, tufted and ferruginous duck nested in confusion, laying large clutches and dropping eggs in each other's scrapes, which communicated by tunnels through the vegetation. I have seen comparable chaos, affecting tufted ducks only, on

Roy's Folly in Loch Leven. Are the fish ponds an
artificially favourable habitat for ducks, resulting in
saturation as in an English covert full of pheasants?

As well as the ducks, there was a colony of common
terns with some thirty nests, some already with
young, in a sort of 'turf' of water crowfoot. But the
black terns, of which we saw about forty, did not seem
to have settled, except for one large floating nest with
two eggs in open sedge; its owners scolded us with the
short *tchik tchik* note when we waded out to it.

The pond, with a muddy shore, was notable also for
waders, of which we had seen few at Radziasz. We
identified eight species between us, including some
ruffs still in fine array and up to a hundred black-tailed
godwits. But the surprise for me was a robin-like bird
that emerged from the thick reed-grass *Glyceria*,
perched on top of a post, and sang for about twenty
seconds with head and tail up before vanishing into
cover, from which it did not emerge during the next
two hours: my first bluethroat. A fieldfare should also
have surprised us, but we gathered that small numbers
were nesting in the area.

In Milicz Josef & Co duly produced another first for
me, an adult roller. It was quite brilliant in the bright
sunshine and treated us to a quiet repeated rattle, which
we were told was not typical. The supporting programme here was of other birds of mixed woodland:
hawfinch, serin, siskin, golden oriole, several warblers, redstart, buzzard and two middle spotted woodpeckers which stole the show by playing hide and seek
among the old oaks, as we lay on the ground and
watched. Sometimes one gave a whickering call with
wings spread and partly raised, showing their barring.
Sometimes they called in flight. The area of chase
became wider, the calls noisier and the birds perched
momentarily on trunks and branches at all angles;

from the date it seemed to be midsummer madness. But it made a wonderful climax to four days in which we had seen 110 of the 183 species recorded in the Milicz area in the past six years. Close links are still maintained with Polish ornithologists at Wrocław, but our kind host, Professor Szarski, to whom we owed the whole trip, died within a year or so.

In 1960 Margaret and I paid our only visit to the United States. Bill Drury, then director of research to the Massachusetts Audubon Society, had most kindly arranged a Hatheway Fellowship for me, the third and last ever awarded, my predecessors being two very distinguished Europeans, Hans Löhrl and H. N. Kluijver. We sailed early in May on *S.S. Statendam* and on the 7th I had a splendid view of a pale phase pomarine skua close to the ship. Later, far out in the Atlantic, I watched a small party of arctic terns flapping languidly WNW as though each wingbeat would be their last, one of the most deceptive sights in the mysterious phenomenon of migration.

Once welcomed by Bill and Mary Drury and their hospitable colleagues and installed in a comfortable apartment, with blue jays, like outsize blue tits, coming to the windowsill, I tried to settle down to make a survey of the 220 acres of Drumlin Farm, the reserve which also houses the Society's offices. Altogether I proved the breeding of twenty-six species, seven of them in nestboxes, ranging from the rehabilitated wood duck to the black-capped chickadee on which Dr Kluijver had been working. He filled the boxes with shavings to accommodate the excavating drive of this titmouse, which for long was considered to be conspecific with the Palearctic willow tit.

But I cannot claim much accuracy for my Drumlin survey, as the field work was sandwiched between visits to other reserves, a weekend with the Petersons and my film-viewing on behalf of the BBC, which took me as far as Florida and a swim with brown pelicans overhead. So I will epitomize my American birdwatching with a summary of the events of 16 May 1960.

The Big Day is an American concept in keeping with a big country. To have taken part in one with Roger Tory Peterson as leader, driver, and above all, lightning listener is an experience that sticks for a lifetime. Operations began at 4.05 a.m. and continued until 10.45 p.m., though we went on reliving it all beyond midnight – almost a 24-hour stint.

The total was not as big as Roger has clocked up before or since on his home beat in Connecticut: 105 species identified by sight or sound. Eight of these were voices conjured out of the air by RTP alone, from a least bittern on a marsh by the Connecticut Rover (where we opened our score), to yellow-throated vireo and field sparrow.

Our strength varied through the day. Horace and Rebecca Alexander were with us on the dawn to break-fast stint, and Horace came out again until mid afternoon.

The early morning excursion was very much a *tour de force* by Roger, in a grey dawn world of strange sights and sounds. But we came across the only small bird's nest of the day, flushing a song sparrow off four eggs in a grass tussock, the sort of site a meadow pipit would choose in Britain. Pipits are one of the few groups that are poorly represented in North America – the 'sparrows' (buntings to Europeans) seem to take their niches.

After breakfast, on a morning now beautiful and sunny, we went up the north side of the Connecticut River as far as Essex, then back along the south side, visiting the fantastic Gillette Castle. Somewhere on its protruding stones a pair of phoebes, equivalent to our spotted flycatchers, were obviously nesting.

At about 4 p.m. Roger and I went over to Great Island, which straddles the mouth of the river, with Peter Ames who was working that season on the ospreys with Barbara Peterson; my diary records that they had about sixty nests under observation. Looking out of the train from New York to Boston on our arrival a few days earlier, we had seen three nests in little more than a minute. The previous afternoon I had been shown two nests built on cartwheel foundations at the tops of poles in gardens, and another on the transformer box of an electricity supply pylon – a hot seat from which the birds were usually evicted.

The year before our visit the Scottish ospreys had raised young for the first time, and when I told our New England friends that their protection had cost around £2,000, they applauded the sentiment, but plainly could not quite understand how we in Britain felt about it. Ironic that in 1974 Paul Spitzer tells me there was only a single nest on Great Island, though a slow recovery now seems to have begun, with four nests in 1979.

Stupidly I did not keep the stages by which the score mounted, but I was gathering birds new to me at every stop – from double-crested cormorants far out in the widening river to a fine view of a pair of black and white warblers in the woods round Gillette Castle. This little bird climbs trunks like a treecreeper, but makes a domed nest on the ground like our wood warbler. It is a British bird by virtue of a single specimen from Shetland in 1936.

This brings me to an analysis of the day's tally. Mute swan, starling, and house sparrow were European introductions, so probably was the mallard with her brood at Rocky Neck State park, though this is also a native bird. Fourteen species were intercontinentals, from the proud ospreys to the little tern, swallow, and bank swallow (our sand martin). No less than twenty-two more were North Americans that have occurred in Britain and Ireland, some of them since our Big Day, from the brown thrasher to the veery, a thrush with nightingale-like nesting habits. Then there were the 'replacers' – distinct species but obviously closely related to familiar Europeans, or occupying similar niches: ring-billed gull (common gull), tree swallow (house martin), and American crow (carrion crow).

Enough of statistics; let me return to the climax of the day: Great Island and its flocks of waders; a single snow goose that flew in from the sea; a brood of two young horned owls in an old osprey's eyrie towards which Roger and Peter hoisted me over a tangle of poison ivy and enormous briars; above all the lost legion of ospreys, wheeling against the blue sky above their nests, on the ground, on a hunter's blind (hide), in jetsam literally lapped by the tide.

But the last new bird of all was as dramatic as any. We had scored our night herons at Rocky Neck and were driving back through the dusk when Roger pulled up in the precipitate manner to which I was now accustomed. How he heard it I do not know, but down from the sky on its vertiginous display flight dropped an American woodcock, as mysterious and crepuscular as our counterpart. We called it a day.

As we drove through Kidlington towards Oxford on 1 March 1968, I spotted a waxwing on a whitebeam, surely a good omen for our visit to East Africa, where, on Nigel Sitwell's invitation, I was to lead a party on a now familiar circuit, with the advantage that we could then visit Uganda, and enjoy what used to be called the Murchison Falls. The idea was that, not having been in Africa before, I should be on the alert and a move ahead of the others, who in fact included several competent birdwatchers. It was a tremendous experience; but thousands have now enjoyed it, exclaiming with ecstasy at their first lilac-breasted roller on the roadside wires and muttering 'Just another bloody roller' at the end of the day. So quickly do these wonders satiate. But we did stick our Landrover in the Ngorongoro Crater, from which we were rescued by Peter Wake's ingenuity, only to stick again, fortunately temporarily, in the middle of a march of soldier ants. So I have my Africa story, but I have yet to sort out my list of birds.

The only other birdwatching I have done outside Europe is at Skanes in Tunisia, where Margaret, Ròna and I spent a restoring four days in January 1974. To hear a hoopoe and to see two 'life birds' from our bedroom the first morning was a good start. My total list was only fifty-two certain species, but it included one or two which should not have been there, and that is always satisfactory; and I had a moment of minor triumph when I was able to greet a car-load of young Swedish enthusiasts, all beards and binoculars, as they burst out of their car. 'By the way, there's a male *Falco naumanni* in the palm tree over there'. Birdsmanship dies hard.

19
Ireland and England

In previous chapters I have referred a good many times
to parts of these islands outside those in which my lot
has been particularly cast: Hampshire, Argyll,
Lothian, South Wales and Oxfordshire. This, therefore, is a tidying-up chapter and I may as well begin
with Ireland to which I paid eleven visits between 1931
and 1969, spending a total of 70 nights and passing
through or setting foot in all the 32 counties, although
my bird lists for some are conspicuous for brevity, for
example, moorhen and magpie in Co. Longford.

My introduction to the land whence my ancestors
reputedly invaded Scotland some 1500 years ago was a
fortnight's pretty comprehensive tour round its western rim in August 1931 with Bernard Keeling and his
mother in their car. We camped, then quite a novelty in
Ireland, and were tortured by midges but we had some
wonderful weather to climb Muckish in Donegal and
Carn Tual in the Macgillycuddy Reeks. I managed to
identify seventy-six birds, not bad for August anywhere in Britain and Ireland, including ring ouzel,

whinchat and corn bunting (in Achill) which I have not seen again in Ireland; *Atlas* reveals how scarce the first and last of these are. I am also pretty sure that 'a peregrine quartering like a buzzard', seen from the car near Glengarriff, must have been a hen harrier, which I did not then know occurred in Ireland. I had a fine view of a male in Ballyhoura Forest when on a tour with the Royal Scottish Forestry Society in October 1964, on the same day as I claimed to have seen a water vole at Cahir, which raised the mammalogists' eyebrows.

After the 1931 visit there was a big gap until June 1949 when Margaret, David and I went under BTO auspices and stayed with Ivan Goodbody and his parents in Glenageary. Highlights were a trip to Rockabill, to see the colony of roseate terns, in a mature craft whose engine at one critical moment had to be kicked into life again; and a drive to the west to meet Robin Ruttledge and see the great scoter loughs. Nests of merganser and sandpiper reminded me of Argyll as did the common gulls of Lake Cara, though their environment was pleasantly eutrophic. The oddest observation of the tour was at a jay's nest twenty-five feet up in a spruce in Powerscourt demesne. The solitary well-grown young one worked itself into such a paroxysm, evidently at our presence twenty-five yards away, that it fell out of the nest and killed itself on the ground. I have always hoped to have an ethologist explain this to me.

After that came several short visits to the north; on one, in March 1953, I was introduced to the brent geese of Strangford Lough and to a long-eared owl which was betrayed in a dense *macrocarpa* by needling goldcrests. At the Ringdufferin estate was the most accessible rookery I have met. Bill Seaby of the Ulster Museum and I climbed to 88 nests, mostly only 25 to

30 feet up in pines, larches, oaks, hawthorn and even an elder. Three held the large clutch of 6 eggs, there were 25 with 5 and 30 with 4 eggs, but we saw none of the red type that used to be reported. On our way back to Belfast we watched Arnold Benington lowering some of his pupils to look at four big young ravens in a quarry nest, reminding me of my efforts with the Caerphilly and Fochriw boys.

Five years later we tempted providence on a camping holiday with Emlyn Evans in late August by Lake Currane in Kerry. The week was notable for a period of sixteen hours' continuous rain and wind, which did the tents no good, and for our catching the county's first garden warbler in our mist nets. Eventually came a saving telegram from Cynthia Longfield and we took refuge in her cottage at Cloyne in Co. Cork. Best known as a world authority on dragonflies, Miss Longfield is also an experienced ornithologist and, when the rain stopped and the rest of the party did the sights of Cork and Blarney, she took me to the strand at Ballymona, then hardly known to outside birdwatchers. The day's tally, including roadside birds, a 'pure' rock dove and a chough attacking a kestrel, was just over seventy species, eighteen of them waders. We counted no American wanderers; indeed none would be considered rarities, but they ranged from at least fifty sanderlings busying themselves along the tideline, to a spotted redshank showing its elegant paces against its common relative and half-a-dozen greenshanks on Ballymona Pool. As background were little grebes, moorhens, coots, herons, cormorants, several duck, mute swans, gulls and terns, including my first Irish black terns, about two dozen of them for good measure.

Any great gathering of birds is impressive: who can watch a huge starling roost without some wonderment? But at Ballymona the variety of birds, so nicely adapted to exploit the feeding niches of strand, lagoon, bare mud, freshwater pool, and streams was a beautifully illustrated example of an ecosystem at work. And while vast numbers of invertebrate animals and small fish must have been probed, sieved, speared or picked up by all those different bills, the whole atmosphere was essentially peaceful. Nature may be red in tooth and claw, but there are times – especially, I have noticed, at aquatic habitats – when to the human observer she seems to generate tranquillity.

Just as so much of Ireland's landscape is England or Scotland with a difference – a pattern of fields and hedges that must have been imposed but has been quietly hibernicized; moorlands, bogs, and scrub-woods somehow more lush than those you find in the Highlands – so Irish bird life has its distinctive features, though the species are the same as in Britain. Where over here could you watch a cock stonechat hovering over an ivy-covered wall, as I did on this visit to Cloyne? Stonechats may once have been roadside birds in Britain, but cold winters and fast traffic have changed all that.

I suspect that, as the new generation of Irish ornithologists pursue their researches, other, subtler differences may emerge, for example in the proportionate numbers of species: without nuthatch and woodpeckers, has Ireland relatively more titmice, especially great tits, to fill these niches? So far, and rightly, interest has tended to concentrate on the country's importance as the winter home of a good proportion of the world's waterfowl, and on the rare waders such as grace those wonderful pools to which Cynthia Longfield introduced me, and from which I trust the death-kiss of the developer may ever be averted.

I cannot leave Ireland without a glance at the Bann estuary where Peg Pollock, looking through the telescope in her cottage, can have a dozen species, waterfowl, waders and gulls, in view at once. Our visit in August 1969 coincided with a passage of curlew sandpipers, and I crawled to about fifteen yards from a mixed company of small waders, which gave me a good chance to discriminate the few 'curlews' from the masses of dunlins. My notes record that the curlew sandpiper has more pronounced (pale) superciliary and (dark) eyestripes, a point on which I cannot help digressing. The glossary in *The Handbook* defines 'superciliary' as 'referring to the part immediately above the eye', and does not list 'eyestripe'. The bunting head on page 33 of vol. I of *Birds of the Western Palearctic* identifies 'supercilium' with *The Handbook*'s 'superciliary' and marks 'eyestripe' as that running through the eye at the top of the ear coverts. These distinctions can be critical, yet books by good authorities constantly confuse the two terms.

On this argumentative note I must quit Ireland, for which my list is only 137 species, far less than for several British countries. I hope there will soon be a chance to augment it. On the way back to Britain, a glance at the Isle of Man, only visited once with W. B. Alexander in April 1950. The late H. M. Rogers took us over to the Calf and showed us a chough's nest in a window embrasure in the old lighthouse, surely the easiest in the British Isles to see. My list for four days was 59 species and a redstart(?) which we saw flutter against the cliffs of Spanish Head and fall down out of sight while our boatman was bringing us up close to a party of purple sandpipers.

I have looked at birds in every English county but with more time and attention in some than in others. Northumberland is one of these and the cause was

Monks House, the private field centre run with such success by Eric and Dorothy Ennion in the 1950s. The visit that stands out was from 22 July to 5 August 1955 when the north-west was enjoying an unprecedented summer. We paid two visits to the Farne Islands, where we helped Eric to noose the cliff-nesting sea-birds for ringing. We saw not only the now contentious grey seals but on the Wamses the mysterious little flock of greylag geese that comes annually to moult.

On shore a ploy that appealed particularly to David, then thirteen, was trying to catch for ringing the young eiders that came into Monks House bay to bathe and preen in its little burn. By a quick sprint from cover it was sometimes possible to dive into the surf and secure one underwater. To reduce the distance, David dug a big pit well down the beach. This acted as a hide and soon attracted the bird photographers as well. I spent some time in it just watching black-headed gulls pattering the sand at the very edge of the tide. They seemed to move backwards in bursts of 5 to 15 seconds, during which they made one or sometimes two pecks in front of them. As a feeding method this appeared less productive than that of an adult I watched at Budle Bay. It worked over a small area full of worm casts and in one 5 minute period made 52 lightning stabs, 37 of which were followed by a swallowing movement. Whenever I could see the prey it was a small brown worm.

Early mornings were sometimes devoted to watching from the dunes the corn buntings that nested in the fields inland. As usual they led us a dance and it was not until our last morning that we found two nests of young, very well hidden in chickweed in what passed for an oat crop. During the day we sometimes worked the Heligoland trap near Monks House, but migration had scarcely begun and we made no spectacular captures. As a change, Emlyn Evans, David and I climbed Cheviot and saw some of the hill birds which I had been trying to count in the North Pennines in the two previous years.

My visits to Moor House were due to the BTO's contract from the Nature Conservancy to survey the breeding bird life of declared or proposed national nature reserves. Moor House is a chunk of 10,000 acres, two thirds of it boggy moorland on the Tyne side but straddling the Dun Fells and flowing down grass and bracken slopes to the Eden valley. I paid my first short visit in May 1953, crossed the reserve boundary to climb Cross Fell, and was rewarded by a pair of dotterel, evidently on passage because there was no sign of them on a second visit in June. At the end of the season I produced an estimate of the population based on single-handed transects and searches of the courses of the becks where sandpipers, ring ouzels and dippers were likely to be found.

In 1954 I paid another solo visit in May, spending fifteen hours working the becks. In mid June Peter Lewis, one of my Forest of Dean stalwarts, and I spent twelve hours largely dodging the weather; and the following week, with five undergraduate members of the Oxford Ornithological Society, we made twelve strip counts, covering as much of the reserve as possible. By extrapolating from the birds recorded on these counts, I produced figures for the commoner species, while the scarcer ones were estimated from searches of the becks, crags and the buildings at Moor House which, due to the prevailing helm wind and rain, inevitably became known to us as Wuthering Heights. For those who would like some idea of the birds of a classically dystrophic habitat all over 1,000 feet above sea level, here are the 1954 totals in pairs: meadow pipit (800), skylark (250), red grouse (140), wheatear (50),

common sandpiper (13), snipe (10), wren (10), golden
plover (6 to 10), dipper (5), ring ouzel (2 to 3), pied
wagtail, grey wagtail and lapwing (2 each), crow,
starling and curlew (one each): about 1300 pairs of 16
species on 10,000 acres. Swallows and probably yellow wagtails nested at Moor House in 1953. Other
possible breeding species, based on odd sightings in
both years, were buzzard (old nests seen), mallard,
merlin, short-eared owl, cuckoo, dunlin and blackbird.

On our last day Max Nicholson lunched with us.
'And what about the oystercatcher I saw on the Trout-
beck? I hope you got it?' My mouth must have fallen
open, because this was news to all of us. We saw it in
the afternoon, a single bird from nowhere, just sent to
give the Director General a little coup. But two records
did come out of the expeditions; my dipper's nest at the
top of Knock Ore Beck on 7 May is, I believe, the
highest ever recorded in Britain, and so must be the
lapwing with four eggs on the top of Cross Fell on 22
June, found when we were hopefully looking for dotterel again.

The OOS party seemed not too disheartened by our
experiences at Moor House because most of them,
with two new recruits, came with me to Scolt Head in
Norfolk the next season, when we tried some ambitious observations on the common tern colony,
watched over by Bob Chestney as by his father Charles
before him. We lived in the Hut put up for Britain's
first full-time birdwatcher, Miss E. L. Turner, and
which looks out over the marshes and channels to the
mainland and often avoids the rain that sweeps the
distant landscape. I am afraid the fruits of our hours in
the hide were never published but I think the party
found it good training and I did see an oystercatcher
rob a tern's nest. One result was that I developed a

great affection for the Hut and, by agreeing to let the
Nature Conservancy have a copy of all my observations, we were allowed to borrow it for a week's
holiday in 1957, 1958, 1959, 1961 and 1962, though not
all members of the family were enthusiastic about
crossing the saltmarsh from Alfie's boat to *arena firma*
below the Hut.

This period coincided with the arrival of the mist-
net, though we were usually too early for large-scale
migrations. I caught several pied flycatchers and
wheatears, but our triumph was the island's first
barred warbler which I had glimpsed in the *Suaeda*
bushes one afternoon. We cut a trace through them, set
a net across it and one drive by the boys and myself was
enough. Our last two stays were in June, when I found
the island's first gadwall's nest, but the customary
birds were enough for us, with the odd harrier flying
past from time to time and in August the attentions of
juvenile skuas as we made our annual low-tide pilgrimage to the wreck in the sands west of the ternery.

After a break of some years, we came back to Norfolk in June 1976, just as the hot weather began. I was
delighted to find how well the shore-nesting birds
were holding their own even outside the reserves
against increased pressures, though the habit of driving seawards as far as possible and then releasing the
dog for a nice scamper while the morning papers are
read does not appeal to me. I am glad to see that Derek
Goodwin attacks it too in his book *Birds of Man's
World*.

I have many other memories of East Anglia, but will
resurrect just one, my first visit to Minsmere and
Havergate in 1949, with Reg Moreau, one of the best
and most amusing companions anyone could wish for.

My diary described the last lap of our journey. 'Suffolk doesn't give you much hint of its bird-haunts; one

moment you are in normal agricultural scenery, then a swift transition, a river valley with heathy banks beyond, an unmetalled road through new conifers and old oaks where a redstart's tail flashes, an enquiry at a farm, and you bump down to a road-end with the watcher's tent and hut well hidden on the side of an ancient sand-dune, but commanding the sea approach to the sanctuary.'

The RSPB was already managing Minsmere, and the experienced Dick Wolfendale was installed as warden for the breeding season. As he led us off, a solitary male marsh harrier appeared, flopping languidly over the reeds like an old actor mǎking his positively last appearance.

There were no high-rise hides in Minsmere then; Dick took us to an old duck-shooting butt that overlooked the historic pool where the avocets were first found breeding. They had moved to Havergate by 1949 but we soon had a magnificent spotted redshank in full plumage to enjoy, with a greenshank, several ringed plovers, and the forerunner of a party of black-tailed godwits in all shades from the winter to summer dress. Watching them, we were perplexed by a short-legged bird, rufous-bodied but black at the breast and head; it proved to be a ruff, the first I had ever seen in its finery.

A few minutes later I had another 'first', a male bearded tit; however well you know it from the books, it is still hard to believe in that bill: as if a child had modelled a piece of pinkish-yellow plasticine and stuck it on, to offset those black Chu-Chin-Chow moustachios. We hardly had eyes for the fifteen green sandpipers which rose from the pool, but I just managed to glimpse a bittern landing on the other side, one of about six pairs present that year.

We then moved inland to inspect a deeper pool

among the reeds. 'Here', rhapsodizes my diary, 'was a tableau to end bird tableaux: the pond was dotted with mallard and teal, coots and moorhens; along its nearer edge were about half-a-dozen herons in all sorts of postures, and among them the squat white figure of a dozing spoonbill. When the harrier came over again, mobbed by redshanks, lapwings, and black-headed gulls, I almost pinched myself. The spoonbill, like the harrier, looked as if it too "had been retained at enormous expense for the season" to delight bird-watchers.'

On the way back to the hut we flushed a stone curlew from the heathy area. In the wood we had, for variety, seen blue tits and a great spotted woodpecker. A final look at the shingle produced little terns, red-legged partridges and, on a shallow pool, a shelduck fussing over ten ducklings. By the time we reached Orford that night I had recorded seventy-four species.

Next morning we were taken by Captain Groves down river to land at Orfordness, where common terns were trying, not very successfully, to nest, and 'patches of purple-flowered everlasting pea were spots of pleasant colour among the tedious shingle'. Then the gallant captain took us up Butley Creek to the post-breeding haunt of the avocets, and we saw at least twenty-two birds. The avocet was one more first for me – another bird-book portrait come to life. But the most remarkable sight of the day was probably a meadow pipit's nest with three young near our landing place on Havergate. It was built in a patch of fleshy orache right on the tideline. When the eggs were well-incubated, the tide had reached the nest and floated them for 24 hours – and yet they hatched. If they had been newly laid, they would have sunk.

Dorset is the scene of another dip into my English birdwatching. In April 1956 and 1957 we returned for short visits to Swanage, when Wilfrid and Horace and Rebecca Alexander were living there. An account of these visits could easily become simply a catalogue of birds seen, memorable to me but tedious to readers. But how often can you look out of a hotel bedroom window and see a Slavonian grebe in full plumage just off shore? Or go out before breakfast and identify forty-five species, including marsh harrier and peregrine, a 'double' I am not likely often to repeat. The peregrine, a tiercel, made at least two circuits about fifty feet above the beach huts at Studland, searching the shore and taking no notice of me. Probably it came from the Isle of Wight, where it was just about at the end of its breeding tenure.

That afternoon we went to Tillywhim to see the guillemots and razorbills newly arrived, and the odd fulmar on its ledge. This, of course, is the charm and excitement of Purbeck: rapid juxtaposition of habitats each with their characteristic birds. The next day, on a more leisurely early stroll along Swanage front, I suddenly saw a hoopoe undulating gracefully past. This was news for the breakfast table, and 'WBA' and I spent the morning touring likely spots, such as manure heaps, where this elegant stranger might be probing. We got a fine cock redstart out of it but that was about all.

The following morning a cock Dartford warbler was my aperitif, singing almost antiphonally against a whitethroat so that their two phrases could be compared. The rest of the day was taken up by a real break-out west to Abbotsbury, by way of Lodmore and Radipole Lake at Weymouth. I had not seen the famous swannery before; it was then, I think, at a peak of nesting pairs and Fred Lexster was a vivid host, producing as well some waders, early terns fishing in the Fleet and a high-circling short-eared owl.

At Durlston Head, on another early morning, I watched two jays apparently chasing each other. But one, which I took to be the male, soon perched on an exposed dead bough and began to sing squeakily like an unoiled rowlock: *checherchy checercher*, followed usually by a rattling noise, with his bill half open. The second bird answered from cover, generally with a single phrase followed by a cat-call. I have been in on these performances several times and the description of the song in *The Handbook*, provided by H. G. Alexander no less, does not conflict with my impression. We do not think of the crow family as very tuneful or profuse vocalists, and *The Handbook*, attributes to the other members a rather pejorative 'kind of' song. Evolutionally, is it coming or going?

Against the general abundance of bird life on these visits I noted one decrease: twenty years before, corn buntings had been everywhere along the sloping bramble-studded hillsides above the cliffs, from Durlston to St Aldhelm's Head. Now I saw only odd birds. Stonechats, on the other hand, since 1940 so scarce inland, were quite plentiful both on the heaths and in the chalk scrub; and on the second spring visit I saw in the same Durlston area three pairs and two cocks and found two nests, one with large young and one building, on an early walk that remains to me the epitome of Purbeck in April.

For one thing I had at last got the knack of recognizing colonies of spider orchids flowering in the short turf. There were also plenty of the green-winged orchid, always a favourite of mine, milkwort (*Polygala calcarea*, no doubt), and even a spring gentian in bud. Then I had just hit the moment right for the arrival of migrants out of the sea mist. Suddenly a willow warbler would appear on the fence along the lip of the cliffs, or a whitethroat would strike up from a tiny patch of scrub: I noted one 'pale female' – did I miss a fabulous rarity? But a calling cock ring ouzel was good enough for me, intoxicated by the inexpressible impact of spring and by my own conceit at being alone on the cliffs to enjoy it.

Finally I must look in at that wonderful staging post between Oxfordshire and Scotland: Brathay Hall at the head of Windermere, in what is now Cumbria. Our first visit was a family one in 1948 when Dick Faithfull-Davies was Warden of Francis Scott's brain-child, which has now become world-ranging in its expeditions and impact. Nearly twenty years later Brian Ware, now Director of Brathay, invited me to join the advisory committee of the new Field Study Centre and this led to a dozen short visits over the next decade, during which Margaret and I also compiled *Brathay: the First Twenty-Five Years* (1972).

But these visits were not all hard work; there were delightful evening occasions presided over by Marjorie Ware; and there was time to explore Brathay's various habitats, from scrub wood to lakeside, to see the pied flycatchers at their nestboxes, to watch a dipper travelling underwater in the river Brathay, to find my most northerly yellow wagtails' nests, and to spend one glorious midsummer day on the lake with Margaret, watching the perch and eels in the clear water. On a spring visit my species list of birds usually topped the half century; in winter I would get to about thirty. In November 1969 these included a large flock of chaffinches and bramblings feeding under the beeches in front of the Hall, and in October 1975 a juvenile hawfinch made the sudden and brief appearance that characterizes my relations with it.

20
Mainly Islands

And so at last to Scotland again. Is it strange that the first serious birdwatching trip we made away from Ardnamurchan remains after over fifty years not only one of the most exciting but, in terms of nests found, the most remarkable?

When my father offered me a special trip if I won a scholarship to Winchester, I chose without hesitation to go to North Uist, the home of the red-necked phalarope, a bird which to a schoolboy symbolized rarity. We had heard a good deal about it and its remote haunts from George Brooksbank, and through him we arranged to stay with Captain Ranald Macdonald of Balranald (and this only 180 years after the '45!).

All went well with the exam, though the General Strike of May 1926 caused us some apprehension and it was with Britain still in the grip of a coal strike that my father and I left London by train on 6 June. Our progress reads now like one of the leisurely expeditions of Victorian days. We spent the night in Glasgow, went on next day by early train to Mallaig and our tally for this stage – one of the first I kept – was fifty-four species. We spent two nights at Mallaig, visiting islets in Loch Nevis to see a large colony of gulls among the wild hyacinths, and on the afternoon of the 9th embarked on *S.S. Clydesdale* for Kyle of Lochalsh.

The voyage out to the Long Island was nearly too much for me, though the sea was alive with birds, including the first fulmars I had ever seen. After a glimpse of Harris we landed at Lochmaddy about 5.30 p.m. on the 10th and were driven across the island in a T-model Ford. I had not been in a treeless landscape before and was also impressed by the number of horses in use and in the fields – they had nearly disappeared by this time from mainland Argyll. But the wind ruled everything. The belt of elders and fuschias, in which hoodies and twites nested along one side of the lawn at Balranald, hardly poked their shoots above the sheltering wall, and another tall stone wall protected the vegetable garden; in its crevices tree sparrows were fighting a losing battle for nest-sites against house sparrows.

But we hadn't come so far to see tree sparrows. As soon as I decently could, I was out on the bog which lay in wait all round the human settlements. Dunlins reeled and whirred past me maddeningly and at the end of my search in the dusk I had found one deserted egg and a nestful of young skylarks, just enough to fuel my excitement.

Next morning Balranald took us to the phalarope's principal haunt, the edge of a shallow 'bogbean loch'. He was a good guide and we were soon looking at 'two or three pairs, either on the shore or swimming lightly in the loch', as I wrote in my diary; and hardly had our host left us when I 'came on a phalarope's nest with one egg'. I can see it now, a surprisingly large bare scrape for the miniature lapwing-like egg, with a stem of bogbean lying diametrically across it.

The problem of protecting the phalarope in those days was a particularly difficult one. Many nests, it seems, were destroyed by cattle on the way to and from the lochs; in fact, the bird often took a hoofmark as the basis of its nest-scrape. But if the favoured nesting areas were fenced off, so Balranald explained to us, this would attract the attention of those local men who were known as or suspected of being egg-collectors' 'eyes'. Also, in this wide flat landscape, figures were visible a long way off and we had to be careful not to linger by any nest or show too keen an interest in one spot. So it was a look and away which, of course, made observation of the birds anywhere near their nests impossible.

So we did not learn much about the phalarope's home life. But we found a nest with two eggs on the 13th by Loch Paible, where there were at least three pairs; and two nests on the 14th by the bogbean loch. While we were watching and trying to photograph several phalaropes, one attacked another (female and male, we presumed) and sent it flying into the bog, where we flushed it off the full clutch of four. After lunch I found a second nest, with three eggs. Our original nest also had only three eggs on the 14th, which surprised us, but we did not know then that phalaropes often lay at intervals of more than twenty-four hours. Next day we took Balranald to see the Loch Paible nest, which had three eggs in the cup. 'Hello', he said, 'there's an eggshell too', put his finger into the lining and pulled out a whole egg which had been half-buried. 'We hope there will be another young one for it,' says my diary virtuously and Balranald wrote later to tell us that all four nests had hatched without mishap.

My favourite picture of the phalarope is of one on a shallow pool by Loch Paible, swimming 'so beautifully lightly, while a background was formed by three or four dunlin', standing on one foot and looking bulky and almost clumsy by comparison.

But memories may deceive as to numbers; we often feel there was a wealth of birds when we were young, and paucity today. My diary, however, confirms the richness of the Balranald area: during our week's stay we found 40 nests of dunlins, 22 of skylarks and 9 of lapwings, and this in the middle of June when many pairs had young. The voices of these three – with the skylark often mimicking the dunlin's reel – were with us all day, with sun, wind and occasional showers on fields, bog, and machair.

Another voice, more penetrating and almost as frequent, was that of the corncrake. The first nest we found was well-hidden in a clump of nettles in a grass field close to Balranald House. By the end of the week we had found seven more, six of them on the edge of the bog where they were quite easy to see, especially as four had woven canopies of grass stems overhead. Whatever value this may have for the sitting bird, it certainly aided detection by one sort of predator. We also found two dead corncrakes, one hanging on barbed wire.

Two other characteristic birds of Balranald were twite and ringed plover. The plovers, killdeer-like, nested on ploughed fields as well as in more usual sites, and we found a twite's nest with four eggs and three young in a furrow under the turned earth. Corn buntings were also typical of the farmland, but the only nest we found was on a grassy island in the phalarope's loch. Its companions were a few pairs of black-headed gulls and arctic terns. Moorhens, coots and dabchicks also nested round the loch, clear indicators of its 'nutrient-richness'.

In addition, we found nests of snipe, common sand-piper and house sparrow, making a total of 16 species; we saw another 12 possible breeding birds and we hardly explored the western part of what is now the RSPB reserve at all. On our last morning we put up a short-eared owl, and it seems likely that it was nesting somewhere in the bog.

We had a wonderful journey back to Ardnamur-chan, with gannets and kittiwakes diving behind the boat all the way to Lochboisdale and Castlebay, which we reached in the glim of midnight. Next morning we called at Tiree and Coll, passed a great concourse of auks off Ardnamurchan Point and landed at Kilchoan to the corncrake's voice once more.

After such an orgy of nest-finding any other visit was to be an anticlimax and in June 1967, when Bal-ranald had just become a reserve, we were told that phalaropes no longer nested there and the warden rather ruefully showed us a corncrake's nest in Hougarry kirkyard, robbed by an unknown agent after the nettles hiding it had been cut. What surprised me on this second visit was the presence of redshanks and oystercatchers, neither of which we had noted in 1926. Apparently redshanks did not begin to nest locally until some years later, but we must have missed the oystercatchers; perhaps they had not then spread from the shore, which we hardly visited, being engrossed with bog and machair.

Our base in 1967 was Dremisdale in South Uist, overlooking Loch an Eilein to which six pairs of greylags brought their broods after hatching them by the lochs of the moorland. The machair lochs are much richer in feeding and it was my pleasant task to visit them and count the parents and their families, which ranged from two to seven goslings, and the failed and non-breeders. It was exciting to be seeing really wild greylags instead of the feral stock with which Britain is now being impregnated, though I agree that some free-flying geese are better than none at all, and I find the Canada geese which flight almost daily over our house in winter quite acceptable too.

Except for Loch an Eilein, which I could watch from our bedroom in Mrs Macleod's comfortable croft, most of my goose survey was done with the warden of the Loch Druidibeg reserve, the late Murdoch Mac-Rury, a local man of great charm who had done much to get the idea of a nature reserve accepted in the island. Brother Niall, as the Nature Conservancy's Regional Officer, also had a keen interest in the survey and encouraged me as well to have a look at all the breeding birds in the area.

So, in a heat wave unusual even in June in the Islands, we took all South Uist for our oyster, from the miles of shell-sand beach hardly marked by human print to the summit of Beinn Mhor, where Emlyn saw a golden eagle, Margaret may have seen a trip of dotterel and, sitting in the hot sunshine, we all listened to two cuckoos calling in Hellisdale below us, an experience Wordsworth would have envied. But what would he have made of the cuckoos that came to roost in the few trees at Grogarry Lodge with a dozen or so collared doves, still comparative newcomers, and some tens of starlings? As many as seven were reported and, on the evening of 16 June, we saw three, one of them a female, chasing and apparently preparing to roost on a little scrub-clad islet in Loch Ollay beside the main road.

Altogether we listed 71 species in our week, 48 of which were breeding or presumed to breed on the reserve. These included a long-eared owl, which I did not see myself, being entangled in the dense cover of wind-battered spruce on an island in East Loch

Druidibeg as it flew out, and greenfinches in the same area, where I understand they are still to be found as a little isolated group. In contrast to North Uist in 1926, I only came on one dunlin's nest with eggs, although the dates of the two visits were much the same.

Never an island-collector on the James Fisher scale, I have over the years paid visits to most of the main ones round Scotland and may be allowed to summarize these briefly and chronologically. We stayed on Iona in the summer holidays of 1928 and 1929 with our friends the Troups, whose harled house seemed to grow out of the close-cropped sward. They took us to Staffa, to Lunga in the Treshnish, my first big seabird colony, and the intrepid John Macinnes gave us a rock-shaving circuit of Iona itself, bringing out a screaming peregrine in protest. In June–July 1947 Margaret, David and I found the peregrines gone, but I made a survey of the breeding birds which I was able to show Timothy Reed over thirty years later when he was deep in his study of the land birds of Scottish islands.

Mull I have only visited incidentally, mainly travelling to and from Iona, though in August 1953 we watched crossbills extracting rowan seeds near Tobermory in a year of invasion. My one tour of Skye was in September 1930 and chiefly remarkable for meeting Seton Gordon, who showed me the lymphad (long boat) scratched in an embrasure of Duntuilm Castle. On Eigg and Muick I have only made brief landings in 1935 and my visit to Rum in May 1961 with Ken Williamson and Pat Banks has already been mentioned (page 173), though I can add that we established a first breeding record for the redstart. My neighbour Kerr Elliot flew Grant Lee and me to Coll in early July 1962. A successful brood of peregrines was the highlight (I have not seen one since) and with Grant's help I

ringed my first arctic skua chick. Just for the record we
also landed on Tiree.

Thanks to Robin and Dorothy McInnes, Margaret
and I spent a week in their cottage by Scapa Flow in
Orkney in June 1966. Fifty-three of the 72 birds we
identified were the same as we saw in South Uist the
next year, which I suppose is to be expected. Much
more surprising was a telephone call from Eddie Balfour, as a result of which I saw my first bee-eaters with
him in the policies at Binscarth. On a second visit, in
August 1968, when we rented the only house on the
Mainland from which the old Man of Hoy can be seen,
I found a juvenile barred warbler in the little garden
and realized a minor ambition, to land on Eynhallow,
where Eddie Balfour's party was ringing young fulmars. We also ringed some on Rousay with Elaine
Bullard, bringing back from their cliffs a cutting of
honeysuckle which flourished for years by the door of
Hordley.

Shetland was my 'last' county in Britain and Ireland
and to celebrate this I was interviewed for local radio
by Fred Hunter, who started Emlyn Evans and me on
five days of wedding-cake richness in May–June 1969.
When we got to Yell, Bobby Tulloch took over, waft-
ing us to Fetlar, Unst and small islands seldom landed
on. However many others have shared the experience,
it is impressive to gaze on Muckle Flugga, the most
northerly point of Britain, and its adjacent gannetry of
Hermaness, and to have seen the snowy owls at the
nest. We only came on one phalarope, and I snapped
Emlyn photographing it, a traditional ploy. On 1 June
we hired a car and toured Yell, skimming its cream
with nests of whimbrel (my first), golden plover, red-
throated diver, both skuas and black guillemot, which
I suppose should be called tystie in these surroundings.

June of the next year saw Emlyn and me on Islay,

which has about as many breeding species as all Ireland. Thanks to Gordon Booth we located both scoters and choughs. Walking back from the choughs' cliffs, I saw what I thought was a heather-haunting moth. Getting Emlyn's permission to sacrifice it for science, I hit it circumspectly with my cromag and found it was a female marsh fritillary, the first I had ever caught, though not a new discovery for Islay. Ròna and I paid a short visit in April 1977, its most idyllic moment being a lunch-hour stop by Loch Lomond on the drive up. That evening I got locked out of our hotel in Lochgilphead after visiting Mike Gregory, the BTO representative for Argyll, and Ròna, after an evening with her friends the Birtwells, got locked out on Islay, so our adventures were not all ornithological. In more or less continuous rain we drove over most of the island's motorable roads and I can only say that the show of barnacle geese came up to all expectations.

The most hazardous island voyage Margaret, Emlyn and I made was in June 1971. The Masons of Eynsham Park had not only lent us their house at Badachro but put *The White Phalarope*, with Finlay Beaton and Alec Mackenzie, at our disposal. So we decided one fine but blowy day to try for the Shiant Isles. Eric Hunter, the Scottish Wildlife Trust's representative in Wester Ross, joined us and we arrived after two and three quarter fairly lively hours to be met by the immaculately dressed Roger Martin, who was spending a holiday on Shiant Mor. We added nothing to ornithological knowledge of these now well-worked islands, but it was an outing memorable for Finlay's and Alec's seamanship in a Force 7 wind.

So much for islands. But there are two mainland areas I cannot leave entirely out of account. Galloway I will always associate with Arthur Duncan, host on my 1952 pied flycatcher tour, Judy and Walter Champion of Cairnsmore, who took us to the Mull of Galloway in 1963 and on whose drive I had to wait for a golden pheasant to cross, and Donald and Joan Watson whose hospitality we have enjoyed so often. It was Donald who masterminded the outing at my last BTO Regional Representatives' conference, at Dumfries in February 1959. An unexpected marsh harrier nearly caused a motorway-type pile up of our cavalcade *en route* for the lesser white-fronted goose and the bean geese which were just where Donald said they would be. In 1964 he showed me my first hen harrier's nest, which is mentioned in his book (*The Hen Harrier*, Poyser, 1977), a bird monograph in which the roles of author and artist are combined in one man.

The other area is Perthshire, which I have been visiting since my boyhood friendship with George Brooksbank, but more intensively since Niall and Moira went to live near Pitlochry, moving in 1957 to their own Tigh-ur within hail of the Pass of Killiecrankie, where in May I can see and hear some of the most northerly pied flycatchers in Britain. These have now been joined by green woodpeckers, while no great distance away are moors and high tops with hen harriers, dunlin, ptarmigan and dotterel. In 1975 we saw all these during a fourteen-mile walk on the hill. But birdwatching is not always arduous in Perthshire: I have seen an immature eagle from Niall and Moira's doorstep, watched and listened to migrating geese fly over their house, and spotted a great grey shrike from the car with their son Ronald. Perthshire is also the only Scottish county in which I have seen hawfinches; persevering readers will have gathered they are one of my jinx birds. I believe they are still at Scone Palace where I found them with J. M. D. Mackenzie way back in April 1949 on my first Scottish tour as secretary of the BTO.

21
West End Barn

On 17 July 1975 we moved, after nearly twenty-seven years, from Hordley to the little house we had built on the western outskirts of Wootton village and called West End Barn after the old building it has replaced. Although 'WEB' stands only about a hundred feet higher than Hordley, it commands wide views, especially to the west and north-west, which means that, when a strong wind blows from those airts, we feel a little like lighthousekeepers; but there are great compensations, for example at sunset. We also look across the valley of the Glyme to the main part of the village, dominated by its medieval church, and down to the pond excavated by a neighbour and attracting anything from little grebes to a gaggle of Canada geese.

The move meant a great change in my ornithological habits. No longer had I the Hordley census (Chapter 16) to provide me with basic field work on my doorstep. New outlets for my remaining energy were needed but, while I was lucky enough to find one absorbing new area, I am prevented from eulogizing on it by the resurgence of egg-collecting and the need to keep the whereabouts of rare birds as anonymous as possible.

In general, I have found an increasing interest in the bird life of habitats profoundly affected by man and ranging from city centres, through parks and suburban gardens, to industrial sites and, above all in the Thames counties, to gravel pits. I have discovered the private world enclosed by the 'cliffs' surrounding a deep wet pit, which attracts its own community of birds, completely distinct from that of the farmland above and around it. Since it now lies under some fifteen feet of water, I can describe with some freedom my 'Lyonesse' at Lechlade on the borders of Oxfordshire and Gloucestershire. Here Ted Richardson (commemorated by a nature reserve just across the road) and I spent many happy hours in the 1960s in the realm of the little ringed plover, that elegant opportunist who dodges the dumpers and the developers and shows a steadily increasing population as the acreage of gravel workings expands.

The ideal gravel pit is one which may still be working but in which there is an extensive area of shallow pools and of low mounds, both being colonized by appropriate vegetation, from reeds *Phragmites*, reedmace *Typha* and willows to willowherbs *Epilobium*, coltsfoot *Tussilago farfara*, mosses and liverworts. The first bird colonists (as described in B. S. Milne's excellent paper 'Ecological Succession and Bird-life at a Newly Excavated Gravel-pit' in *Bird Study* 21:263–77 (1974)) may be little ringed plover, on the floor, and sand martins, in the 'cliffs', in as little as seven months. Although Milne's pit was in (former) Huntingdonshire, the similarity with the breeding birds of Lyonesse is close. Little grebe, mallard and tufted duck (nesting under the great leaves of coltsfoot), mute

swan, moorhen and coot were the 'waterfowl' shared
by both pits; redshank and lapwing were the waders
that joined the 'lrps'; skylark, yellow wagtail, sedge
and reed warblers and reed buntings formed the common passerine element. At Lyonesse pied wagtails
sometimes nested under coltsfoot like the yellow wagtails. Milne's pit attracted one or two pairs of several
other species, including blackbird and robin, which I
would regard as secondary, appearing when the vege-
tational succession has proceeded to thicket.

Lyonesse was maintained only by constant pump-
ing. Once this ceased, the water level rose and a completely new habitat was formed, a 'lake' which
attracted great crested grebes and retained little grebes,
coots and moorhens while providing a wintering place
for wildfowl and a passage stop for black terns, but
only a little marginal ground for most of the original
community. Pathetically the little ringed plovers clung
on for a couple of years and even hatched young. But
the old magic had gone, though the conditions that
allowed it are continually recurring elsewhere as the
search for gravel goes on.

On our way back from the Camargue in 1962, John
White and I spent a night in a camp site on the edge of
the Bois de Boulogne. The sight of swallows over its
artificial lakes struck me as something not to be
expected in London parks, and aroused my interest,
but it was not until 26 October 1976 that I was able to
spend most of a day there, seeing 28 species, eight
more than I found in the much more parklike Bois de
Vincennes two days later. In early April 1978 I was
able, while Margaret and Ròna continued their cultural
attack on Paris, to spend about fifteen hours in the Bois
de Boulogne. The programme of active *reboisement*
ensures that it will remain woodland rather than park-
land, but how the natural ground flora survives the

intense human use is remarkable. I do not know what the full species list for the Bois may be; Robert Etchecopar recorded 47 one April morning. My list so far is only about 40 and includes great and lesser spotted woodpeckers, short-toed treecreeper, nuthatches in numbers, goldcrest, blackcap, serin and tree sparrow. I have yet to see the hawfinches which Guy Mountfort watched there. Contrary to the bunkum that is spread about birds in France, I found those in the Bois easy to approach (so are the red squirrels) and I wonder how long the two occupied nests I found – blackbird and dunnock – would have survived in a similarly 'exposed' British park. No doubt devotees of Regents Park and Hampstead Heath can make comparable claims and it is true that London's birdlife has become much richer in recent years. *The Endless Village* (published by the Nature Conservancy Council) demonstrates that, brought to light by Bunny Teagle's survey in 1975, the Birmingham conurbation has a diverse wildlife, and M. J. Bayliss has recently shown that 70 to 80 species of bird breed annually within the admittedly partly rural limits of the city of Oxford (Oxford Ornithological Society Report for 1977).

All this reminds me that I have written very little about conservation in this book. This is deliberate: the problem of the environment is always with us and I have thought it appropriate not to look at it too hard, but to dwell on the watching and enjoyment of birds rather than their protection. Nor have I attempted to deal with the committees of all kinds on which I have sat. Committees are essential for the democratic conduct of affairs but their activities make dull reading unless there is a blazing row, which in my view is best forgotten once time has softened its rugosities. But I must just mention my years with the Council for Nature, first as Chairman of its Youth Committee, when we ran 'A Taste of Nature' courses for youth leaders, and later as a joint hon. secretary, which brought me into close touch with Sir Landsborough Thomson, then the Council's chairman. The last of my father figures, I consulted him on all sorts of matters, from the sermon I was asked to preach at Selborne as part of the first National Nature Week in 1963 to the revision of his editorial *magnum opus, A New Dictionary of Birds*. This discussion took place the last time I saw him, a great ornithologist, administrator and Scotsman.

Obviously West End Barn's third of an acre, after three and a half years gradually becoming a garden with a central sward, is completely different to Hordley's bosky charms. But, to the end of 1978, fifty species of bird have perched in it or on the house and we have seen another 43 over or from it. The river valley and our neighbour's pond help and so does the wide view, but the combination of grass, stone walls and a wire fence just outside probably accounts for redstart, stonechat, whinchat and wheatear – all scarce birds in Oxfordshire – and for the cock ring ouzel whom I saw early one April morning just before the resident blackbird saw him off. Somehow I felt that those old walls would one day attract another chat and on 16 March 1978 a dull-looking 'robin' on a pedestal within a few feet of our patio window was revealed as a hen black redstart, who continued to honour us for the next eleven days and then – from its behaviour it must have been the same bird – was seen by grandson Benedict on the west wall of the garden on 14 October, reappearing next day to be watched by seventeen members of the Banbury Ornithological Society having tea after our annual Blenheim walk.

The most spectacular of the 'over or from' birds must be the female goshawk who floated above me on the first anniversary of our move, during the 1976 heat wave. Some people are suspicious of all goshawks as possible escapes and one was reported lost in Witney, not very far away, about this time. But I could see no jesses or other signs of captivity on my bird. Sparrowhawks frequently, hobby and buzzard are other birds of prey on the list but the only percher is the kestrel, spotted on top of the garden shed by James Ferguson-Lees, who was staying for the night after giving the Bernard Tucker Memorial Lecture in November 1978.

Coincidental with our move from Hordley, Tony Soper introduced me to Ian and Polly Mayman, owners of the Talland Bay Hotel between Looe and Polperro in south-east Cornwall. After a preliminary visit in November 1975, when Ian pointed out to me a black redstart sitting on a noticeboard by the East Looe River, we arranged to hold mid-week 'Holidays for Birdwatchers', with me as guide and based on the hotel. In the autumns and early springs of 1976–8 seven of these events took place, introducing me both to some enthusiastic observers and to a part of England I hardly knew. Altogether 106 species have been recorded, including my earliest ever swallow, on 7 March 1977 over the hotel car park. There is a good variety of woodland, estuarine and sea coast species on the list and I have learned not to be surprised at green woodpeckers on the cliffs at Talland Bay and Rame Head, where I saw an evidently migratory Dartford warbler in October 1977 and an evidently robbed raven's nest in April 1978, just where my father found one some seventy years earlier. But I think our only notable observation has been of tree sparrows, which are very scarce in the south-west.

At the other end of Britain a week in May 1976 in cousin John Letts's most comfortable cottage at Blairmore near Kinlochbervie enabled Margaret, Emlyn

Evans and me to reach Cape Wrath (only by minibus) and have one of the most superb island views in Britain: from the Butt of Lewis by way of Sula Sgeir and North Rona, last seen on the seal flight in 1947, to the hills of Hoy in Orkney. We also made a pilgrimage to Desmond Nethersole-Thompson's greenshank study area and had him sign his four monographs beside the river where his children catch the breakfast trout. In June 1977, at family strength, we spent a week near Pwllheli, where on Morfa Abererch I found a tiny machair with nesting oystercatchers and skylarks; on a trip to Aberdaron we gazed at the hump of Bardsey, now saved for the future, in pouring rain. A similar family venture to Twynholm in Galloway in 1978 was blessed with a heat wave and some wonderful cliff scenery plus flowers and seabirds at Meikle Ross: somehow people do not associate Solway with cliffs. But, again, tree sparrows nesting in the village were my most interesting find; perhaps no one else looks for them in places where more spectacular birds are to be sought.

These largely coastal visits are necessary when living about as far from the sea as it is possible to get in England. But every year teaches me how little I know of Oxfordshire even after thirty years. Indeed, I am sure there are still discoveries to be made in Wootton parish although, thanks to the enthusiasm of Pat Williams and Trevor Young, we have now a pretty good grapevine. But ought we not to be getting down to studies more demanding than augmenting the nest record card totals of the BTO each season? Fifteen long-tailed tits' nests in 1978 suggest a good opportunity to watch for the communal breeding behaviour which seems to be characteristic of this species. Or what about the woodcock, that bird of mystery, to which sustained as opposed to anecdotal attention is at last being paid?

But the future is not really my concern in this book, in which I have tried to recall, on the whole, the lighter side of a lifetime of birdwatching. In 1948 my Ph.D. was the first ever awarded for a study entirely of British birds in the field; in 1978 there were seventeen D.Phil. students at the Edward Grey Institute in Oxford alone. I have been privileged to live through a period of intense growth in scientific as well as popular ornithology and to know most of the leading British and a good many of the foreign protagonists in this development.

I once asked John Markham if he would go on taking photographs of wildlife, even if he knew no one else would ever see the results. 'Yes', he replied. If I were asked the same question about my notes and diaries, I am afraid I would not be so categoric: keeping them up is certainly a private ritual I enjoy; but if other people are entertained by the extracts I have assembled here, the better I shall be pleased.

Appendix
The Hordley Censuses

Although I attempted some sort of breeding bird census for every spring we were at Hordley (1949–75 inclusive), those for the first two were very much prentice efforts and, on close examination, those for 1951–5 are not comparable in accuracy to the final 20 years. In the table that follows, therefore, I have simply shown in the first column after the species names the number of the first seven seasons in which each species was proved to nest on the census area.

The annual totals for 1956–75 show the estimated number of 'breeding units' (usually pairs) for each species (see p. 196). But no census is as tidy as its maker would like it to be and I have had to introduce a few other categories. 'B' indicates a brood seen, usually of mallard, and is not absolute proof of breeding on so small an area; a juvenile cuckoo also comes slightly oddly into this category. '?' indicates suspected nesting, based on several but inconclusive observations, while '♂ ♀' means that a pair was seen on the area but no nest found; '½' is a pair on the edge of the area,

264

probably or certainly nesting, but not counted in the
totals. '♂' indicates a probably unmated male, present
for some weeks. [1] refers to kestrel's nests in successive years just outside the area. The clutches in the two
red-legged partridge nests in 1965 were probably laid
by the same hen, and the two chiffchaff nests in 1966
by the mates of a bigamous cock.

	49–55	56	57	58	59	60	61	62	63
Mute swan	1	—	—	—	—	—	—	—	—
Mallard	2	—	2B	1	—	?	—	—	1
Kestrel	1	—	—	—	—	—	—	—	—
Red-legged partridge	—	—	—	?	—	—	—	—	—
Grey partridge	3	1	—	2	2	♂♀	—	♂♀	—
Pheasant	5	3	4	4	?	2	2	3	3
Moorhen	7	2	2	1	1	3	2	1	2
Coot	—	—	—	—	—	—	—	—	—
Stock dove	7	2	2	1	3	1	—	—	1+
Woodpigeon	5	4+	3	3	5	8	4	4	2+
Collared dove	—	—	—	—	—	—	—	—	—
Turtle dove	4	1	—	—	2	1	1	♂	2♂♂
Cuckoo	—	1	—	—	—	—	—	—	—
Barn owl	5	1	1	—	1	1	1	—	—
Tawny owl	2	—	—	—	1	—	—	—	—
Great spotted woodpecker	—	—	—	—	—	—	—	—	1
Swallow	2	2	2	1	1	1	1	3	3
Pied wagtail	—	—	—	1	♂♀	1	—	—	—
Wren	5	3+	6	6	6	6	11	—	♂
Dunnock	7	5+	7	10	8	12	9	10	7
Robin	7	2	4	5	6	7	6	3	4
Blackbird	7	10+	14	15	23	20	21	27	15
Song thrush	7	6+	11	10	12	11	13/14	9	3
Mistle thrush	6	2	2	2	2	1	2	1	1
Sedge warbler	2	1+♂	1	—	1	—	1	—	—
Lesser whitethroat	1	—	—	—	—	—	♂	—	1
Whitethroat	4	2+	?	2	1	—	1	♂	♂
Garden warbler	4	2	1	—	2	♂	—	—	♂
Blackcap	4	1	?	?	♂	1	1	2	1
Chiffchaff	3	1	1	♂	1	1	♂	♂	♂
Willow warbler	5	2	—	—	♂	♂	1	1	1

64	65	66	67	68	69	70	71	72	73	74	75
—	—	—	1	1	1	1	1	1	1	1	—
—	1	—	B	?	1	1	1	—	?	?	?
—	—	—	—	—	—	—	—	—	[1]	[1]	—
—	2	—	—	—	1	—	1	?	—	—	—
?	♂♀	—	—	—	B	—	1	1	—	—	—
1	3+	5	5	5	4	5	5+	12	5+	7	6+
1	3	4	2	4	3	4	5	3	4	4	2
—	—	—	—	—	—	—	1 bird	—	—	—	1 bird
1	4	4	3	1	3	2	3	2	3	2	2
4	7	8	8	6	10	14	13	7	8/9	7	6+
—	—	—	—	—	—	?	?	2	?	?	2
1	♂	1	2	1	2	1	1	2♂♂	1+♂	2♂♂	1
—	B	—	—	—	—	—	1	1	1	1	1
—	—	—	—	—	—	—	—	—	—	—	—
—	—	—	—	—	—	—	—	—	—	—	—
—	♂	—	—	—	—	—	—	—	—	—	1
3	3	2	1	2	1	3	3	2	2	3	1
—	—	—	—	—	—	—	—	—	—	—	1
4	5	4	2	4	4	3	5	6	9	10	8
9	13	12	10	11	10	14	12	11	9	10	12
7	6	7	4	6	6	4	5	7+	7/8	6	6
20	21	19	23	24	20	23	17/18	23	18/19	21	20
9	15	12	11	16	17	11	14+	15	11/12	10+	16
1	1	1	1	1	2	2	1	1	1	1	1
—	2	1	—	?	—	—	—	—	—	—	—
♂	—	1	—	1	1	—	♂	—	1	—	1
—	½	1½	—	1½	—	—	—	—	—	—	—
—	♂	♂	—	—	—	—	—	—	—	—	—
1	♂	1	1	1	2	1+♂	1+	2	2	2	2
1	1	2	1	1	1	1	1	1	♂	1	—
—	1	2	1	?	2♂♂♂	1+♂	2♂♂♂		1+♂	1+♂	2

	49-55	56	57	58	59	60	61	62	63
Goldcrest	—	—	—	—	—	1	—	—	—
Spotted flycatcher	6	2	2	1	1	—	2	?	2
Long-tailed tit	4	—	1	1	—	1	1	1	—
Willow tit	—	—	—	—	—	—	—	—	—
Coal tit	—	—	—	—	—	—	—	—	—
Blue tit	7	1	4	2	2	3	5	2	4
Great tit	7	3	3	3	1+	3	3	?	1
Nuthatch	—	—	1	—	—	—	—	—	—
Jackdaw	7	5+	7	7	5+	5+	7	9	10
Rook	—	—	—	—	—	—	—	—	8
Starling	5	5	8	2	3	3	7	6	6
House sparrow	7	18	26	16	c.30	30	20+	25	25
Tree sparrow	6	—	2	3	1	1	1	2	1
Chaffinch	7	5+	6	8	7	11	9	5	5
Greenfinch	7	1+	5	1+	4	8	2	2	1
Goldfinch	6	1+	1+	2	♂♀	1	7	2	2
Linnet	3	—	—	1	3	?	—	3	1
Bullfinch	1	1	1	2	1	?	2	2	2
Yellowhammer	3	1	2	—	—	—	—	—	—
Species proved to nest		32	30	28	32	27	28	22	28
Minimum 'breeding units'		97	130	113	136	144	143	123	114

64	65	66	67	68	69	70	71	72	73	74	75
—	—	—	—	—	1	?	1	?	1	1	1
2	4	3/4	3	3	2	?	2	2	5	3	3
—	—	1	—	1	1	1	1	1	1	1	2
—	?	1	—	→	—	—	—	—	—	—	—
—	—	—	—	—	—	—	—	—	—	1	—
4	4	2	3	3	4	6	6	3	5	3	3
2	3	5	3	3	2	2	2+	3	3	3	3
—	♂	—	—	—	—	—	—	—	—	—	—
9	12	12	8	14	12	11	9	5+	5+	7	6
3	1	—	—	—	—	—	—	—	—	—	—
10	6	6	7	11	10	8+	7	5+	8	8	10
20+	27	27	26	30	c.30	24+	11+	11+	18+	8	8
4+	1	3	—	1	3	2	6	4+	2	1+	1
6	7	6	6	5	6	7	4	6	5	7	6
2	2	2	4	5	5	7	4	5	4	8	7
3	3	2	3	4	4	2+	2	7	4	5	4
3	2	1	2	—	—	—	—	1	—	—	—
2/3	2	3	3	1	1	2	3	2	3	1	1
1	1	2	2	1	2	1	2	♂	♂	♂	♂
28	30	33	28	30	32	29	33	30	30	30	32
134	163	163	146	168	172	164	151	152	148	144	146

Index

Index

271